# Hail! Hail! Rock'n'Roll

John Harris was a writer at the NME until 1995, and went on to be the editor of Select magazine. He now works across a range of subjects for The Guardian, as well as writing for Mojo, and is a Contributing Editor at Q magazine, with his own monthly column. His acclaimed first book, the Britpop history The Last Party, was published in 2003. He is also a regular panellist on BBC2's Newsnight Review. For more information, visit www.johnharris.me.uk

Hywel Harris is a designer, web developer, illustrator and photographer whose work has been published in the NME and The Guardian, and appears both online and in print. His website is at www.hywel.biz

# Hail! Hail! Rock'n'Roll

## JOHN HARRIS

### DESIGNED AND ILLUSTRATED
### BY
### HYWEL HARRIS

sphere

SPHERE

First published in Great Britain in 2009 by Sphere

Copyright © John Harris and Hywel Harris 2009

The moral rights of the authors have been asserted.

A CIP catalogue record for this book is available
from the British Library.

ISBN 978-1-84744-293-2

Printed and bound in Great Britain by
Clays Ltd, St Ives plc

Papers used by Sphere are natural, renewable and
recyclable products sourced from well-managed forests and certified in
accordance with the rules of the Forest Stewardship Council.

**Mixed Sources**
Product group from well-managed
forests and other controlled sources
www.fsc.org Cert no. SGS-COC-004081
© 1996 Forest Stewardship Council
FSC

Sphere
An imprint of
Little, Brown Book Group
100 Victoria Embankment
London EC4Y 0DY

An Hachette UK Company
www.hachette.co.uk

www.littlebrown.co.uk

**Essex County
Council Libraries**

# CONTENTS

For Liz Harris

# INTRODUCTION

Do you remember the first time? Someone put on a record, or a CD – or, if you were unlucky, a cassette, maybe put together by a weird friend of your older brother – and though you had probably heard rock'n'roll music on plenty of other occasions, you actually listened, realising that something fantastic was afoot and that you would probably never be the same again. A lot of people mark that moment by frantically jumping up and down; others stay perfectly still. Whatever: you know it when it happens.

Now, this is only paragraph two, and maybe too early to be conjuring up the presence of that scowl-faced, unspeakably aloof operator Lou Reed, but bear with me. On The Velvet Underground's fourth album – Loaded, much of which is sung by their long-forgotten alumnus Doug Yule, and unfairly damned by their hard-bitten fans as being far too polished and polite – there is the brilliant Reed song that he somewhat unsubtly called Rock & Roll. It's all there: a precocious suburban unfortunate called Jenny – about five years old, apparently – who's unconvinced that 'two TV sets' and 'two Cadillac cars' are going to do much for her, and who chances on a New York radio station, hears the music, and is changed forever – 'She started dancing to that fine, fine music/You know, her life was saved by rock'n'roll.' It's icky and sentimental, of course, but not a bad picture of exactly what this stuff can do to you.

Alternatively, you could go straight to School Day, the Chuck Berry hit released in 1957, which portrayed the drudgery of a formal education and the liberating possibilities offered by a jukebox. The title of this book is taken from its last verse, which gets close to the heart of why even the simplest noise can make all the difference: 'Hail! Hail! Rock'n'roll/Deliver me from the days of old/Long live rock'n'roll/The beat of the drum is loud and bold/Rock, rock, rock'n'roll/The feelin' is there, body and soul.' Not that such sentiments sit comfortably in our age of cynicism and endless irony, but that's surely about right.

Now, once you've been hit by the music, something else occurs, when you realise that just beyond it, there's a whole other world. If you've picked up this book, you surely know the drill: who plays which guitar, which musicians got religion or a drug habit, which Rolling Stones album is the most pointless, who is guilty of playing 'landfill' indie, whether the British Parliament once had a debate about the Beastie Boys' hydraulic penis. Such is a never-ending universe of fascination that leads overqualified obsessives to take low-paid jobs in record shops, doting fathers to beat a weekly retreat to the loft conversion, and otherwise sensible adults to spend hours shouting at each other in the pub – and, really, who can blame them?

After all, stick this and the music together, and you get something that has defined whole lives. Here, it's perhaps best to quote the great rock writer Nik Cohn, who wrote a fabulously impressionistic, rollercoaster history of rock he titled Awopbopaloobop Alopbamboom, after the incantation invented by Little Richard. It was published in 1969, just over a dozen years after rock'n'roll decisively arrived, and among its best passages is this one: 'Myself, I was ten when it started, I'm 22 now, and it has bossed my life. It has surrounded me always, cut me off, and it has given me my heroes, it has made my myths. Almost, it has done my living for me. Six hours of trash every day, and it's meant more to me than anything else.'


Hail! Hail! Rock'n'Roll is built from all that. You can make your way through it in any order you like but, by the end, you will probably know more about the glorious tangle that comes to mind every time a song hits the correct spot: the history, the talk, the records, the gigs, the clothes, the hair, the finer points of the music, and the endless myths and legends. When the basic idea was being developed, it was aimed at being a cross between a scientific field-guide and a vintage edition of Rolling Stone magazine – which is to say that we somehow wanted it to feel as if just about everything was present and correct: as the hoary old Spinal Tap song would have it, 'The majesty of rock/The mystery of roll/The ticking of the clock/The wailing of the soul.'

There's a story underneath it all, though it's probably far too complicated to nail down. It pings across continents, from grand American hotels to British 'toilet venues', and from there to Japanese arenas and auditoriums in Finland.

Its characters include heavy metal singers from Birmingham, Jamaican production gurus, high-achieving musicians routinely compared to God, and a cast of supporting players that takes in everyone from an LA 'rodeo tailor' to the people who invented skull-crushingly loud amplifiers, one of whom was based in a shop near Heathrow Airport. And, naturally, the saga goes on: from your Elvises and Lennons and Rottens, the torch has inevitably passed into the wobbly grip of such latter-day icons as the infamous female singer from North London who sounds a bit like Billie Holiday marooned in a British off-licence, and has perhaps fallen for a little too much of the aforementioned mythology.

That said, reading through the 200 or so pages that follow, you may pick up the strong aroma – cigarette smoke, bad food, cheap soap – of a time that has now gone: when songs had to be bought in the form of physical objects, musicians occasionally looked like creatures from other worlds, and people swearing on television could still make the headlines. Just to make this clear: the modern world still hurls forth plenty of great music, and allows miracles that no one stranded in music's supposed golden ages would have believed – thousands of songs in your pocket, and inventions that have allowed untold millions to tap into an infinite jukebox whenever they fancy. Self-evidently, this is all great. Some of us, however, cannot help but feel the odd pang of longing for the days when everything was that bit more difficult. So, even if it contravenes Chuck's insistence that rock was there to push us beyond 'days of old', forgive us our nostalgia – and bear in mind that if people in their teens now happily queue up to buy records made several decades before they were born, it's obviously contagious.

Besides, the 'n' word is often a signifier for liking something so much that you can't let it go, which is surely completely understandable. You have to know this behaviour's limits, obviously: there is surely no point in paying good money to see such real-life spectacles as Thin Lizzy without Phil Lynott, a version of Queen devoid of Freddie Mercury, or musicians playing along – to packed houses! – with old films of Elvis. But go to the right kind of records, and you're easily in the clear: to paraphrase Nik Cohn, if your chosen six hours of trash would include – and these are random names, but anyway – Public Enemy, Mott The Hoople, Janis Joplin and Happy Mondays, why worry? It's a very common disease: completely benign and usually life-enhancing. It might even make you a better person (possibly).

Of course, there have been many attempts to decry our beloved rock, from the squealings of people convinced it heralded the beginning of civilisation's terminal decline, to the work of musicians who have fallen prey to self-loathing and found themselves cut off from music's undeniable wonders (if you've got two hours to spare and want to drill into rock'n'roll's supposed heart of darkness, listen to Pink Floyd's The Wall – though it may take you several years to recover). Even if you've long been in love with it all, you can perhaps imagine a world made up of rock's less edifying aspects: Jack Daniel's mirrors, cracked snakeskin boots, people who look like Ron Wood. Awful? Maybe, but even at its most tawdry, what's not to like?

The author of this book has probably spent far too long trying to figure all this out: not just what it is that makes you jump up and down, but why it is that somewhere in all that noise there might lurk the key to a better way of living, or something. God knows what links such dreamy ideas to some of the absurd and/or horrific stuff detailed in what follows: Sid Vicious destroying himself onstage, Van Halen being spectacularly obnoxious, the guy from Slipknot who apparently puts nails in his own head, Duran Duran's album of cover versions. But if you've ever found yourself thinking such thoughts, you can take comfort in the fact that some of history's finest minds have done the same.

In 1977, for example, the renowned American music writer Lester Bangs went on tour with The Clash, around such glamorous places as Derby, Cardiff, Bristol and Birmingham, and wrote this: 'Don't ask me why I obsessively look to rock'n'roll bands for some kind of model for a better society…I guess it's just that I glimpsed something beautiful in a flashbulb moment once, and perhaps mistaking it for a prophecy have been seeking its fulfilment ever since…'

…Or, as another devout believer once put it: 'Hail! Hail! Rock'n'roll…'

# Chapter 1

# THE TALK

I magine this. You are a musician, with the songs to make an entire generation swing. You hair is cut just so; some cutting-edge outfitter has supplied you with the correct kind of spangly jumpsuit. Hits, it seems, are only a breath away, with the high life not far behind. The limo is rumbling away outside your flat, the plane tickets to New York have been booked, and you are living the dream something rotten.

And then, guess what? Some impudent, clever-clever, poorly-dressed journalist with a tape recorder turns up at your record company's office, escorts you to a bar, and asks you a most terrifying question: as people who work in airports would have it, have you anything to declare? With the right quips, statements and waspish one-liners, your chances of success will only increase; get things wrong and, even if the music can easily do the talking, you may not be quite the dead-cert you thought.

Now, we are about to start 20 or so pages full of brilliant examples of rock mouth-offery, but it has to be said: though it is just about preferable to working in a coalmine, interviewing even the most talented musicians can be no fun at all. Very often they will stare at the floor, fidget and only break the silence with the emptiest of clichés. Even booze will fail to liven things up and, while the person from the PR company hovers fretfully in the corner, out will come what might be elegantly called boring tripe. One particularly dread example will put your thoughts in the correct place: 'We just make music for ourselves, and if anybody else likes it, that's a bonus.'

From time to time, however, musicians come good – and whether from the stage, on television, or clustered around a recording device in a pub, they utter things that are not just entertaining but positively headline-grabbing. Sometimes, what they say will benefit their career no end, but the wrong kind of quote can create a stink and precipitate what is known these days as a Career Wobble (for particularly grisly proof, go online and have a quick rummage around the words 'Eric Clapton' and 'Enoch Powell'). But such crises are their problem, not ours; because whether outrageous or remarkable quotes nudge careers in the right direction or send them tumbling into The Dumper – or, as is usually the case, simply keep everything ticking over – they are usually a right old scream.

Part of this is down to the fact that, since the mid-1960s or thereabouts, musicians have been encouraged to hold forth about no end of stuff that should arguably sit well out of reach: politics, religion, the existence of aliens, you name it. And, of course, all this can sometimes go a little too far. Not so long ago, the author of this book interviewed the estimable British rock writer Nick Kent, who cast his mind back to the 1980s and remembered a chilling realisation indeed: 'We reached a point where you had bands who were thinking harder about their interviews than the music,' he said. If you're of a certain age, you might remember this: a trip to the newsagents to buy NME or Smash Hits, your attention tweaked by some raffishly-attired no-mark giving it the old 'I have genius coursing round my underpants, and if I see that guy out of Blue Zoo, you better hold my coat'. And then the sighing comedown: 85p wasted on their latest single, and the realisation that they would never be able to walk the walk.

Thankfully, this chapter is about the good stuff, usually uttered by people with the talent to back it up. Here you will meet the Gallagher brothers, drunk and supercharged in a Glaswegian hotel room at 2am, desperately arguing over the true meaning of rock and about to throw each other out of the window. Over there: the great Sly Stone, out of his mind on a US chat show, excusing his lateness by telling the host that he spent the afternoon breaking into his own house. There is a guide to the multiple ages of rock by that great campfire raconteur Joe Strummer, and admirable verbal material from Lee 'Scratch' Perry and Keith Richards. There are very entertaining words from Courtney Love, Shaun Ryder and Little Richard – and also a condensed history of a phenomenon that has an ever-increasing impact on the way musicians talk about themselves and the world: the shrill, shrieking coverage of music by the tabloid press, and the pantomimic horrors – 'The Filth And The Fury!', 'Amy On Crack' - it has spawned.

Anyway, one last cast-iron guarantee. In the course of the what follows, no one says, 'We just make music for ourselves', nor the soul-destroying nine words that always follow it. And that, surely, is a definite bonus.

# BOB DYLAN'S BORN-AGAIN SERMONS

**In late 1978, Bob Dylan became a born-again Christian, was duly baptised, recorded an evangelical album entitled Slow Train Coming and eventually set out on the road to spread the good news. Though his audiences seemed sceptical, he kept on keeping on**

'I'd like to say we're presenting the show tonight under the authority of Jesus Christ.'
*San Francisco, California, 11 November 1979*

'You know, we read in the newspapers every day how bad the world is getting. The situation in Iran, the students rebelling, you know, even over here they're rebelling. They don't let the Iranians sneak into the whorehouses. But that don't matter much because we know this world will be destroyed. God will set up his kingdom for a thousand years. So there's a slow train coming, but it's bound to pick up speed.'
*San Francisco, California, 13 November 1979*

'Satan's called the god of this world and as you look you see he really is god of this world. But for those of you who don't know...I'm curious to know how many of you don't know and how many of you know that Satan himself has been defeated at the cross. Does anybody know that? [Applause] Alright. At least we're not alone.'
*Santa Monica, California, 18 November 1979*

'The world as we know it now is being destroyed. Sorry, but it's the truth. In a short time – I don't know, in three years, maybe five years, could be ten years, I don't know – there's gonna be a war. It's gonna be called the War of Armageddon. It's gonna be in the Middle East. Russia's gonna come down first. Anyway, we're not worried about that. We know there's gonna be a new kingdom set up in Jerusalem for a thousand years. That's where Christ will set up his Kingdom, as sure as you're standing there. It's gonna happen.'
*Tempe, Arizona, 25 November 1979*

'Hmmm, pretty rude bunch tonight, eh? You all know how to be real rude! You know about the spirit of the Anti-Christ? Does anybody here know about that? Well, the spirit of the Anti-Christ is loose now.'
*Tempe, Arizona, 26 November 1979*

'Don't matter how much money you got, there is only two kinds of people: there's saved people and there's lost people. Now, remember that I told you that. You may never see me again. I may never be through here again. You may not see me. Sometime down the line, you'll remember you heard it here – that Jesus is Lord. And every knee shall bow!'
*Tempe, Arizona, 26 November 1979*

*Dylan: Every knee shall bow!*

'No matter what you read in the newspaper, that's all deceit. The real truth is that he [Jesus] is coming back already. And you just watch your newspapers...maybe two years, maybe three years, five years from now, you just watch and see. Russia will come down and attack in the Middle East. China's got an army of 200 million people, they're going to come down to the Middle East. There's going to be a war called the Battle of Armageddon. Which is like some war you've never even dreamed about. And Christ will set up his kingdom. He will set up his kingdom and he will rule it from Jerusalem. Now I know, as far out as that might seem, this is what the Bible says.'
*Tempe, Arizona, 26 November 1979*

'I told you The Times They Are A-Changin' and they did. I said the answer was Blowin' In The Wind and it was. I'm telling you now Jesus is coming back, and he is!'
*Albuquerque, New Mexico, 5 December 1979*

# Keith Richards on drugs
## How come they taste so good?

'I don't know if I've been lucky or it's that subconscious careful, but I've never turned blue in someone's bathroom. I consider that the height of bad manners.' *1980*

'I must say, in fairness to the poppy, that never once did I have a cold. The cure for the common cold is there, but they daren't tell anybody because they would have a nation full of drug addicts.' *1978*

'Half the reason I got drawn into it was because I didn't have a lot of freedom and time off. If I'd had the freedom I could have dragged myself off to somewhere remote for three months and cleaned myself up and pulled myself together. But in this business, there's always a new tour to do, and before you know it, five years have gone. I started getting hooked ten years ago. That was when I was squeezing blackheads – now I'm pulling out grey hairs! Ha ha! But now, I can remember what each show was like afterwards, without having somebody tell me.' *1978*

'There was a knock on our dressing room door. Our manager shouted, "Keith! Ron! The Police are here!" Oh man, we panicked. Flushed everything down the john. Then the door opened and it was Sting and Stewart Copeland.' *1982*

'Actually, I really think the quality's gone down. All they do is try and take the high out of everything. I don't like the way they work on the brain area instead of just through the blood system. That's why I don't take any of them any more. And you're talking to a person who knows his drugs.' *2006*

'I don't take drugs unless I have to under great duress with my brain open. I've had a couple of weeks on morphine. I did try to squeeze a little bit extra out of the night nurse. She was very accommodating.' *2006*

'I looked at my dad's ashes and thought, What am I gonna do? Do I desecrate them with a dustbin and broom? So I wet my finger and I shoved a little bit of Dad up my hooter.' *2008*

# The wisdom of Lee 'Scratch' Perry
## Jamaican reggae musician, producer, visionary and godhead

'When I left school there was nothing to do except field work: hard, hard labour. I didn't fancy that. So I started playing dominoes. Through dominoes I practised my mind and learned to read the minds of others. This has proved eternally useful to me.' *1984*

'I am LSP – I am the inheritor of the pound, the shilling and the pence; I am the inheritor of the dollars and I am also the inheritor of the Euro. So it will be Lee 'Scratch' Perry running the economy. LSP be showing you L for pound, the American dollar for S and the P for Mr Perry. The P for the Mr Perry is also for Mr Pyramid. My memory's very good and I remember the days in Egypt very good, and I am Mr Pyramid. It may have changed a little to Mr Perry, but I am Mr Pyramid.' *2004*

'My performance style? I am imitating Jesus. Performing means spiritually healing, healing the brain of the sick people, who are dread, and who are dead. So I have to come back and heal their brain, and heal their head. Save some from cocaine reggae, and from cancer reggae, and from death reggae.' *1999*

'I would like to be remembered as a fish – an angelfish who come to feed the nations with one Bob Marley loaf of bread and two fishes. I'm Lee 'Scratch' Perry, right? And I'm a Piscean. My sign is two fish – one facing east and one west. Bob Marley was an Aquarian and he go by the water. The bread come from Heaven and the fishes come from the sea and I feed the nations with music.' *2009*

'I think Switzerland is most cool and you don't see gun boys. I make the punky reggae party but then it get too dread, so I have to leave Jamaica. I go to Switzerland, but I am still the punk and so others follow: Tina Turner, David Bowie.' *On his adopted homeland, 1997*

*Noel and Liam Gallagher, 1994*

# WIBBLING RIVALRY: THE BEST BITS

**On 7 April 1994, the author of this book interviewed Liam and Noel Gallagher in a hotel in Glasgow. Two months before, Oasis had crash-landed in the music press when all of the band apart from Noel were detained on a ferry en route to Holland and sent back to the UK, forcing the cancellation of a gig in Amsterdam. That incident sat at the heart of the following conversation – the best bits of which were eventually released on a single that reached No 52 in the UK charts…**

**John Harris**: How do you feel about the fact that, already, Oasis have attracted a reputation for being rock'n'roll animals?

**Liam**: I'm into it, me. I'm into it. But at the end of the day…I go home and get a clip off me mam, know what I mean? And I do. She clips me round the head and goes, 'What are you like, you little tinker?'

**Noel**: It's not a reputation, right, that I…

**L**: I like the way it's bubbling up. It's reminding me of the Roses all over again. I like that, me. I want to get 2000 people in a nice fuckin' gaff who are there to see *me*, not fuckin' go…

**N**: Woah. Hang on a minute. That's not what he's on about.

**L**: He is.

**N**: He's on about a reputation about getting thrown off fuckin' ferries.

**L**: Yeah, but that's part of it, that's what…

**N**: The thing about getting thrown off ferries – blah, blah, blah – and getting deported is summat that I'm not proud about…

**L**: Well I am, la.

**N**: Yeah, alright. Well, if you're proud about getting thrown off ferries, then why don't you go and support West Ham and get the fuck out of my band and go and be a football hooligan, right? Cos we're musicians, right? We're not football hooligans.

**L**: You're only gutted cos you was in bed fuckin' reading your fuckin' books…

**N**: No, not at all. Listen. No, listen. He says, right…Here's a quote for you from my manager, Marcus Russell, right…

**L**: He's a fuckin'…'nother fuckin'…

**N**: Shut up you dick. Right. He gets off the ferry after getting fuckin' deported. I'm left in Amsterdam with me dick out like a fuckin' spare prick at a fuckin' wedding…

**L**: It was a bad move, you know…

**N**: Shut up! Shut up!…This lot think it's rock'n'roll to get thrown off a ferry…Do you know what my manager said to him? He said, 'Nah. Rock'n'roll is going to Amsterdam, doing your gig, playing your music…and coming back and saying you blew 'em away.' Not getting thrown off the ferry like some fuckin' scouse schlepper, being handcuffed. That's football hooliganism, and I won't stand for it. And listen: they all got fined a thousand pounds each.

**L**: We didn't at all.

**N**: Yes you fuckin' did.

**L**: You can stick your thousand pounds right up your fuckin' arse 'til it comes out your fuckin' big toe.

---

*Noel goes to the toilet. When he returns the conversation examines the connection between classic rock'n'roll groups and bad behaviour…*

**JH**: Would the Stones have done anything without getting arrested and getting people's backs up?

**L**: No, would they fuck! That's why they were so good!

**N**: *[Super-indignantly]* What? Cos they got arrested? Because The Rolling Stones got arrested they were a great rock'n'roll band? Fuck off! Bullshit! Bullshit!

**L**: No, but they had…summat else there.

**N**: What? An edge? Is that what you're

16

saying? An edge?'

L: No, they had a life, you dickhead. They had a life, man…

N: We've got a life! We've got a life!

L: Not if you start going on like that. *[Begins to mince up and down bedroom]* Do you want to walk around like that? Like that?

N: No, not at all…You think it's rock'n'roll to get thrown off a ferry, and it's not.

L: I don't think it's rock'n'roll.

N: That was your quote, you prick! That was your quote! 'It's rock'n'roll! It's rock'n'roll!' That's what you *said*!

L: I was laughing about it. I'm into it…It happened. That was reality, mate.

---

*Some minutes later…*

N: Right. This band is about fuckin' music. It's not about getting thrown off fuckin' ferries. *[To Liam]* Why don't you go downstairs and smash the bar up and say you're the singer of Oasis?

L: Cos I don't want to. If I did, if I was gonna go down and smash the bar up, I'd do it and there's nothing would stop me.

N: Then why don't you go and make a scene? Why don't you do a Keith Richards? Throw the TV out of the window!

L: Cos I'm not Keith Richards.

N: Throw the TV out the window!

L: I don't want to do that. If I wanted to do it, I'd just go like that and do it, and do it. But I don't want to do that. I'm not about that.

N: What are you about?

L: I'm about being…I'm about going down the fuckin'…I'm about…*[takes long slug of gin and tonic]* That's what I'm about.

N: Right. That's what you're about. Right…

L: Sit down, man. You're getting into a state. You've had too many G&Ts. Sit the fuck down.

N: See, you're not a spokesman for the band.

L: I'm not – are you?

N: Yeah, I am.

L: Are you?

N: Yeah, I am.

L: You might be in your little world, but as far as I'm concerned, if you think what I'm saying is bullshit, I think what you're saying is fuckin' bullshit, man.

N: Right. Well, fine. But you don't speak for the band.

L: You don't speak for the band.

N: I do speak for the band.

L: You do, yeah, because you're fuckin', yeah…I fucking speak for the band, I'm speaking now for the band. And I'm into it. I'm into all that fuckin' shit. *[Referring to Noel]* He's teetotal. He's a fuckin' priest. He was born to be a priest.

---

*Further debate about Liam's naughtiness ensues, until the inevitable mention of The Beatles…*

L: It's not doing anyone any harm. That's just me. John Lennon used to fuckin' burn about doing little mad things, and that…

N: Do you know John Lennon?

L: Do you know him?

N: I don't, but do you?

L: Yeah.

N: Well, you must be pretty old. How old are you? 21?

L: No. About fuckin' thousand and five fuckin' one.

N: You're 22.

L: No, I'm 21.

N: Right. And remember, I watched you being born. And I don't even know John Lennon.

---

*Five or so minutes later…*

JH: The Who hated each other as well.

L: Yeah, well I hate this bastard.

JH: Is that important to you? Is that what fires this band up?

L: Yeah. That's what it's all about. That's why we'll be the best band in the world, because I fuckin' hate that twat there…And I hope one day there's a release where I can smash fuck out of him, with a fuckin' Rickenbacker, right on his nose, and then he does the same to me, cos I think that we're stepping right up to it now. There's a fuckin' line there and we're right on the edge of it.

JH: How often do you have arguments like this?

L: Every fuckin' day.

N: Hourly.

JH: Do you have any recurring dreams?

N: Yeah. Just the one.

L: *[Menacingly]* I take over the band.

# THE THOUGHTS OF SHAUN WILLIAM RYDER
**Twenty years of quotable brilliance, from Happy Mondays to Black Grape and beyond**

'I got fired from the Post Office because I was distributing amphetamines and acid for absolutely no profit, just giving it to my fellow postmen just to see what fun I could have with them delivering to totally the wrong street with the wrong numbers…to see what kind of mayhem we could create.' *2001*

'We didn't get into the music biz and discover drugs. We discovered drugs and got into music.' *Looking back on Happy Mondays, 1995*

'I've seen fucking hundreds and hundreds of spacecraft flying across the sky over Salford. I mean hundreds of them. There's obviously other planets like this and other life. Anyone who thinks there isn't is a dickhead.' *1990*

'You live in Natty Twang Town on Doubledecker Bus Avenue, and it's fucked. Full of fucking EastEnders, Coronation Street people and pogo sticks and platforms and lots of different fucking coloured Smarties and toffees. Then you fuck off, right, and go on a plane and live on a park bench next to a tree and stay there with a towel and a beach and a ski slope – all sorts of different bollocks, where it's double normal. You have it there for five years, but then you go back to Doubledecker Close and think, Fuck me, this is mad here! She did what? He did what? You go, Fuck me, that was already mad, how the fuck did your egg not fry in there?" *On the experience of fame, 2007*

'Vegetarian? Me? Animals just exist to be chopped up and eaten, pal. Especially cows. I fucking hate cows. They freak me out.' *1988*

'I stopped tripping a while back, though I did have some wild stuff in America. It ended up with me in the middle of a highway, flagging

*Shaun Ryder: he lived in 'Natty Twang Town'*

down a juggernaut and shouting to these two black geezers, "I'm an Englishman and I'm tripping, so take me home." They gave us a lift to Cleveland, which was cool.' *1989*

'Selling some crap to the papers is better than burgling some old woman's house or mugging somebody, or even selling bags of heroin. I like some nice clothes or a car, so if someone's going to offer me £6000 just because he wants me to say I smoke pot and I've done a bit of Borstal and community service, then fair enough, man. It's just showbusiness.' *1992*

'I just thought Kurt Cobain was a fucking great fucking artist man, y'know what I mean? But to blow his head off for a bit of a drug problem and a bit of a chick problem was just fucking ridiculous, man. I mean, fuck me, it's not as if he couldn't afford his gear or anything. He could have stayed a smackhead for years and just got on with it.' *1995*

'I'm not with Catholics or Protestants. I think everybody should live in peace. It's ridiculous that we're still arguing over religion in this fucking century. Religion was the first rule-book…like, if you live in the desert don't eat pork cos it will kill your insides, and get rid of your foreskin…these fucking things like, "Thou shalt not do this, thou shalt not do that." Basically, the Bible was the first fucking police force.' *1995*

'There's a rumour I was doing 50 rocks *[of crack]* a day and that each rock contained 20 grams of coke, so I'd be doing 600 grams a day. That's rubbish. I think I was only smoking about 15 or 20 rocks a day, man.' *1992*

'I'm really looking forward to playing America again, it's going to be great. Especially Seattle. The first time I went to Seattle, in 1988, I caught chlamydia.' *1997*

18

# 'A BLESSING AND A LESSON'

## No one – but no one – does a career-retrospective interview like Little Richard

'I've heard people call me the Quasar, the Architect, the Originator, but I never heard nobody in the audience saying such a thing. I don't carry myself that way, never have. I'm very much a gentleman in what I do. And I don't get down on nobody else for doing whatever else they do. To each his own. I try to be a guide for people, to make their darkness bright and to make the pathway light, and never to condemn or control or criticise. I've tried to let my life be an example. I'll be 62 this year, and I've lived too long, come too far, to be considered a misfit.' *1994*

'I've never been paid. Twenty-five years, and they've never given me a dime. My songs are continuing to be recorded over and over. Waylon Jennings had a hit with Lucille not long ago in the country charts. It went to Number One, my name was in the Billboard charts, and yet I never received a quarter…They just had three movies with my songs in them, and they don't even send me a Christmas card or even talk to me on the phone.' *1985*

'They shoulda called me Little Cocaine, I was sniffing so much of the stuff. My nose got big enough to back a diesel truck in, unload it, and drive it right out again.' *1984*

'He was a star. When I got him, he was a star. Sly *[Stone]* told you that everybody is a star. The only problem is, people haven't been put in the dipper and pulled back on the world. That's what the answer is. You've got to be placed into the dipper and pulled back down on the world, and then men will see your good works and glorify God Jehovah.' *On Jimi Hendrix, a former member of his backing band, 1973*

'People go, Oooo! They masturbate! Why they goin', Oooo!, when they do it? Some people get three or four a night – I got nine! When I was doing it, I enjoyed doing it. In fact, some nights I couldn't go to sleep until I did it. It's just like a baby with a pacifier. And I don't see why people frown upon it. It's the truth!' *1985*

'I gave up rock'n'roll in 1976. I had a lot of death in my family. My brother fell dead…I had another friend got shot in the head. Another friend of mine got cut up with a butcher knife. Another friend of mine had a heart attack. Then my mother died. Then my nephew shot himself in the head. So I decided that I would give my life to being an evangelist.' *1985 – he returned to rock'n'roll in the late 1980s*

'When I see my old friends, they're on walkers, some of 'em are in wheelchairs, some of 'em got a stick. And they hit you with it, too. I'm just glad that I'm able to still get around. And I can be found, and I'm sound. It's a blessing and a lesson…I'm just glad to be wrapped up and tied up and hooked up with the right force. The power of love.' *2003*

'One night I forgot some words to a song, and those words came to me. It was my first big hit: "Tutti frutti, aw rootie." I thank God for those words…And I'd like to give my love to everybody, and let them know that the grass may look greener on the other side, but believe me, it's just as hard to cut. And I'd just like to leave them with "Awop-bop-a-loo-bop-a-lop-bam-boom!"' *1994*

*Little Richard: the Qasar, the Architect, the Originator*

19

Sly Stone:
'not so bad',
apparently

# 'IN ORDER TO GET IT, YOU'VE GOTTA GO THROUGH IT'

**Sly Stone interviewed by chat-show man Dick Cavett on US telly in July 1970: a cut wrist, a lot of face-chewing, the same out-there vibes that defined his warped 1971 masterpiece There's A Riot Goin' On – and six minutes of TV heaven. Or, if you look at it another way, sheer hell…**

*Enter famous US chat-show host Dick Cavett and Sly Stone (aka Sylvester Stewart), leader of multi-racial funksters Sly & The Family Stone. Cavett is dressed in a sober grey suit; Stone is attired, head to foot, in what appears to be red velvet. His hat is a kind of super-fedora with feathers in it, and he sports spangled britches. He chews the inside of his mouth a lot. He is also anxiously examining his left wrist.*

**DC:** You've cut yourself. Did you have trouble getting here?
**SS:** I got my house broken into.
**DC:** Why are you injured there? Was that during a performance?
**SS:** I broke into my house. *[Uproarious audience laughter]*
**DC:** Caught yourself breaking into your house, did you?
**SS:** Actually, I caught myself trying to repair it. I *cut* myself, yeah…
**DC:** It's an actual wound. I think it's just a flesh wound…
**SS:** *[Looking momentarily hostile, and beginning to slur words]* Is that sympathy I'm getting? Is it…*symmmmy?*
**DC:** Sympathy, yeah. Considering you were almost late getting here, it's as much sympathy as…
**SS:** Why? You understand a house being broken into. If it was your house, you'd be a little late.
**DC:** Right. That's right. You were going to be here another time and you never got here.
**SS:** I was here.
**DC:** I mean *physically* here.
**SS:** I was here. Marching *[laughs]*…No, I wasn't here.
**DC:** Had I said something?
**SS:** No. You were great, man. You are great. You are great.
**DC:** *[With some weariness]* I'm great.
**SS:** Right on. For real. *[Looks at Cavett]* For real. Hey Dick. *Dick.* Hey Dick.
**DC:** You have my entire attention.
**SS:** You're *great. [Audience applauds]*
**DC:** I find it hard to keep the conversational ball in the air, but it's nice of you to say that.
**SS:** You are. Really, though.
**DC:** Well, you're not bad yourself.
**SS:** Well, I am kinda bad. But I'm not *so* bad. You're right. I'm not so bad.
**DC:** You're straight on.
**SS:** I am straight *in. [Pause]* In order to get to it, you've gotta go through it. That's really the truth.
**DC:** Who said that? Was it Emerson? Or Thoreau?
**SS:** Jimmy Ford *[Texan jazz musician born in 1927]*…Jimmy Ford's in LA, beating up people…No, not really. Actually, he's writing beautiful songs. And he's destroying the minds of people who've been led to believe that the world is flat. Hey Dick! Dick. One more thing…
**DC:** *[Looking mid-way between amused and nervous]* Our relationship will continue right after this message!

*Commercial break begins*

**DC:** We're back. We had a brief message from our local stations, but we're back.
**SS:** We're back. We're *black.*

DC: You're a magician with words. Listen: I want to ask you a straight question. Bill Graham *[legendary '60s West Coast concert promoter]* was here – the man who closed the Fillmore East and the Fillmore West.
SS: *Who?*
DC: You know Bill Graham. He got fed up dealing with the…
SS: *[Loudly]* Gramme, man! I know him so well, he's such a nice guy, I call him…
DC: What is that, exactly?
SS: I can't tell you. *[Pause]* Gramme-cracker. Are you hip to the Gramme-cracker?
DC: *[Sarcastically]* Oh yes, yes.
SS: He'll never let us play.
DC: Do you think Graham was right in his complaints about some acts being hard to work with?…He said that the reason he got out was that the acts were incredibly ungrateful, they demanded an incredible amount of money…the only fun in it for him was the money.
SS: *[Thoughtfully]* It's kinda hard for Bill Graham to make a final analogy about what he doesn't do when he's sweating onstage.
DC: *[Obviously humouring him]* He did a lot of sweating onstage. Sometimes the audience would heckle him.
SS: Well, that's because he had an ulcer. Or something probably equivalent.
DC: Your relationship with him was not pleasant?
SS: Fine! That's why I'm telling you the truth.
DC: *[After a long pause, theatrically waves at Stone]* I like that! Tell me another story! *[Stone looks, with some curiosity, at Cavett and his other guest]*
SS: Hey! How come you two have got the same legs crossed? *[Camera zooms out to illustrate his point]* I do it like this. *[Stone leans back and crosses legs]*
DC: That's supposed to be more masculine, if you cross your legs like that.
SS: You know what happens?
DC: No, what?
SS: *[Slowly and slurred]* You…just… change…positions. *[Pause]* We have a brief message from our local stations…
DC: You're right! And that's where it's at, baby!

*Cue commercial break. Exit Stone.*

# Lear jets, kettles, porn…

## Rubbish catchphrases that only musicians – and roadies – could utter

### 'No ass, no pass'
A completely lairy instruction that crystallises the sex/backstage access exchange common to countless touring rock bands – and, obviously, their road crews. The original source is lost in the mists of time, but it was used as the subtitle for the American porn film Backstage Sluts 2 in 1998. Which was nice.

### 'Love 'em and Lear 'em'
A cringe-inducing and not un-boastful rule that links lovers and private jets, attributed to The Eagles' Don Henley circa 1977. According to his sometime squeeze Stevie Nicks, 'It's something he would have said. He once sent a little cranberry-red Lear jet to pick me up from a Fleetwood Mac gig somewhere and fly me to New York.' Says Henley: 'Once in a while we would do something completely over the top like that, and it was simply our way of coping with the absurdity of making so much money and being so famous at such an early age. We had to do absurd things sometimes just to be able to put it all in perspective.' Of course you did.

### 'When on tour-o, drink Sapporo'
A catchphrase used regularly by Paul Weller's touring party in Japan, in tribute to the nationally-ubiquitous beer brand that comes in pint glass-like cans. An article in Q magazine in 1994 traced it to a colourfully-named lighting engineer called Alf Zammit.

### 'No kettle, no metal'
A very arcane one, this. Uttered on tour by the long-lost, fleetingly popular Brit-rock band Three Colours Red circa 1997, as a crisp statement about the necessity of tea-making facilities in dressing rooms. Slightly more adventurously, 3CR – or rather Geordie guitarist/singer Chris McCormack, younger brother of one of UK metallers The Wildhearts – were also fond of the mantra 'no spliff, no riff'.

# I READ THE NEWS TODAY, OH BOY

**Glorious highlights of the ongoing hysteria spasm that is red-top rock reporting**

## POP IDOLS SNEER AT DYING KIDS

*Daily Mirror, 14 May 1987*

The Beastie Boys were in Montreux, Switzerland, for its annual TV pop 'festival', and due to arrive in the UK within days, bringing their 'hydraulic penis' (see Chapter 3). Cue a 'scoop' – entirely fabricated, said the band – alleging grim behaviour involving a party of terminally ill children, replete with such 'quotes' as, 'Who cares about a bunch of cripples anyway?' By way of a standard act of Fleet Street warfare, The Sun then jumped in with contrary testimony from one of the kids' mums: 'The Beasties were very kind to the children and signed autographs for them.'

## AMY ON CRACK

*The Sun, 22 January 2008*

One of many backhanded tributes to North London's version of Billie Holiday, replete with her fondness for 1)'the pipe', and 2)late-night visits to the 7-11. The soaraway Sun got hold of footage of La Winehouse 'smoking hit upon hit of crack after a 19-minute binge in which she snorted powdered ecstasy and cocaine'. They forecast nothing less than a 'nosedive to oblivion'. Which, to be fair, is probably what she was after.

## BAN THIS SICK STUNT

*Daily Mirror, 25 September 1995*

Subtitled 'Chart stars sell CD with DIY kids' drugs guide'. Packaging for the Pulp single Sorted For E's And Wizz/Mis-shapes contained origami instructions for the creation of a bog-standard 'cocaine wrap', and the Mirror got in a right tizz. Thanks to the fuss, the offending CD booklets were recalled and – oh yes – pulped. NB: the front-page story was written by future orange-skinned TV bod Kate Thornton, and accompanied by a promotion for the lovely-sounding cod-bingo game Mirror Instant Scratch.

## JACKO PULPS LOUT COCKER

*Daily Mirror, 20 February 1996*

Another Pulp one, included as an object lesson in how the red-tops nimbly jump from one standpoint to its complete opposite. The morning after Jarvis Cocker had so brilliantly interrupted Michael Jackson's Artist Of A Generation vom-fest at the Brit Awards, the Mirror claimed that his 'loutish' antics had 'brought terror' to the kids used in MJ's performance (there's irony here somewhere, obviously). But within days, with the British public taking a firm pro-Jarv stance, the paper was leading a 'Justice for Jarvis' campaign, assisted by such names as Patsy Kensit, Zoe Ball and Barbara Windsor. Consistency, as they say, is the hobgoblin of small minds.

## DOHERTY IN HIS CELL

*The Sun, 16 April 2008*

'And guess what,' said the good old Currant Bun, 'he's on heroin.' From the top, then: 'Jailed rocker Pete Doherty stares vacantly in his cell – amid revelations he is shooting up heroin in the prison's Detox unit. The junkie singer, 29, has been injecting smack smuggled into London's tough Wormwood Scrubs slammer.' Surely the very definition of 'not exactly front-page news'.

*Pete Doherty: on drugs, apparently*

## KICK THIS EVIL BASTARD OUT!

*Daily Star, 12 February 1994*

Laboured outrage about a UK tour by Snoop Doggy Dogg, with the obligatory quote from a rent-a-quote Tory MP (soon to be superseded by rent-a-quote New Labour MPs). Said Terry Dicks, the member – in both senses, perhaps – for Hayes and Harlington: 'He should be put on the first plane back.' He wasn't.

## THE FILTH AND THE FURY!

*Daily Mirror, 2 December 1976*

A treat. The unknown Sex Pistols were a last-minute booking on ITV's teatime programme Today, where they got roaring drunk, rose to host Bill Grundy's bait, and swore like troopers. In around 12 hours, they thus became notorious, forever. Best bits: guitarist Steve Jones's use of the very '70s insult 'rotter', and the madness of 'Lorry driver James Holmes, 47', so outraged that he kicked in the screen of his TV. 'It blew up and I was knocked backwards,' he said. D'oh!

## MYSTERY OF ELTON'S SILENT DOGS

*The Sun, 28 September 1987*

More red-top bollockry, which ended with a successful libel suit. Dogs guarding EJ were alleged to have been made barkless by a 'horrific operation' that turned them into 'silent assassins'. He sued, and got a million, much to the annoyance of then-editor Kelvin MacKenzie. 'Bloody Elton John,' he said in 2006. 'Libel can only have a value if there has been some kind of damage, right? Where is the damage? There's nothing wrong with him!'

## ROYAL ROW AS FRANKIE GO TOO

**FAR** *Daily Star, 28 December 1984*

Frankie Goes To Hollywood's much hyped debut album Welcome To The Pleasuredome had been out for a full two months when a Star staffer suddenly discovered that it featured 'a Prince Charles impersonator talking about orgasms and ejaculation'. The splash went on: 'Scores of angry mums complained to the Daily Star after buying Frankie's album' – presumably as a Christmas present, but the piece still reeked of fibs. Who, after all, phones the Daily Star to complain about anything?

## PHIL: I'M FAXING FURIOUS

*The Sun, 30 September 1994*

Phil Collins's marital bust-ups were not just reflected in lachrymose hit singles. According to the Sun, the supposedly mild-mannered Genesis singer also sent his estranged missus Jill a long fax including the words, 'You are slowly making me hate you' and 'Man, I'm so fucking angry with you'. And to think: she was the only one who really knew him at all, etc.

## JAGGER WEDDING DAY ROUGH

**HOUSE** *Daily Mirror, 13 May 1971*

A very Mirror-type move: the portrayal of Mick'n'Bianca's nuptials in St Tropez in terms that rather suggested the life of the paper's in-house mascot Andy Capp. Note: according to the Oxford English Dictionary, the term 'rough house' denotes 'a disturbance or row', which was what happened when French law's insistence on open-access weddings meant that the world – and his wife – got in. While we're here, on page 30 of that day's Mirror was a boxing story, pricelessly sold as 'Bugner answers Boo Boys'.

## OASIS: WE ARE BIGGER THAN GOD

*Daily Mirror, 9 July 1997*

What larks. At the height of his band's imperial phase, Noel Gallagher needed little encouragement to give an affirmative answer to a question from an NME interviewer: 'Do you think Oasis are more important to the youth of today than God?' Given his fondness for a life that occasionally suggested a school play about The Beatles, the echoes of John Lennon's 1966 'bigger than Jesus' controversy were obviously irresistible, and the papers duly played the required role. 'Noel's amazing claim stuns Church', was the sub-heading – but God, as far as anyone knew, was unbothered.

## ELVIS IS ALIVE

*Sunday Sport, 9 October 1988*

An archetypal headline from the paper that was launched as a meld of the USA's National Enquirer and a low-end soft-porn title (with sport), before essentially becoming a low-end soft-porn title (with sport). 'Incredible photographs' apparently proved that the King was alive, if still fat, and thereby 'rocked the world', though we remain more taken with two inside stories: 'Sex swap stars wild nights with Bowie and Sting' (page 13) and 'Mars baby slung out of UFO' (page 7).

*Johnny Rotten: 'Filth and fury' (with chips)*

23

# ROGER WATERS VS DAVID GILMOUR

**A masterclass in rock feuding, over 20 years and six rounds. Ding ding!**

## ROUND 1: Is it Pink Floyd without Roger Waters?

**Waters**: 'Pink Floyd has become a spent force creatively, and this should be recognised in order to maintain the integrity and reputation of the group name…It is only realistic and honest to admit that the group has in practical terms disbanded and should be allowed to retire gracefully from the music scene.' *From a legal deposition, 1986*

**Gilmour**: 'I don't understand why Roger is doing this…If he'd put all that time and energy into his own career instead of trying to fuck us up, he might be in a stronger position than he actually is. He's lost all sympathy, it seems to me, with the press and a lot of the public too, judging by some of the things we see at the concerts: kids wearing "Fuck Roger" and "Roger Who?" T-shirts.' *1988*

## ROUND 2: Stadium rock: evil, or what?

**Waters**: 'I wrote The Wall as an attack on stadium rock – and there's Pink Floyd making money out of it by playing it in stadiums! That's for them to live with. They have to bear the cross of that betrayal.' *1992*

**Gilmour**: 'I see no reason to apologise for wanting to make music and earn money. That's what we do…I personally think that our music is suited to larger venues.' *1994*

## ROUND 3: And what about 1994's The Division Bell, eh?

**Gilmour**: 'I really like The Division Bell, although I wouldn't say it's an immediate album. You have to put a bit of work in to get out of it the riches that are there.' *1994*

**Waters**: 'It had got totally Spinal Tap by then. Lyrics written by the new wife *[writer Polly Samson, who Gilmour married in July 1994]*. Well, they were! I mean, give me a fucking break! Come on! And what a nerve: to call that Pink Floyd. It was an awful record.' *2004*

## ROUND 4: Who's the best musician?

**Gilmour**: 'What we miss of Roger is his drive, his focus, his lyrical brilliance, many things. But I don't think any of us would say that music was one of the main ones…He's not a great musician, our Rog. God bless him. He just isn't.' *1994*

**Waters**: 'That's crap. There's no question that Dave…is a great guitar player. But the idea, which he's tried to propagate over the years, that he's somehow more musical than I am, is absolute fucking nonsense.' *2003*

## ROUND 5: So, any chance of you two making up then?

**Gilmour**: 'I think he's got my phone number and I've got his. But I have no interest in discussing anything with him. He's told too many lies and too many bad things have happened.' *1990*

**Waters**: 'I don't miss Dave, to be honest with you. I don't think we have enough in common for it to be worth either of our whiles to attempt to rekindle anything.' *2003*

## ROUND 6: Hell freezes over – the reunion at Live 8, July 2005

**Waters**: 'It was terrific. I really loved it. I hope we do it again. It was more than good…Live 8 was *so* great.' *2005*

**Gilmour**: 'The Live 8 thing was great, but it was closure. It was like sleeping with your ex-wife. There's no future for Pink Floyd.' *2006*

*Dave and Roger, 2005: "Do you fancy doing this again?" 'No, you bastard.'*

# BOLLOCKS!

## Bob Geldof, Margaret Thatcher, iPods and Sting: the collected targets of Paul Weller

'People like Bob Geldof, setting themselves up as spokesmen for the kids, make me spew.'
*1977*

'When did punk go wrong? When The Clash became just like any other rock band. All those pictures of them in biker jackets with their hands in their pockets, like, "We might be holding a gun." Or a fucking water pistol.'
*1995*

'I think U2 are a load of wallies. If they had long hair and wore headbands, no one would look twice at them.'
*1983*

'I don't understand what Bono – or Bow-now, or however you pronounce it – is trying to tell me. Is it that the world is shit and false? Well, I knew that already. Why is he always swaggering? Why that mock rock star arrogance? What's the concept? Why not just be a rock star and get on with it?'
*1994*

'I haven't got the internet in my house…I think it's the Devil's Window.'
*2008*

'It's like a mini fridge. With no fucking beers in it.'
*On the iPod, 2008*

'I'd rather eat my own shit than do a duet with James Blunt.'
*2006*

'How do I feel about being called the Eric Clapton of the 1990s? Bollocks. Fucking bollocks. I've still got an edge in my music, hopefully always will

have – and if my music ever got as laid-back and mellow as Eric Clapton's, I pack it in. Or shoot myself.'
*1995*

'I think they were absolute fucking scum – especially Thatcher, who I think should be shot as a traitor to the people. I still think that, and nothing will ever change my opinion.'
*On the Conservative governments of the '80s and '90s, 2008*

'I can't stand Q *[magazine]*. It's a load of intellectual bollocks.'
*1994*

'I don't like the crappy slogans Wham! have got: "Make it big" and "Go for it". Go for fucking what? An all-year suntan?'
*1985*

'The Style Council records sound a lot better than fucking Wake Me Up Before You Go-Go. I think we won. Mods rule.'
*1995*

'He's a fucking horrible man. Not my cup of tea at all. Fucking rubbish. No edge, no attitude, no nothing.'
*On Sting, 2007*

'You can't blame me for the New Romantics. I'm an old romantic. Terrible, wasn't it? There seemed to be a lot of the old punks involved. They went underground for a while and resurfaced in frills. I've never lived in North London, you see. That's quite important.'
*1995*

'I talk a lot of shit a lot of the time, and people should remember that.'
*1996*

*Paul Weller: won't be getting an iPod, then*

# LEMMY THINK...

The worldly opinions of the King of Motörhead – amazingly, all taken from one interview (January 2000, Sunset Strip, Los Angeles)

## On losing his virginity

'It was on a beach in Anglesey. Just starting to rain, it was. I didn't realise how much moisture you'd create, and how you'd pick up all that sand. It took me weeks to get it out. It must have been hell for her.'

## On violence

'Fighting doesn't mean shit to me. My last fight was probably on Portobello Road, years ago. Oh, and I took a gun off a geezer over here *[in LA]*. He drove by in a van, and me and this bird were waiting for the lights to change. He shouted something, and she said, "Fuck off, creep", and the van pulled over and he got out with this big silver .45 automatic. He looked like he was going to shoot her. So I just reached out and took the gun out of his hand. What are you gonna do? See the chick get shot? I just grabbed it. He was half drunk anyway. Then again, so was I, or else I'd never have done it. I was thinking, I'm going to die now. Fucking hell. What did I do with the gun? Threw it down the grid. It's probably still there. But don't print that. Put, "It happened on Portobello Road, ten years ago".'

## On being in legendary spacerockers Hawkwind

'It was like fucking Fellini's Satyricon half the time. We had one chick who was double-jointed dancing with us. She was really dainty and little and blonde, but a sexual pervert of the first order. She'd skip out in this little white dress, and roll all her bones out of the joints and assume this impossible position. And everyone would go, "Aaaaargh!", cos they were all tripping.'

## On Saturday morning kids' TV

'I never got in the cage on *[classic ITV show]* Tiswas. Phil Taylor *[Motörhead drummer]* went in and dragged our manager with him. Me and Eddie *[Clarke, guitarist]* only got buckets of water thrown over us. That was a great fucking show, man. Sally James? She was there. Tasty to look at on TV, but in the flesh…pleasant enough, I suppose. I was on Tiswas twice.'

## On his infamous Nazi memorabilia collection

'Did I really get Adolph Hitler's autograph from Ozzy Osbourne? Yeah. He gave it to me cos he knew I collected that sort of thing. He got it off Bob Daisley, who was his bass player. It's on the wall in my apartment, just as you walk in. It says, "Merry Christmas and Happy New Year, Adolph Hitler". What's it worth? Very little. He signed a lot of shit, man.'

## There's more…

'What's the most valuable item I own? My Damascus steel Luftwaffe sword. I'm not going to tell you how much it cost. It made me wince to write the cheque. It's a beautiful thing, though. They made the best shit. It's not my fault. If the Israeli army made the best shit, I'd collect their stuff. But they don't.'

## On teaching Sid Vicious to play the bass

'I tried, but he was impossible. It was before he joined the Pistols, when he was living on the couch in the squat we were in, in Holland Park. Nice house, man. Leopardskin couch. Vish *[i.e. Sid]* saw it and immediately commandeered it, with Viv from The Slits, who he was having an affair with. He was alright, Sid. He was always a gentleman with me. I got quite upset when he died. He never had a chance. He was trying to be all the people he admired and it was impossible for him. But that fucking Nancy Spungen…I'd have strangled her if he hadn't have knifed her. She was the Courtney Love of her day.'

## On recording the 1980 single Don't Do That with the one-off Young & Moody Band, featuring a handful of hard-rock royalty (e.g. drummer Cozy Powell), and the Nolan sisters on backing vocals – and suggestions that he might have 'got off' with one of the latter…

'Two hours in a recording studio's hardly enough to build up mutual trust, is it? And there's four of them. It's very hard to crack four. You can crack two, three's difficult, and four's impossible. I fancied a couple of them. The Nolan blow-job rumour? I'll tell you what that was. We were at Top Of The Pops, and our manager was stood talking to one of them. He dropped his lighter on the floor and he went down for it, and she said, "While you're down there." You don't expect one of the Nolan sisters to say that.'

## On Mark Lamarr, Never Mind The Buzzcocks, and why Lemmy walked out (in March 1998)

'He's a stand-up comedian? Well, he's not very funny. For a start, I noticed him rehearsing all the ad-libs for an hour before the show. And I wouldn't join in: I said, "Fuck it, if it's an ad-lib you don't practise it – it's *ad-libbed*." So they didn't like that; they had the knives out. And then these four birds came on, one of whom was that chick out of – what was it? – Brotherhood Of Man? No, Bucks Fizz. And they fucking laid into them chicks, and the chicks hadn't even got a mike to defend themselves. "Didn't I see you down the whorehouse", and all this shit. Really neanderthal stuff. And I just said, "Fuck it – cutting edge of British comedy? I don't have to sit here on this rubbish fucking show." I got up and fucked off. They cut the show to make it seem that I didn't split. But I did.'

## On sexual adventure, kind of thing

'I went with a sex change once, who'd had his dick removed. He was female – as long as there isn't a dick, you know what I mean? It was convincing, believe me. Nice tits. Better than most of the girls at the time. It was at the Embassy Club in Old Bond Street. Tasty, she was. Really pretty.'

## On drugs

'What's the longest I've ever been awake? Two weeks. That was the old days, when you could get the good stuff. You know that "Speed kills" thing? Bullshit. It doesn't kill anybody. I'll always prefer speed to cocaine: cocaine makes you think you're gonna throw up, wears off too quick and you go to sleep on it. What's the point of that?'

## On whether the rumour that he now shuns the full sexual picnic is true

'It has been for the last nine or ten years. Laziness, I think. All that humping and jumping around, shifting positions…you get the chick's foot up your nose. A knee in the groin always calms the ardour. I just got lazier. I like to be pampered more. Is it alright with the women concerned? Well, either that or they go. But I return the favour. You've got to be a gentleman.'

## On the prospect of getting his legendary facial appendages removed

'I've thought about it – but then I found out the price. Do I have warts anywhere else? I used to have 19 on this hand *[holds up right hand]*. And that proves that these ones are moles.'

*Lemmy: 'You've got to be a gentleman'*

# 'I DELIVER THE GODDAMN GOODS'

## Courtney Love: the quote machine made of 100 per cent rock'n'roll fibre

'He thought I was too demanding, attention-wise. He thought I was too obnoxious. I had to go out of my way to impress him.' *On Kurt Cobain, 1992*

'I'm laying in our bed, and I'm really sorry, and I feel the same way as you do. I'm sorry, you guys. I don't know what I could have done. I wish I'd been there. I wish I hadn't listened to other people. But I did…I have to go now. Just tell him he's a fucker, OK? Just say, "Fucker, you're a fucker." And that you love him.' *From the taped message played to the Seattle vigil following Cobain's suicide, 1994*

'My goal keeps me alive. And no personal issue is going to interfere with that. If people try and put me in the crazy box – "crazy fucking Courtney"– go ahead. But if you think you're going to stop me from where I'm going, you're not going to do it. I work my ass off. I deliver the goddamn goods. And I will deliver them again.' *In her first interview after the death, 1994*

'She's going to grow up in Seattle, in a really good neighbourhood. Peter Buck lives behind us, and there's this coffee shop next door…yes, it's a poncey neighbourhood and rich kids can be so awful, but I am not going let her get above herself. She was awful on the plane coming over here and I decided right then, "Two years of boarding school for you." Boarding school was good for me. So was jail.' *On her daughter Frances Bean Cobain, 1994*

'In my parallel universe, the No 1 album would always be Captain Beefheart's Trout Mask Replica. Kurt and I fucked to that record once. It was amazing sex.' *1994*

'This thing about me being crazy actually works sometimes. Let them think I'm crazy! In business, if they think I'm crazy, they'll fill out the fucking cheque.' *2002*

'I did take heroin when I was in the very beginning of my pregnancy. I did. Otherwise I could have sued the hell out of them. *[But journalist Lynne Hirschberg was]* completely

wrong, She made it seem like I was taking drugs into my *second* trimester.' *1995, on a 1992 Vanity Fair story she said 'ruined her life'*

'When Madonna did that Rolling Stone cover with me and Tina Turner, she took me to her office and she said, "You don't have photo approval?" "No." "You don't sign your own cheques?" "No." "You're a fucking idiot! This is how you do it." And she has this ledger, and once a week she sits and signs her cheques and she has a red pen and she writes, No! or Fuck off! And that's how you keep control.' *2002*

'I was at the V&A *[museum]* and got talking to Vivienne Westwood, Dame Vivienne, and I said, "Great to meet you. I'm a huge fan," and she said, "We've met before. And we talked on the phone for three hours one time." I had zero recollection of it. I said, "Was I horrible? Was I boring?" She said, "No, I would have hung up on you if you had been. You were terribly amusing."' *2007*

*Courtney: 'too demanding, attention-wise'? Surely not*

# John Lydon
## The Q Awards, November 2001.
### Roll the tapes...

'America's a fantastic country. It's new, it's undiscovered, it's undeveloped. They're mad, but they have a great openness to new things, which you don't get in England any more. Here, everything new is hated and resented. You're happy with that scratchy toilet paper. I'm sorry – I like a bit of aloe vera on my bum now.'

'Where was I on September 11? I was with my very good cousin, Bin Lydon.'

'My misdemeanours 30 years back still haven't been taken off the record. And that buggers up my visas and anything else you care to mention. My only crime in life is – what? Amphetamine sulphate. For fuck's sake. That's a mediocre version of viagra, isn't it? And the way they cut it up in London at the moment, it might as well be valium.'

'When did I last walk around *[his native]* Finsbury Park? You don't walk around Finsbury Park – you run.'

'I burned Sid Vicious's suicide note on TV because that's what Sid would have liked. That's not disrespect; Sid's my fucking friend. A suicide note – he'd have realised that was corny. And the idea that it'd be worth money to someone? This is embarrassing shit. Some collector who knows nothing about either of us having that in his private drawing room? It's terrible. We didn't do this shit so wealthy people could collect our underwear.'

'Paul McCartney: I've met him a few times over the last couple of years, and I really like the bloke. I was quite chuffed to know that. He doesn't present himself too well on TV – he comes over too dopey. But he's much better when the cameras are off. We trade tapes. I like Elton John, too. What a bang-on bloke.'

'Who the fuck wrote the rules about music? Why are we following this slavish idiocy? Actually, that was the difference between me and Glen Matlock. He thought music ended when Chuck Berry declared that rock'n'roll was four to the bar. For me, it's 22 of my mates *at* the bar.'

# Mark E Smith
## A pub in Notting Hill, April 1993.
### Your fourth pint, sir...

'It's all take the fuckin' money and run at the moment, isn't it? I mean. I'm no socialist but they're trying to apply an American system over here and they haven't got the fuckin' guts to push it through. I mean, you can't even smoke in lifts anymore.'

'I think Nirvana are a load of wop; biggest heap of crap I've ever seen. They're just fuckin' college kids who are lucky enough to have the money to sit around all day wearing sweaty check shirts.'

'It's really not that bad in Britain. From the last few European tours we've done, I reckon it's a lot worse over there. I mean, I always wish the bastards who talk about Europe would fuckin' wake up. When John Major's going on about how great Europe is, I'd like to get him on our fuckin' tour bus and dump him in Valencia or somewhere and say, "Go and have a walk round and have a fucking look", you know what I mean? He'd see worse litter than around here. He reminds me very much of Chamberlain in the '30s. Very similar. I mean, Europe is completely unstable, so what does he do? He cuts the army by half and closes the coal mines down. It's exactly what Chamberlain did. And when the Nazis went off we were fucking zapped. He's got the same shopkeeper attitude. Lions led by fucking donkeys. It's true.'

'When I was 13, the only concerts you could go to were Emerson Lake & Palmer or fuckin' Yes. You'd turn on the radio and get Whispering Bob Harris. And that's part of what frightens me, cos now, I get back from the pub and switch on the radio and Bob Harris is back! I fought a revolution to get rid of people like him. I did! I had ashtrays thrown at my head by longhairs. And now all these groups are playing Led Zeppelin tunes – that's what groups like The Fall were formed to fight against.'

# STATUS QUO: AN ORAL HISTORY
### It's like Spinal Tap! Only real!

Starring: Francis Rossi (vocals/guitar), Rick Parfitt (guitar/vocals), Alan Lancaster (bass/vocals) and John Coghlan (drums)

## LONDON, 1970

*First called The Spectres, the great British institution that is 'the Quo' released their first single in 1967: a cod-psychedelic Top 10 hit titled Pictures Of Matchstick Men. By the end of 1969, however, things were on the move: blues-influenced 'boogie' was the new thing, along with a reinvented image, as seen on the cover of the 1970 album Ma Kelly's Greasy Spoon.*

**FR**: When it came to doing the photo, we knew about it in advance. We drove, did a gig, didn't wash. Did the next night's gig, didn't wash or shave, and then drove to London overnight. It had to look like that. From then on, I'd always shave at night, so there'd be a bit of stubble the next morning. *[Pause]* Fucking hell – that's how designer stubble was invented.

## THE CASTLE, TOOTING, 1970

**RP**: This was a heads' gig: trench coat, pint, album under your arm, sitting on the floor. It was the first time we'd played to an audience that was sitting down, and we were thinking, Blimey, this is weird. The stage was only three inches high, but I remember the audience being down *there*. You had to get down to the audience – so this is how the legs apart, head down thing happened. And they were all nodding their heads, so we thought, Do the same, copy the audience – you can't go wrong. We only looked up between numbers. And the Quo stance was born.

*Rossi (left) and Coghlan: 'didn't wash or shave'*

## BIELEFELD, WEST GERMANY, EARLY 1970s

*The West German town served as Status Quo's base during extensive European touring. There were rum goings on…*

**FR**: One of the guys we knew had a Cine 8 projector, with these films. Everyone would check into the Central Hotel in Bielefeld, get a towel, and come back to one of the rooms. The projector was set up so it'd go on to the net curtains – but it would also project across the street. We didn't know this. People would walk down the street seeing huge tits and knobs on this wall. Everyone would be on the bed, having a polish. You did everything in each other's company, so having a polish was nothing to worry about. I remember a German girl in among all this – these blokes who were clearly aroused – saying, 'English man? Shag?' It was like, 'Shut up! I'm trying to have a polish'.

## FRANCIS ROSSI'S HOUSE, 1973

*Their run of peak-period hits began with Paper Plane in January 1973, followed later that year by an LP titled Hello!, which opened with Roll Over Lay Down, a song – as with 1974's Down Down – with domestic inspirations…*

**FR**: I had problems with my wife. She'd sit up on my side of the bed, waiting for me to come in. I have to sleep on my side of the bed, so I'd try and move her over. So that was it: 'Roll over lay down, let me get in' – as in 'for fuck's sake'. People still think it's about sex. The same with Down Down. It didn't mean *going down*. The idea of going down on someone in the '70s – no chance. People weren't hygienic in this country, let me tell you. You weren't going to go near *that*.

## VARIOUS LOCATIONS, 1974 ONWARDS

*And so the Quo's imperial phase began: hit after hit, a good deal of touring, and very nice houses…*

**JC**: I must be the only person who's been to Venice and not seen any water. We did the gig in the dark, left in the dark, and went straight from the hotel to the bus. Ridiculous.

**FR**: My wife used to love booking me

into these holidays. She was a funny girl like that. I remember coming back *[from tour]* one time, putting my bags down, and there was another set of bags in the hall. We were going out the following day to the Canary Islands – on a package tour. I went, 'Oh no – you haven't booked us on a package?! Why didn't you just book us a flight?' Two weeks of, 'You're in Status Quo, aren't you?' Non-stop. I was dying.

**RP**: I had a couple of big houses: one in West Byfleet, and another one in Hambledon *[Hampshire]*. Snooker table, swimming pool, 24-track recording studio, five cars, all the trappings. A rock star's house. I had a bar in the reception room, and the driveway was fucking miles long. Life had changed.

**AL**: I had a big swimming pool, the round bath with the mirrored ceilings, cocktail bar. Tastefully done, mind.

## SWEDEN, 1977

*Status Quo's tenth studio album was Rockin' All Over The World, recorded in Gothenburg with producer Pip Williams, who would go on to work with ex-Rainbow singer Graham Bonnet, The Moody Blues and Richard O'Brien from The Rocky Horror Show.*

**AL**: In comes Pip Williams, and in come the strings, the chick singers, the brass, the keyboards, the triple-tracked solos. What he did to us ruined us. He raped us.

**FR**: We had loads of letters from fans saying 'What the fuck have you done?' I think it's a poxy record, I really do.

**RP**: I loved it. I completely disagree with him: that was a fantastic album. We do half that fucking shit on stage. What a great album.

## VARIOUS LOCATIONS, 1980

*Somewhat improbably, the group didn't discover cocaine until the end of the 1970s, when Parfitt and Rossi took, shall we say, a great deal.*

**RP**: I'd be away from home for two or three days at a stretch, doing coke, sleeping in top hotels. I couldn't go out unless I had some with me. You start living life at that level, and anything below it is a grey, boring place to be. I suppose I was doing two or three grand a week on coke and booze. You turn into an animal – and the real drag about it is that you don't know it.

**FR**: I'd get up, have a toot, get in the shower. If I didn't have a toot till lunchtime, what a good lad I'd been. I was doing two-and-a-half, three grams a day, for ten years. That's how I blew my nose out. When did that happen? I don't know. I just noticed there was a hole one day.

## LIVE AID, 1985

*John Coghlan left in 1980. In 1984, Status Quo announced their retirement from touring and live performance, but were persuaded to open Live Aid, starting with Rockin' All Over The World.*

**JC**: Live Aid was hard for me. Alan Lancaster said, 'We should get John back for this'. I'd gladly have done it. The original four should have been back together. But I thought, Oh fuck it – if they can't be bothered to phone me up, then bollocks.

**FR**: Live Aid was pretty grim. I thought we were crap.

## AN UNSPECIFIED BRITISH AIRPORT, 2000

*Rossi and Parfitt formed a new Status Quo without Alan Lancaster (who now lives in Australia) in 1985. John Coghlan has been known to occasionally sit in with a Quo tribute band called State of Quo. Meanwhile, the show goes on…*

**FR**: I was arriving at the airport back from Amsterdam recently. The guy said, 'Where've you been?' I said, 'You know where I've been – it's on the luggage label, and that's why you've pulled me in.' This carried on until I said, 'Amsterdam'. He said, 'What did you go there for?' I said, 'Well, not that it's your business, but to shag the wife, get away from the children, eat some fantastic food and smoke some dope.' He said, 'You admit it then.' He looked up my arse and everything – 'Can you lift your testicles up?' I was there for two or three hours. And at the end he said, 'I'm a great fan of yours – I'm coming to see you in Brighton with the girls from Debenhams.'

*Lancaster and Parfitt (right): big houses – 'tastefully done, mind'*

# THE JOE STRUMMER GUIDE TO MUSIC HISTORY
## From Henry VIII to Acid House

**① The pre-rock era**

'Do you know who the first DJ was? He was the highest paid official in the court of Henry VIII, and his job was to assess the king's mood and then to choose what wood to put on the fire. So if Henry was fucking pissed off and about to have another of his wives' heads chopped off, he'd lay on some pine, say, to bring him down a bit, chill him out. But then if Henry was getting drunk and rowdy, he'd choose the oak to mellow him out. He'd order in stock, trying to guess how things would be in the weeks ahead – "I'll have some beech and a double load of oak – oh, and an extra bit of pine, just in case." So he was like the first DJ, man: the original selector.' *1997*

**② Early rock**

'I saw a TV programme where they were taking the piss by reading out the lyrics of Be Bop A Lula: "She's my baby…I don't mean maybe." They didn't understand that it's Gene Vincent and that's it – the meaning of life is revealed immediately.' *1979*

'People can get caught thinking it's all about technique, when in fact it's not really about technique at all. It's about something even more exciting and unidentifiable. Everybody else was playing 12-bar blues at the time *[Bo Diddley]* kicked off, so he said to himself, I have to do something different if I want to make it in this town. So he came up with something even more African than the blues is: the Bo Diddley style. Also, he taught Mick Jagger how to sing. I think Jagger's a great singer, but when you listen to his American accent inside his songs, it's actually Bo Diddley's.' *1979*

**③ The '60s**

'Not Fade Away *[by The Rolling Stones]* sounded like the road to freedom. Seriously. It said, "Live! Enjoy life! Fuck chartered accountancy!"' *1988*

'The reason that Motown brought out so many great records is because there was a really heavy structure there. They wouldn't stand for any pop star-ism, right? Their writers – they were just writers who were writing, and if they came up with a duff song, the management would turn round and go, "That's a duff song." That's why only the good songs came through. The singers? They realised they had to really sing it well: "If you can't sing it, we'll give it to this lot who are waiting in the hallway." Lack of preciousness: "If you can't do it, we'll get someone else." That made people really jive to it.' *1984*

'Bob Dylan, right? Like A Rolling Stone. Heavy song, number one, worldwide smash. Bob Dylan was *there*: the radical beat poet was there, to take the jewel crown of pop and make the world something different. And, of course, he came out with Can You Please Crawl Out Your Window? I've read accounts of him playing it to his friends, going, "Well, isn't it great? Don't you think it's great? This is my latest masterpiece. Isn't it great?" And they were kind of going, "Mmmmm…well…it's…er…erm…" "Shut up. It's great." He wouldn't have it, that it wasn't great. Whereas if you play Like A Rolling Stone now and play Can You Please Crawl Out Your Window?, you can see that Can You Please Crawl Out Your Window? is a half-baked load of mish-mash, nich-nach nothing.' *1984*

**④ The pre-punk '70s**

'It's got nothing to do with them *[The Kids]* anymore, when, like, Rod Stewart gets up there and starts going on with his string orchestra. It's not what you feel like. So you've got to have music what you feel like *[sic]*. Otherwise you go barmy, don't you?' *1976*

**⑤ The punk wars**

'Yesterday I thought I was a crud. Then I saw the Sex Pistols and I became a king and decided to move into the future.' *1976*

'After they *[the Pistols]* sacked *[Glen]* Matlock, that was the end, because Matlock was the tunesmith. That shows how crazy they were – just because he liked The Beatles, they sacked him.' *1988*

'We just happen to dig Tapper Zukie and Big Youth, Dillinger and Aswad and Delroy Washington. We dig them and we ain't scared of going into heavy black record shops and getting their gear. We even go to heavy black gigs where we're the only white people there.' *On The Clash's love of reggae, 1976*

'We thought we could make pop real again… We didn't realise what a lonely road it was going to be. We didn't know the punk movement was going to fall apart, that Siouxsie And The Banshees would become like Led Zeppelin, that the Pistols would fall apart so fast, that Rotten would get a Holiday Inn band and The Damned would become comedians.' *1984*

'I've met the people whose attitudes punk changed. Literally – I feel like I've met every single one of them! And the story is the same for all of them: we changed their minds individually and that affected the decisions they made in their own lives. It wasn't a mass thing; the mob storming the palace. It was lots of individuals who grasped some of the things we were honking on about.' *2001*

⑥ **The '80s and after**
'Adolescents make the best records. Except for Paul Simon. Except for Graceland. He's hit a new plateau there, but he's writing to his own age group. Graceland is something new. That song to his son *[That Was Your Mother]* is just as good as Blue Suede Shoes: "Before you were born, dude/ When life was great." That's just as good as Blue Suede Shoes, and that is a new dimension.' *1988*

'Boy George: everybody in the world falling over themselves, saying how wonderful he can sing. He can't even begin to sing. I don't even pretend I can sing, but he pretends he can. And half his material should have been dumped before it was even thought of…I don't buy these records, cos I've got more sense, but I hear them over the radio. Sometimes they play a few album tracks of his, and it's like…an audible Kleenex. It's about as worthy as a Kleenex.' *1984*

'Standing in a kitchen listening to rave music, I couldn't understand it. I had to go to a rave to understand it. And after about four hours we were supposed to go into a trance. In fact, I *was* going into a trance. And I thought, Say we were in a forest, and there was nothing to do, apart from these big empty logs. Say we were pygmies or something. All we'd be doing by lunchtime – we'd be standing round these logs with big sticks, going, Dumm-dumm-dummm!' *1989*

*Strummer: the world's only expert on Henry VIII (far left) and Big Youth (above)*

33

# Chapter 2

# THE STAGE

I n musical terms, the summer of 1985 was memorable for two things: Live Aid, and an inescapable, teeth-grindingly bad single called Live Is Life, made by an Austrian group called Opus. They're still going, apparently, with ten original albums to their name, and a drummer called Günter Grasmuck.

But anyway. That song was not exactly high art. Its opening four lines were, 'Nanananana/Nanananana (all together now)/Nanananana/Nanananana', and the lyrics were apparently about very little at all. Trying to nail exactly what it was doing to people was hard then and is even harder now, but here are two possible clues: it was recorded in front of a paying audience, and its title was Live Is Life. Somewhere in those two facts – along with the 'nanananana' bit – lay the explanation for the reason that it loitered around the British charts for fifteen weeks. Fifteen weeks!

'Live is life,' then. We should now cut Günter Grasmuck and his friends a bit of slack, and acknowledge that they were on to something. It would be nice to think that what they meant was this: that somewhere in the crackle of amplifiers and screech of feedback, the clack of trampled plastic glasses, some moron jumping onstage and shouting 'Hello Northwich!' – well, that way lies the essence of rock music's magic.

Time was, this was very nearly forgotten. Because of the problem of playing to thousands of screaming adolescents using tiny amplifiers and the Public Address systems used for announcements at baseball games, The Beatles quit the live stage in 1966. At around the same time, The Rolling Stones came close to doing the same thing. Then, fortunately, someone invented Big Speakers, the screams died down a bit, and the live experience really got going: tours became year-long affairs, outdoor spectaculars became bigger and more bombastic – and by the 1980s, for better or worse, we were in the age of Stadium Rock. Meanwhile, the public fondness for absorbing rock music in more cosy surroundings never went away, and despite serial ups and downs, the British institution we know as The Toilet Venue is still with us, and prospering.

Still, behind even the most thrilling spectacles, there is a lot of less glorious stuff. If you have ever been to a drum soundcheck ('Duh-duh-duh'; 'That's good, Barry – now the hi-hat'), you will be aware of this. From a distance, touring the world may look like a never-ending thrill, but you will be lucky to find many musicians who relish every last moment. Just before I wrote this, I read an interview with Kings Of Leon, in which their bass player said, 'I hate touring more than anything in the world.' What with homesickness, a great deal of boredom, too much booze and the certainty of bad gigs, you can just about see his point.

There again, what really is the problem? Never let it be forgotten: quite apart from the fact that the hoop-la surrounding live performance can actually be a scream (motorbikes ridden through hotel foyers, the obligatory 'aftershow' etc.), when everything is going right, there are few more thrilling things than a great rock concert. You could look in any number of places for a poetic portrait of all this, but my own favourite is in Lipstick Traces, a book by the American writer Greil Marcus that finds him rhapsodising about the Sex Pistols' final concert at the Winterland ballroom in San Francisco, on 14 January 1978.

From the top, then. 'With the Sex Pistols onstage, everything changed. Slumping like Quasimodo under heavy air, Johnny Rotten cut through the curiosity of the crowd with a twist of his neck. He hung on to the microphone stand like a man caught in a wind tunnel: ice, paper cups, coins, books, hats and shoes flew by him as if sucked up by a vacuum…Sid Vicious was there to bait the crowd…and Sid Vicious was begging for it, for the absolute confirmation that he was a star…Paul Cook was hidden behind his drums. Steve Jones sounded like he was playing a guitar factory, not a guitar; it was inconceivable there were only three instruments onstage. The stage was full of ghosts; song by song, Johnny Rotten ground his teeth down to points.'

And so to business. The Sex Pistols are in this chapter. So are James Brown, and The Doors, and a couple of hundred of the groups who've played Glastonbury Festival. There is stuff about a venue in Tunbridge Wells located in a converted public convenience, the story of how the ex-Velvet Underground man John Cale decided to decapitate a chicken in Croydon, and a reminder of some of the great rock props, from a giant pig to a replica World War II bomber, now retired, and reckoned to be 'holding up a shed' in Norfolk.

Just about every aspect of the human zoo is here; like the Austrians said, Live is life. Nananananana.

# THE BRITISH TOILET CIRCUIT

A guide to the UK's more intimate – and legendary – indie-rock venues

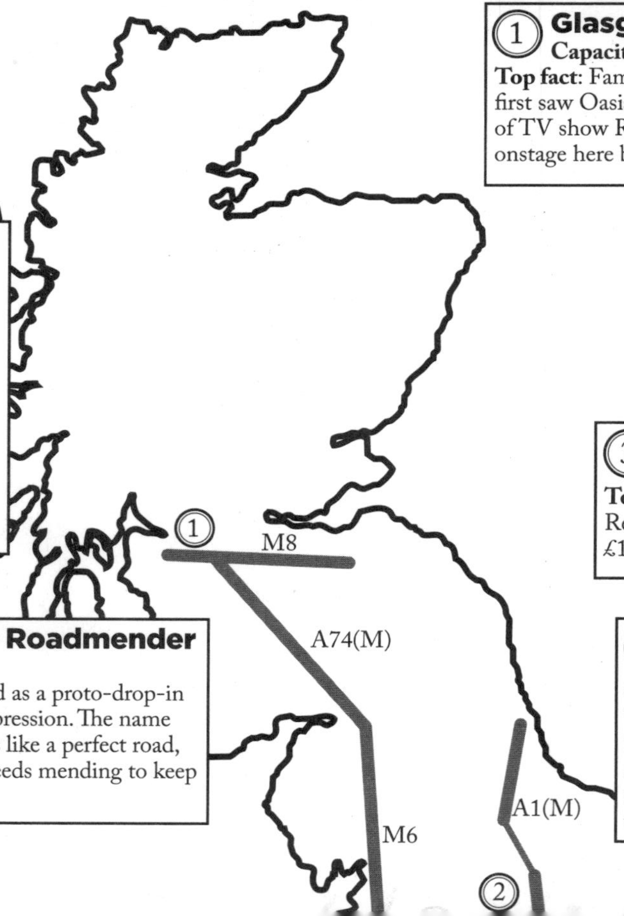

## ① Glasgow King Tut's Wah Wah Hut
**Capacity:** 300
**Top fact:** Famously, where Creation Records boss Alan McGee first saw Oasis, which is getting boring. So try this: In 2006 the star of TV show Rock School, Chris Hardman (Lil' Chris), was joined onstage here by the show's host, Kiss's Gene Simmons.

## ② Leeds Cockpit
**Capacity:** 500 (main room)
**Top fact:** Hosted Brighton Beach, the Britpop club night that catalysed the formation of local fellas Kaiser Chiefs.

## ③ Sheffield Leadmill
**Capacity:** 900
**Top fact:** Culture Club played here the week Do You Really Want To Hurt Me? reached No 1. Entry price: £1. A year later they declined to book Madonna.

## ④ Leicester Charlotte (formerly Princess Charlotte)
**Capacity:** 200
**Top fact:** Location for what Noel Gallagher sees as Oasis's fourth best-ever gig: 'I put my guitar down and set the delay pedal going, then ran for my life. I ended up in the dressing room with one shoe.' At time of writing it was under threat of closure.

## ⑯ Hull Adelphi
**Capacity:** 200
**Top fact:** Cleverly situated in a former housing terrace.

## ⑮ Manchester Roadhouse
**Capacity:** 250
**Top fact:** The entire membership of Elbow have worked here at one time or another. Singer Guy Garvey was initially a barman before being deemed 'not very good' and reassigned to duties on the door.

## ⑭ Northampton Roadmender
**Capacity:** 900
**Top fact:** Originally opened as a proto-drop-in centre during the 1930s depression. The name refers to the idea that 'life is like a perfect road, but one that occasionally needs mending to keep in shape'.

A1(M)

M6

A74(M)

M8

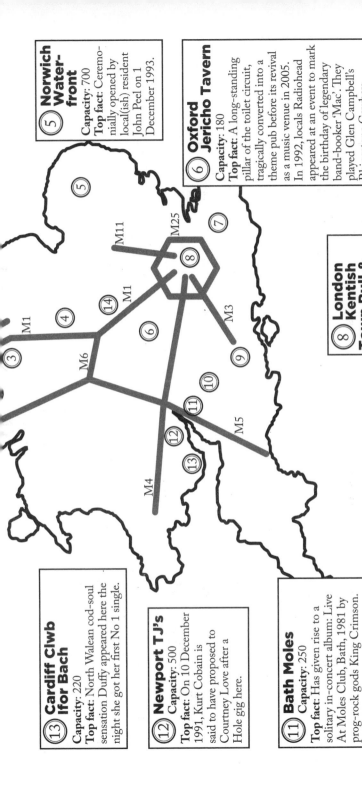

**⑤ Norwich Waterfront**

Capacity: 700
**Top fact:** Ceremonially opened by local(ish) resident John Peel on 1 December 1993.

**⑥ Oxford Jericho Tavern**

Capacity: 180
**Top fact:** A long-standing pillar of the toilet circuit, tragically converted into a theme pub before its revival as a music venue in 2005. In 1992, locals Radiohead appeared at an event to mark the birthday of legendary band-booker 'Mac'. They played Glen Campbell's Rhinestone Cowboy.

**⑦ Tunbridge Wells Forum**

Capacity: 250
**Top fact:** An actual, real life toilet venue, converted from a former public loo. No joke.

**⑧ London Kentish Town Bull & Gate**

Capacity: 150
**Top fact:** A genuine indie institution. According to the people currently in charge, neo-prog trio Muse once played here 'to two people'.

**⑨ Southampton Joiners**

Capacity: 150
**Top fact:** Local legend claims that Jimi Hendrix played here en route to the Isle of Wight Festival in 1970.

**⑩ Trowbridge Psychic Pig**

Capacity: 300 (though shifted location)
**Top fact:** Tragically defunct since 2006, but hosted first gig by Radiohead in 1991. Says co-manager Mark Johnston: 'I was offered this band called On A Friday for £50. When they turned up they insisted that we billed them as Radiohead.'

**⑪ Bath Moles**

Capacity: 250
**Top fact:** Has given rise to a solitary in-concert album: Live At Moles Club, Bath, 1981 by prog-rock gods King Crimson.

**⑫ Newport TJ's**

Capacity: 500
**Top fact:** On 10 December 1991, Kurt Cobain is said to have proposed to Courtney Love after a Hole gig here.

**⑬ Cardiff Clwb Ifor Bach**

Capacity: 220
**Top fact:** North Walean cod-soul sensation Duffy appeared here the night she got her first No 1 single.

Map road labels: M1, M11, M25, M6, M1, M3, M11, M4, M5

# GLASTONBURY: A COMPLETE HISTORY

**1970** *Line-up:* T.Rex, Al Stewart, Stackridge, Roy Harper, Steamhammer, Quintessence, The Amazing Blondel, Duster Bennet, Sam Apple Pie, Ian Anderson, Keith Christmas
*Attendance:* 2000
*Entry:* £1

**1971** *Line-up:* Traffic, David Bowie, Henry Cow, Hawkwind, Gong, The Crazy World Of Arthur Brown, Brinsley Schwarz, Family, Joan Baez, Melanie, Fairport Convention, Help Yourself, Edgar Broughton Band
*Attendance:* 12,000
*Entry:* Free

**1979** *Line-up:* Gong, The Sensational Alex Harvey Band, Steve Hillage, John Martyn, The Pop Group, Peter Gabriel, UK Subs, The Only Ones, Leyton Buzzards, Sky
*Attendance:* 12,000
*Entry:* £5

**1981** *Line-up:* New Order, Hawkwind, Matumbi, Aswad, Taj Mahal, Supercharge, Gong, Roy Harper, John Cooper Clarke, Ginger Baker, Gordon Giltrap
*Attendance:* 18,000
*Entry:* £8

**1982** *Line-up:* Van Morrison, Jackson Browne, Judie Tzuke, U2, Richie Havens, Steel Pulse, The Blues Band, Randy California, John Cooper Clarke, Sad Cafe, The Chieftains
*Attendance:* 25,000
*Entry:* £8

**1983** *Line-up:* The Beat, Marillion, Fun Boy Three, Dennis Brown with Aswad, Curtis Mayfield, UB40, The Enid, The Chieftains, Melanie, King Sunny Ade & His African Beats, A Certain Ratio, Incantation
*Attendance:* 30,000
*Entry:* £12

**1984** *Line-up:* The Smiths, The Waterboys, Billy Bragg, Fela Kuti, Dr. John, Black Uhuru, Howard Jones, Joan Baez, Ian Dury, Weather Report, Fairport Convention, Amazulu
*Attendance:* 35,000
*Entry:* £13

**1985** *Line-up:* The Pogues, The Style Council, Gil Scott Heron, Hugh Masekela, Ian Dury & The Blockheads, James, The Colour Field, Echo And The Bunnymen, Green On Red, Billy Bragg, Joe Cocker
*Attendance:* 40,000
*Entry:* £16

**1986** *Line-up:* Psychedelic Furs, The Cure, Level 42, The Housemartins, The Waterboys, Madness, The Pogues, Half Man Half Biscuit, Loudon Wainwright III
*Attendance:* 60,000
*Entry:* £17

**1987** *Line-up:* Elvis Costello, Van Morrison, The Communards, New Order, Julian Cope, Robert Cray, Los Lobos, Pop Will Eat Itself, The Soup Dragons, Hüsker Dü,
*Attendance:* 60,000
*Entry:* £21

**1989** *Line-up:* Suzanne Vega, Fela Kuti, Throwing Muses, The Bhundu Boys, Pixies, The Wonder Stuff, Ozric Tentacles, Van Morrison, Hothouse Flowers, Elvis Costello, Donovan, The Waterboys
*Attendance:* 65,000
*Entry:* £28

**1990** *Line-up:* The Cure, Happy Mondays, Jesus Jones, De La Soul, Sinead O'Connor, Ry Cooder, Aswad, Lush, Ladysmith Black Mambazo, World Party
*Attendance:* 70,000
*Entry:* £38

**1992** *Line-up:* Carter USM, Shakespear's Sister, Youssou N'Dour, Primal Scream, The Levellers, Blur, The Orb, Lush, Spiritualized, Television, PJ Harvey, Lou Reed, Tom Jones
*Attendance:* 70,000
*Entry:* £49

**1993** *Line-up:* Suede, Spiritualized, The Black Crowes, The Velvet Underground, Teenage Fanclub, Belly, Robert Plant, Midnight Oil, Lenny Kravitz, The Kinks
*Attendance:* 80,000
*Entry:* £58

**1994** *Line-up:* The Levellers, Rage Against The Machine, Björk, Blur, Beastie Boys, Paul Weller, Manic Street Preachers, Elvis Costello, The Pretenders, Johnny Cash, Peter Gabriel, Oasis, Radiohead, Pulp, Inspiral Carpets
*Attendance:* 80,000
*Entry:* £59

**1995** *Line-up:* Oasis, Pulp, The Cure, The Prodigy, The Black Crowes, PJ Harvey, Page & Plant, Jamiroquai, Orbital, Elastica, Supergrass, The Verve, Jeff Buckley, Menswear
*Attendance:* 80,000
*Entry:* £65

**1997** *Line-up:* The Prodigy, Radiohead, Beck, Supergrass, Ray Davies, Dodgy, Smashing Pumpkins, Ocean Colour Scene, Van Morrison, Sting, The Divine Comedy, Ash, Super Furry Animals, Cast
*Attendance:* 95,000
*Entry:* £75

**1998** *Line-up:* Primal Scream, Blur, Pulp, Foo Fighters, James, Robbie Williams, Stereophonics, Bob Dylan, Tony Bennett
*Attendance:* 100,000
*Entry:* £80

**1999** *Line-up:* R.E.M., Manic Street Preachers, Skunk Anansie, Kula Shaker, Hole, Blondie, Joe Strummer & The Mescaleros, Travis, Kula Shaker, Texas
*Attendance:* 100,000
*Entry:* £82

**2000** *Line-up:* Chemical Brothers, Travis, David Bowie, Pet Shop Boys, Basement Jaxx, Nine Inch Nails, Moby, The Beta Band The The, The Flaming Lips, Death In Vegas, Coldplay, David Gray, Cypress Hill
*Attendance:* 150,000
*Entry:* £87

**2002** *Line-Up:* Coldplay, Stereophonics, Rod Stewart, Garbage, Orbital, The White Stripes, The Vines, Roger Waters, Mercury Rev
*Attendance:* 100,000
*Entry:* £97

**2003** *Line-up:* R.E.M., Radiohead, Moby, Manic Street Preachers, The Flaming Lips, David Gray, The Darkness, Will Young, Interpol, Feeder, The Polyphonic Spree, The Coral, Doves, Goldfrapp, Dave Gahan, Primal Scream, Love, The Libertines
*Attendance:* 150,000
*Entry:* £105

**2004** *Line-up:* Oasis, Paul McCartney, Muse, Kings Of Leon, Morrissey, Supergrass, Chemical Brothers, Basement Jaxx, Orbital, Wilco, Scissor Sisters, PJ Harvey, James Brown, Goldfrapp, Franz Ferdinand
*Attendance:* 150,000
*Entry:* £112

**2005** *Line-up:* The White Stripes, Coldplay, Basement Jaxx, Fatboy Slim, Razorlight, Ian Brown, The La's, New Order, The Killers, Primal Scream, Kaiser Chiefs, Brian Wilson, Elvis Costello, Kasabian, Babyshambles, Kaiser Chiefs, Keane
*Attendance:* 153,000
*Entry:* £125

**2007** *Line-up:* Arctic Monkeys, The Killers, The Who, Björk, Iggy & The Stooges, Chemical Brothers, The Kooks, Manic Street Preachers, Kaiser Chiefs, Paul Weller, Kasabian, Lily Allen, Amy Winehouse, Arcade Fire, Editors, The Gossip, Hot Chip, Bloc Party, Dirty Pretty Things
*Attendance:* 175,000
*Entry:* £145

**2008** *Line-up:* Kings Of Leon, Jay-Z, The Verve, Amy Winehouse, Leonard Cohen, KT Tunstall, Crowded House, Neil Diamond, Massive Attack, Panic At The Disco, Shakin' Stevens, Kate Nash
*Attendance:* 177,500
*Entry:* £155

**2009** *Line-up:* Neil Young, Blur, Bruce Springsteen, Franz Ferdinand, The Specials, The Ting Tings, Fleet Foxes, Lily Allen, Status Quo, Kasabian, Nick Cave & The Bad Seeds
*Attendance:* 177,500
*Entry:* £175

*Glasto King Michael Eavis*

39

# HEY JUDO!

### The legendary Budokan arena – a by-word for being 'big in Japan'

Aside from Madison Square Garden – and, just possibly, London's gleaming new O₂ – there are not many huge indoor auditoriums that truly symbolise all the magic and wonder of the live experience. If you doubt this, think of two grim words: 'Wembley' and 'Arena'.

Thankfully, there is one other exception: Tokyo's Budokan. Built in 1964 for judo bouts in that year's Olympics, it eventually became an obligatory stop-off for Western musicians, and was etched into myth by a handful of live albums: **Deep Purple**'s Made In Japan (1972), **Bob Dylan**'s Dylan At Budokan (1979), **Eric Clapton**'s Just One Night (1980), Heavy Metal man **Michael Schenker**'s One Night At Budokan (1982), **Blur**'s Live At The Budokan (1996), and, perhaps most famously, At Budokan by the American power-pop quartet **Cheap Trick** (1979).

The Trick – made up of knobbly-faced drummer Bun E. Carlos, extrovert guitarist Rick Nielsen, and the cherubic Robin Zander (vocals) and Tom Petersson (bass) – played the Budokan on 28 and 30 April 1978. Though struggling at home, they were – oh yes – big in Japan. When At Budokan was released in the USA, it sold three million copies and belatedly introduced Cheap Trick to their home crowd, thanks in part to the sterling live version of I Want You To Want Me, which reached No 7 on the US singles chart.

What chiefly gave At Budokan its frantic feel was the sound of a surprisingly hysterical Japanese audience – rumoured to have been transformed via studio sophistry, though the group have always denied anything of the kind, including overdubbing some of their parts.

'My memories are kinda sketchy,' Nielsen later recalled, 'but I can remember that it was about 60/40 girls to guys. There were these security guys, who we called the Tokyo Patrol, grabbing all these fainting girls and dragging them out. It all looked like what used to happen to The Beatles.'

Talking of whom, not all Budokan experiences have been quite as glorious as Cheap Trick's. Aside from **Dean Martin** and **Frank Sinatra**, the first Western artists to visit its 15,000-capacity environs were **The Beatles**. Between 30 June and 2 July 1966 they turned in five shows, in front of a terrifyingly polite crowd, that were videotaped by Japanese TV. As the footage reveals, Beatlemania had made them a live travesty, so poor that George Harrison was reduced to inciting audience screams to drown out their awful harmonies (a simple matter of waving his right arm). So let's forget about the Fabs, and think instead of such past Budokan attractions as **Abba**, **Happy Mondays**, **Led Zeppelin**, **Guns N' Roses**, **Pearl Jam** – and, once again, the mighty Trick.

'Last time we were in Tokyo,' Nielsen said in 1995, 'we couldn't do Budokan because Aerosmith were doing five nights there. Fair enough, man – but if you wanna play my house, you better pay me some rent!' Musicians, eh?

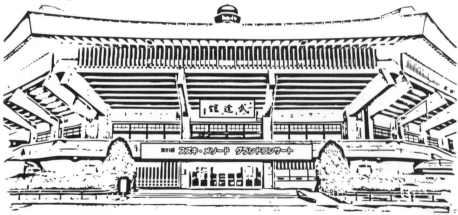

*The Budokan arena: Cheap Trick's 'house'. But only in Cheap Trick's heads*

# Everybody talk about...prop music!

**Classic on-stage visual aids, from hydraulic willies to motherships**

### Funkadelic's Mothership *1976*

Thanks to a production budget of $275,000, the P-Funk Earth Tour by George Clinton's Parliament/Funkadelic collective introduced US black music to the same OTT aesthetics as stadium rock. By way of enacting the themes of Parliament's Mothership Connection LP, a flying saucer would descend on the stage, and Clinton would emerge, recast as Dr Funkenstein. And fair play to him: it must have been a bit more exciting than, say, Razorlight.

### Pink Floyd's pig *1977*

The sleeve of the Animals LP featured a giant pig hovering over Battersea power station (during an aborted photo shoot, it drifted off over the Home Counties, but that's another story). For the tour that followed, the Floyd took along a 30x15 foot helium-filled swine. After Roger Waters departed the group in 1985, he demanded $800 per show for the use of the original pig, only to be outmanoeuvred: his former colleagues slipped free of copyright by adding a nice pair of testicles.

### Kraftwerk's robots *1978*

While making The Man Machine – which featured the classic song The Robots – the 'Werk commissioned their own doppelgangers from a Munich mannequin firm. They were taken on the road in 1981, having spent a few years being used for photo shoots. Record company staff later recalled having to buy plane seats for the dummies and, for at least one early '80s show, the band bought seats for them in the front row. 'Yes,' commented senior Kraftwerker Ralf Hütter, 'they were quite pleased with our performance.' Ker-azy guys!

### Motörhead's bomber *1979*

Everybody's favourite raddled and supercharged metal trio flagged up their 1979 album Bomber with a 40-foot aluminium replica of a Heinkel He 111, a model much beloved of the Luftwaffe (and thus in keeping with bassist/singer Lemmy's rum fondness for Nazi memorabilia). Its current whereabouts are unknown, though Lemmy claims that it's now 'holding up a shed in Diss *[in Norfolk]*.'

*Pink Floyd's pig (non-testicular version)*

### AC/DC's cannons *1981*

Following their mind-bogglingly successful comeback album Back In Black, the legendary Anglo-Scots-Australian hard rockists came up with For Those About To Rock (We Salute You), the title track of which approximated the sound of a 21-gun salute. For the accompanying gigs they commissioned six stage cannons, which joined the huge bell used during Hells Bells. Showcasing a sense of humour presumably rooted in the Newcastle pubs beloved of singer/shrieker Brian Johnson, thus was born the 'Cannon and Bell' tour. (Note to younger readers: it's a reference to a long-lost Northern comedy duo; ask your dad.)

### The Beastie Boys' penis *1987*

A glorious example of the absurd joys of British life in the 1980s: facing the imminent arrival in the UK of three middle-class Jewish boys from New York, the tabloid press rebranded them as apocalyptically anti-social louts, and rent-a-quote Conservative MPs obediently worked themselves into a right old lather. The focus of much of their ire was a vast mechanical male member, unleashed from a black box during renditions of (You Gotta) Fight For Your Right (To Party!). 'There were debates in parliament,' Michael 'Mike D' Diamond later marvelled. 'I've always had this image of people in wigs discussing a hydraulic penis.'

# LIVE AID: THE COMPLETE SETLIST

Come on! Union Of The Snake, Maneater, Don Quixote, Vienna – and, to be fair, the odd classic. Saturday 13 July 1985 went something like this…

[All times shown are in British Summer Time. Philadelphia is five hours behind]

**12.00-12.02 The Band of the Coldstream Guards**: *Royal Salute, God Save The Queen*

**12.02-12.16 Status Quo**: *Rockin' All Over The World, Caroline, Don't Waste My Time*

**12.19-12.34 The Style Council**: *You're The Best Thing, Big Boss Groove, Internationalists, Walls Come Tumbling Down*

**12.44-12.59 The Boomtown Rats**: *I Don't Like Mondays, Drag Me Down, Rat Trap*

**13.00-13.04 Adam Ant**: *Vive Le Rock*

**13.17-13.34 Ultravox**: *Reap The Wild Wind, Dancing With Tears In My Eyes, One Small Day, Vienna*

*Mercury (RIP): 'Day-oh!'*

**13.47-14.04 Spandau Ballet**: *Only When You Leave, Virgin, True*

[At this point, concert at JFK Stadium, Philadelphia begins. Key: PHL = Philadelphia, LDN = London]

PHL **13.51 Bernard Watson** [an 18-year-old unknown from Miami Beach who persuaded promoter Bill Graham to let him open the show, after sleeping in the stadium's parking lot for a week]: *All I Really Want To Do, Interview*

PHL **14.02-14.08 Joan Baez**: *Amazing Grace, We Are The World*

LDN **14.07-14.11 Elvis Costello**: *All You Need Is Love*

PHL **14.10-14.21 The Hooters**: *And We Danced, All You Zombies*

LDN **14.22-14.40 Nik Kershaw**: *Wide Boy, Don Quixote, The Riddle, Wouldn't It Be Good*

PHL **14.32-14.41 The Four Tops**: *Shake Me, Wake Me (When It's Over), Bernadette, Motown medley: It's The Same Old Song, Reach Out I'll Be There, I Can't Help Myself (Sugar Pie, Honey Bunch)*

PHL **14.45-14.53 Billy Ocean**: *Caribbean Queen, Loverboy*

LDN **14:53-15.09 Sade**: *Why Can't We Live Together, Your Love Is King, Is It A Crime*

PHL **14.55-15.10 Black Sabbath**: *Children Of The Grave, Iron Man, Paranoid*

PHL **15.12-15.19 Run DMC:** *Jam Master Jay, King Of Rock*

LDN **15.18-15.47: Sting & Phil Collins** [with **Branford Marsalis**]: *Roxanne, Driven To Tears, Against All Odds (Take A Look At Me Now), Message In A Bottle, In The Air Tonight, Long Long Way To Go, Every Breath You Take*

[Whereupon **Phil Collins** is transported, in a helicopter piloted by **Noel Edmonds**, to Heathrow for a flight to Philadelphia]

PHL **15.27-15.37 Rick Springfield**: *Love Somebody, State Of The Art, Human Touch*

PHL **15.47-15.57 REO Speedwagon**: *Can't Fight This Feeling, Roll With The Changes*

LDN **15.50-15.54 Howard Jones**: *Hide And Seek*

LDN 16.07-16.25 **Bryan Ferry** [with band including **David Gilmour**]: *Sensation, Boys And Girls, Slave To Love, Jealous Guy*

PHL 16.12-16.28 **Crosby, Stills & Nash**: *Southern Cross, Teach Your Children, Suite: Judy Blue Eyes*

PHL 16.29-16.44 **Judas Priest**: *Living After Midnight, The Green Manalishi (With The Two-Prong Crown), You've Got Another Thing Comin'*

LDN: 16.38-16.59 **Paul Young**: *Do They Know It's Christmas [a cappella excerpt], Come Back And Stay, That's The Way Love Is* [with **Alison Moyet**], *Every Time You Go Away*

PHL 17.02-17.19 **Bryan Adams**: *Kids Wanna Rock, Summer Of 69, Tears Are Not Enough, Cuts Like A Knife*

LDN 17.19-17.39 **U2**: *Sunday Bloody Sunday, Bad [including legendary 'Bono gets stuck in crowd' incident, and snatches of Satellite Of Love, Ruby Tuesday, Sympathy For The Devil and Walk On The Wild Side]*

PHL 17.40-17.56 **The Beach Boys**: *California Girls, Help Me, Rhonda, Wouldn't It Be Nice, Good Vibrations, Surfin' USA*

LDN 18.00-18.19 **Dire Straits**: *Money For Nothing* [with **Sting**], *Sultans Of Swing*

PHL 18.26-18.44 **George Thorogood & The Destroyers**: *Who Do You Love* [with **Bo Diddley**], *The Sky Is Crying, Madison Blues* [with **Albert Collins**]

LDN 18.44 – 19.05 **Queen**: *Bohemian Rhapsody, Radio Ga Ga [followed by Freddie Mercury's 'Day-oh' audience participation segment], Hammer To Fall, Crazy Little Thing Called Love, We Will Rock You, We Are The Champions*

[After which, Bob Geldof, impatient with the £1.2 million raised in the UK thus far, appears on the BBC's coverage and becomes impatient with co-host David Hepworth's suggestion that they remind viewers of a postal address for donations before repeating the relevant telephone numbers. The resulting quote – 'Fuck the address, let's get the numbers' – fuses with his instruction to 'give us the money NOW', and enters the popular consciousness as 'Give us the fucking money'.]

PHL 19.05-19.21 **Simple Minds**: *Ghost Dancing, Don't You (Forget About Me), Promised You A Miracle*

LDN 19.23-19.41 **David Bowie**: *TVC 15, Rebel Rebel, Modern Love, "Heroes"*

[Whereupon a video of the Ethiopian famine is shown, soundtracked by **The Cars**' Drive]

PHL 19.41-19.56 **The Pretenders**: *Time The Avenger, Message Of Love, Stop Your Sobbing, Back On The Chain Gang, Middle Of The Road*

LDN 19:59-20:21 **The Who**: [during first two songs, BBC coverage interrupted] *My Generation, Pinball Wizard, Love Reign O'er Me, Won't Get Fooled Again*

PHL 20.21-20.40 **Santana**: *Brotherhood, Primera Invasion, Open Invitation, Medley: By The Pool, Right Now* [with **Pat Metheny**]

LDN 20:50-21:15 **Elton John**: *I'm Still Standing, Bennie And The Jets, Rocket Man, Don't Go Breaking My Heart* [with **Kiki Dee**], *Don't Let The Sun Go Down On Me* [with **Wham!**], *Can I Get A Witness*

PHL 20:57-21:08 **Ashford & Simpson**: *Solid, Reach Out And Touch (Somebody's Hand)* [with **Teddy Pendergrass**]

*Bono, pre-'stuck in crowd' interlude*

☞

PHL 21:27-21:47 **Madonna**: *Holiday, Into The Groove, Love Makes The World Go Round* [with the **Thompson Twins**]

LDN 21:47-21:51 **Freddie Mercury & Brian May**: *Is This The World We Created?*

LDN 21:51-21:57 **Paul McCartney**: *Let It Be [song goes on for some time, and includes infamous 'broken microphone' interlude. Also features impromptu backing vocals/shouting by* **Bob Geldof, Alison Moyet, Pete Townshend** *and* **David Bowie***]*

LDN 21:57-22:02 **Assembled cast**: *Do They Know It's Christmas?*

[Whereupon London concert closes, and everything that follows is from Philadelphia]

22.02-22.20 **Tom Petty & The Heartbreakers**: *American Girl, The Waiting, Rebels, Refugee*

*Run DMC's Jam Master Jay (RIP)*

22.30-22.34 **Kenny Loggins**: *Footloose*

22.39-22.56 **The Cars**: *You Might Think, Drive, Just What I Needed, Heartbeat City*

23.06-23.27 **Neil Young**: *Sugar Mountain, The Needle And The Damage Done, Helpless, Nothing Is Perfect, Powderfinger*

23.42-23.52 **The Power Station**: *Murderess, Get It On*

00.21-00.33 **Thompson Twins**: *Hold Me Now, Revolution* [with **Madonna**, Billy Idol's guitarist **Steve Stevens** and **Nile Rodgers**]

00.38-00.55 **Eric Clapton** [with band including **Phil Collins,** freshly arrived via Concorde]: *White Room, She's Waiting, Layla*

01.00-01.10 **Phil Collins**: *Against All Odds (Take A Look At Me Now), In The Air Tonight*

01.10-01.32 **Led Zeppelin** [with drummer **Tony Thompson,** bassist **Paul Martinez**, and **Phil Collins** on drums, who conspicuously introduces each of them by name, avoiding mention of the 'L' and 'Z' words]: *Rock And Roll, Whole Lotta Love, Stairway To Heaven*

01.39-01.45 **Crosby, Stills, Nash & Young**: *Only Love Can Break Your Heart, Daylight Again*

01.46-02.08 **Duran Duran**: *A View To A Kill, Union Of The Snake, Save A Prayer, The Reflex*

02.20-02.40 **Patti LaBelle**: *New Attitude, Imagine, Forever Young, Stir It Up, Over The Rainbow, Why Can't I Get It Over*

02.50-03.12 **Hall & Oates**: *Out Of Touch, Maneater, Get Ready* [with **Eddie Kendricks** of The Temptations] *Ain't Too Proud To Beg'* [with **David Ruffin** of The Temptations], *The Way You Do The Things You Do, My Girl* [latter two songs with Kendricks and Ruffin together]

03.15-03.35 **Mick Jagger**: *Lonely At The Top, Just Another Night* [both with **Daryl Hall**], *Miss You* [with **Hall & Oates**, **Eddie Kendricks** and **David Ruffin**], *State Of Shock, It's Only Rock 'n Roll* [last two songs with **Tina Turner**]

03.39-03.53 **Bob Dylan, Keith Richards & Ronnie Wood** [during which Dylan utters the oft-misquoted words, 'I hope that some of the money that's raised for people in Africa…maybe they could just take a little bit of it…and use it, say, to pay the mortgages on some of the farms that the farmers here owe to the banks']: *Ballad Of Hollis Brown, When The Ship Comes In, Blowin' In The Wind*

03.55-04.05 **Assembled cast, led by Lionel Richie** [with **Harry Belafonte, Cher, Sheena Easton,** obligatory children's choir and incredible ad-libbed warbling from **Patti Labelle**]: *We Are The World*

# GLOBAL BORING?
### Other, less glorious stadium-based/via-satellite spectaculars, aka 'crap Live Aids'

## Farm Aid
*Champaign, Illinois, 22 September 1985 (and 19 other locations since, plus a US tour in 1989)*
Bob Dylan's off-the-cuff Live Aid comments may have sounded like a call to divert cash from the starving millions to tractor-driving Americans, but some musicians sympathised – hence Farm Aid, brought into being by **Willie Nelson** and **Neil Young**, who have both appeared at every annual Farm Aid show since. Inevitably, the wider world has remained uninterested, though two points of interest spring to mind: 1)Live Aid may have underplayed black performers but, by comparison with this, it was a multi-culti global love-fest, and 2)since when was **Lou Reed** (who has done three) the farming type?

## Nelson Mandela 70th Birthday Tribute
*London, 11 June 1988*
Starred the likes of **Stevie Wonder**, **Youssou N'Dour**, **UB40**, **Dire Straits** – and **Tracy Chapman**, given an extra 'spot' thanks to technical problems for **Stevie Wonder**, which assisted the effective launch of her career. In the USA, its bland rebranding (via careful TV editing) as 'Freedomfest' robbed it of the essential point. One more Wembley show followed on 16 April 1990 – after Mandela's release from prison, at which he gave a frenziedly-received speech. And Tracy Chapman played. Again.

## NetAid
*London, New York and Geneva, 9 October 1999*
Long-forgotten event, chiefly aimed at raising cash and awareness to assist the cancellation of third world debt. In the days when the internet still had sexy/futuristic vibes, much emphasis was placed on its online aspect. Performers included **Bush**, **David Bowie** and **Robbie Williams** (London); **Sheryl Crow**, **Mary J. Blige** and **Puff Daddy** (New York – note commendably higher black representation than Live Aid); and good old **Bryan Ferry** (Geneva, naturally). The gigs raised only around $1 million, explained by the US promoter thus: 'We're seeing a disaster a week…People have gotten used to it, unfortunately.'

## Live 8
*London and Philadelphia (plus nine other locations), 2 July 2005; Edinburgh, 6 July*
Much-hyped de facto successor to Live Aid, organised to put pressure on world leaders about to gather in Scotland for the annual G8 summit, and secure a breakthrough for the developing world. Despite Bob Geldof's insistence that it was not 'Live Aid 2', endless comparisons with the original inevitably created an anti-climax, though the **Pink Floyd** reunion was quite good. Much controversy followed, about: 1)huge sales uplifts enjoyed by bands afterwards (**Keane**, **The Who** and the Floyd were among those to surrender their royalties to the requisite charities); 2)the shortage at the London event of black performers ('If you're holding a party on behalf of people, then surely you don't shut the door on them,' said Damon Albarn); and 3)the fact that the G8 decided to hang on to their countries' zillions.

## The Concert For Diana
*London, 1 July 2007*
Fairly depressing spectacle that marked the 10th anniversary of the much-mourned royal, staged on her hypothetical 46th birthday. A rum line-up of performers included **Status Quo**, **Joss Stone**, **Rod Stewart**, **Lily Allen**, **Bryan Ferry** – and, *naturellement*, **Elton John**. Frequent camera-cuts to Princes Harry and William, plus friends, decisively proved that bluebloods have no sense of rhythm.

## Live Earth
*London and Washington DC (plus nine other locations), 7 July 2007*
Deeply underwhelming 'Live Aid, only about climate change' event, fronted by self-styled global warming prophet Al Gore. In the UK, television coverage drew only a third of the audience for the previous week's Concert For Diana, and the main subsequent story involved complaints to the BBC about swearing – by **Johnny Borrell** of Razorlight, comedian **Chris Rock**, **Ricky Gervais** and **Phil Collins**, who said 'fuck' mid-way through **Genesis**'s otherwise respectable rendition of Invisible Touch, at just gone 2pm.

# GUMMI BEARS, CHILDREN'S CHOIR, $25,000 CASH...

**The insane world of the backstage 'rider': from filet mignon to 'malt balls', edited highlights of what musicians demand if the show's going to happen...**

### Red Hot Chili Peppers

'24 one-litre bottles of still Glacier water. Glacier is a type of water. Note: no Evian/Crystal Geyser or any other local bottled spring water, please. [They] prefer Glacier brands such as Music, Fiji, Smart or other Hawaiian or Australian water (served at room temp)...[plus] small bowls: yoghurt and carob covered peanuts, raisins and malt balls.' *2000*

*No eau, no show*

### Paul McCartney

'To minimise any disruption caused by the receipt of real or hoax phone calls, and/or the discovery of suspicious packages, a properly trained canine search team will be required to conduct a sweep of the stage and backstage area at 5pm.' *2002*

### Celine Dion

'Children's choir: the Presenter must provide a choir that will be required to perform with the Artist, subject to confirmation by the Artist's representative. If so, the Presenter will engage the service of the best local children's choir available for the date of the performance...The choir should be approximately 20-24 children between the ages of seven and 12. The choir should include an equal ratio of boys and girls, of all races...The choir members are asked to wear comfortable, colourful clothing of their own, preferably no long dresses or robes.' *1998*

### Aerosmith

'Absolutely no alcoholic beverages are allowed anywhere in the backstage area at any time. This specifically includes all house crew.' *1997*

### Aretha Franklin

'On the night of the engagement, with reference to the balance of payment due...Aretha Franklin is to receive from the promoter $25,000 in cash. It is understood that this money shall be presented...direct to Ms Franklin. Delivery of this amount may be done at a mutually agreed upon time and place, on the date of the engagement.' *2002*

### Jane's Addiction

'The use of laser pointing devices of any kind or anything that can produce a focused beam of light found on any person in the venue will result in assault charges and ejection from the venue without refund.' *2001*

### Marilyn Manson

'24 bottles Evian water, 1 Champagne (Cristal, Moët), 1 Pernod, 6 Henson's root beer, 6 Henson's cherry vanilla, half gallon of 2 per cent milk, 2 absinthe, 1 bag of Ruffles chips, 1 jar of ranch dip or dressing, 1 Doritos, 1 Pace salsa (medium), 1 bag of assorted chocolate, 2 bags Haribo Gummi Bears... Please make sure that air conditioning works. This is REALLY important! Thanks!!!' *2000*

*A gummi bear: No candy, no band(y)*

### 50 Cent

'50 Cent's dressing room hot meal should consist of boneless, skinless chicken breast or a steak dinner – Porterhouse or filet mignon well done; baked potatoes w/American cheese. This meal should be served each evening in 50 Cent's dressing room. In additional *[sic]* to this, meal for ten persons: a buffet-style set-up reflecting the evening's entrée and sides should be served in chafing dishes at the proper temperature. China, glass and proper silverware should be provided. No plastic, paper or Styrofoam cups will be accepted. Presentation is very important.' *2007*

## ZZ Top

'The promoter acknowledges that s/he is promoting a worldwide "superstar" artist, and that each and every element of such promotion, production and other arrangements shall be first class in nature and commensurate with the stature of a "superstar".' *1999*

## James Brown

'Ground transportation: 1 stretch limousine, black or white, 186 inches long, current year model…Mr James Brown and entourage MUST have two hot meals a day…As close

*James Brown: 'wardrobe Mistress', please*

to Mr James Brown's dressing room as possible, a room must be provided for James Brown's wardrobe mistress…There MUST be an oxygen tank and mask onstage at all times.' *2003*

## Prince

'Coffee and tea set up (include honey, lemon, sugar, cream, fresh ginger root), 1 box Yogi Cocoa Spice Tea, 1 box Celestial Seasonings Herbal Tea Sampler, 12 bottles Fiji water (6 at room temperature), 6 small bottles organic freshly-squeezed orange juice, 6 individual bottles cranberry juice, 6 cans Pepsi, 6 cans ginger ale, 1 sliced fruit tray, 1 bag trail mix, 1 bag pita bread, 1 container of hummus, 1 bag Jensen's orchard veggie chips, 1 bag tortilla chips, 1 jar salsa, 1 box Kleenex…2 scented candles (spice, jasmine, lavender), 6 towels… All items in this dressing room must be covered by clear plastic wrap until uncovered by main artist. This is ABSOLUTELY NECESSARY.' *2004*

# 'Are you ready to testify?'
### Great – and not-so-great – onstage introductions

'You wanted the best, you got the best – Kiss!'
*Kiss's standard introduction, c.1972 to the present*

'Some artists' work speaks for itself. Some artists' work speaks for its generation. It's a deep personal pleasure to present to you one of America's great voices of freedom. It could only be one man – the transcendent Bob Dylan!'
*Jack Nicholson, Live Aid, 13 July 1985*

'Is everybody ready? For the first time in three years, the greatest rock'n'roll band in the world – The Rolling Stones! The Rolling Stones!'
*Roadie and aide Sam Cutler's stock introduction on their US tour, November 1969*

'Ladies and gentlemen…Honoured by their country, decorated by their Queen, and loved here in America. Here are…The Beatles!'
*US TV host Ed Sullivan, Shea Stadium, 15 August 1965*

'I'd like to introduce a very good friend, a fellow countryman of yours. A brilliant performer, and the most exciting guitarist I've ever heard – the Jimi Hendrix Experience!'
*Brian Jones, Monterey Pop, California, 16 June 1967*

'Who said there were no more heroes? Ladies and gentlemen – The Sex Pistols!'
*Footballer Stuart Pearce, Finsbury Park, London, 23 June 1996*

'I wanna hear some revolution out there… You must choose, brothers…It takes five seconds, five seconds of decision…Are you ready to testify? Are you ready? I give you a testimonial – the MC5!'
*The MC5's associate 'Brother' J. C. Crawford, Detroit, 29 October 1968*

'Who the fuck am I? Who the fuck are you? Who the fuck is he? Paul Weller!'
*His father and manager introduces his son, Dublin, 19 March 1994*

# ONSTAGE OUTRAGE
## Turn up, play, and get paid. Or, alternatively, do something a bit more interesting

### 1 Sid Vicious: 'A living circus'

What a scream the Sex Pistols' US tour of January 1978 must have been. Convinced that the most mayhem would be created by sending his charges through the American South, their manager-cum-provocateur Malcolm McLaren spurned your New Yorks and LAs, and arranged gigs in Atlanta, Memphis, San Antonio, Baton Rouge, Dallas and Tulsa (with their last-ever gig before splitting in San Francisco to finish). All of this is documented in the Pistols film The Great Rock'n'Roll Swindle, with one obvious sub-plot: by now, Sid Vicious was the Pistols' nominal bass player, and a paid-up member of that school of thought whereby the rock'n'roll lifestyle is a matter of self-harm, crass stupidity and problems with heroin.

Roadies-cum-minders employed by the group's American record company tried to keep the lid on Sid – according to one witness, to the point that 'they'd beat him up, but not so he couldn't work'. Onstage, however, he was free – and no end of tomfoolery occurred.

In San Antonio, where the band were pelted with popcorn, hot dogs and beer cans, Sid convinced a would-be assailant to back off by clubbing him with his bass. In Dallas – where three of Sid's four bass strings were broken, not that it mattered – he looked out at the crowd and uttered the greeting, 'All cowboys are queers.' That night, in tribute to his heroin addiction, magic-markered on his chest were the words 'Gimme a fix', and, when one audience member headbutted him, he let blood gush down his face before slashing his chest with a broken bottle.

'Look at that: a living circus,' said Johnny Rotten, to Sid's left. Just over a year later, Vicious was dead.

### 2 Jim Morrison: Knob out? Or in?

On 1 March 1969, The Doors played at the Dinner Key Auditorium in Miami. It was their first ever gig in Florida, organised because they'd come top of a popularity poll at Miami's University. By now, Jim Morrison was bearded, starting to run to fat, and apparently permanently drunk, and the gig quickly tumbled into a mixture of chaos in the crowd and somewhat bollocksome pronouncements from the man most of them had come to see.

'I'm lonely,' he said at one point. 'I need some love, y'all. Come on – I need some good times. I want some love-ah, love-ah. Ain't nobody gonna love my ass? Come on.'

To quote from one report, crazy old Jim also 'peppered the crowd with questions, obscene requests and four-letter words. He called for a revolution among the spectators.' Then, according to some accounts, a man since cracked up to be a true poet came up with the killer line: 'Do you want to see my cock?'

Whether Morrison's gonads were actually put on show has always remained unclear. The account of the show in the definitive Morrison biography No One Here Gets Out Alive portrays him wearing 'boxer shorts so large he had them pulled up and over the top of his leather pants' (what might, in fact, be called the proto-John Major look). It claims that he only planned to take off his trousers, and suggests that no knob-out intrigue transpired. Thirty-seven years later, after Morrison had been convicted of indecent exposure (the initial sentence was six months in jail; he later appealed and was released on $50,000 bail), one witness who had testified against him changed his story: 'I didn't see anything come out of his drawers,' he told the Miami Herald.

But 59-year-old ex-cop Theodore Jendry was having none of that. 'He pulled out his business and started whirling it,' he said. 'He should have been arrested right there.' By way of splitting the difference, Morrison's then-lawyer subsequently claimed that he'd been the innocent victim of what is now known as a 'wardrobe malfunction' (yeah, right).

Whatever, the incident did for The Doors. Lest their singer should once again think of dropping his drawers, terrified American promoters increasingly refused to book them – and they managed just one more show before the group splintered and the doomed Morrison moved to Paris.

### 3. L7: 'Eat my tampon, fuckers!'

In the summer of 1992, the all-female, LA-based quartet L7 released an impressive single titled Pretend We're Dead. It reached No 21 in the UK, which doesn't sound like a massive achievement, but this modest success fleetingly made them stars of the British indie-rock circuit.

They duly appeared on the 'post-pub' Channel 4 show The Word – an occasion guitarist Donita Sparks marked by lowering her trousers and allowing millions of viewers a brief glimpse of her genitals. Then, on 28 August 1992, they appeared at the Reading Festival, where the audience happily threw all kinds of detritus onstage.

Sparks decided on a truly gut-churning response: pulling out her tampon and hurling it into the crowd. 'Eat my used tampon, fuckers!' she cried, which bagged a week or so of infamy, before L7 began a quick slide back towards nowheresville.

One last bit of notoriety awaited, however: on a UK tour in April 2000, the band raffled an 'intimate meeting' with their drummer, Dee Plakas. After their performance in London, one happy – or desperate – male ticket-holder reportedly claimed his prize on the tourbus.

---

### 4. John Cale: The Chicken Incident

In 1977, the Velvet Underground co-founder John Cale was on a UK tour, heading for a well-trodden venue called the Croydon Greyhound. Cale was in the midst of a period best described as 'unhinged': while in Germany a few days before, he had picked up a large meat cleaver and he was suddenly struck by an idea. The tour-van stopped at a farm, where Cale convinced the owner to sell him a solitary chicken. His four-piece backing band queried why he'd done so and whether he had any hostile plans for the bird, but no answer was forthcoming.

Once they got to Croydon, Cale instructed a roadie to kill it, and put in on a 'wooden platter'. The plan was to then pass it on to the stage during his beautifully deranged version-cum-demolition of Heartbreak Hotel, whereupon Cale would decapitate the carcass and chuck both the resulting bits into the audience, which was full of punks who Cale thought were in need of 'a little voodoo'. 'I threw the body into the slam dancers at the front of the stage,' he later recalled, 'and I threw the head past them. It landed in somebody's Pimm's.'

As he saw it, it was 'the most effective show-stopper I ever came up with', though some of the band were disgusted. His bass player and drummer were vegetarians; both instantly left the stage, and the latter quit the tour. 'Afterwards, they told me I lied to them,' said Cale. 'I said, "I didn't hurt it – I killed it. It didn't feel a thing."' The essentials of the story were quickly poured into a Cale song that mocked the musicians' queasiness. Charmingly, he titled it Chickenshit.

*John Cale, master rock butcher: this chicken has seconds to live*

# 'THIS IS A BEAUTIFUL DAY'
## Wattstax: history's most underrated festival

### ① The basic story
On 20 August 1972, around 100,000 people crammed into the Los Angeles Coliseum – then the home of the LA Rams American football team – for a one-day gig-cum-festival put on by Memphis's Stax label. It served as the finale to that year's Watts Summer Festival, an annual event put on to mark the anniversary of the 1965 Watts riots. As was reflected in its name, the idea was to adopt the festival spirit then chiefly associated with Woodstock, and celebrate not just music but the black liberation struggle (the organisers even cut a deal with the authorities whereby the requisite police presence would be completely made up of African-American cops).

*Isaac Hayes: everyone got Shafted*

Wattstax was the first outdoor spectacular with the now-standard charity-gig format – a huge range of performers, most restricted to no more than three songs (though, as against your modern stadium spectacular, the pitch on which the stage stood was officially out-of-bounds). The show's co-sponsors were those well-known liberationists the Schlitz beer company, tickets were a mere $1, everybody performed for nothing, and the proceeds went to the Sickle Cell Anaemia Foundation, Watts's Martin Luther King Hospital, and future Watts Summer Festivals. A feature-length film was released in 1973; in 2004, it was released in a restored and expanded version on DVD. And, of course, it's worth seeing.

### ② The bill
Around 24 Stax acts played. They included: Kim Weston (who opened the show with both Lift Ev'ry Voice And Sing – aka The Black National Anthem – and the Star Spangled Banner), The Staple Singers, The Emotions, The Rance Allen Group, Mel & Tim, The Soul Children, David Porter, Albert King, Little Milton, Carla Thomas, Rufus Thomas, William Bell, The Temprees, Little Sonny, Deborah Manning, Louise McCord, Lee Sain, The Newcomers, The Bar-Kays, Eddie Floyd, Jimmy Jones, and Isaac Hayes, who appeared in his regulation gold get-up, and delivered an hour-long finale including Soulsville, the inevitable Theme From Shaft, and a 17-minute meld of Bill Withers' Ain't No Sunshine and the Ray Charles hit Lonely Avenue.

### ③ Jesse Jackson's opening address
*This was extensively sampled on Andrew Weatherall's 1990 mix of Primal Scream's Come Together; also, Jackson's later shout of 'Brothers and sisters, I don't know what this world is coming to' (which preceded a song by The Soul Children) was used as the opening to Public Enemy's 1987 hit Rebel Without A Pause.*

'This is a beautiful day. It is a new day. It is a day of black awareness. It is a day of black people taking care of black people's business. Today we are together. We are unified, and of one accord. Because when we get together, we got power, and we make decisions. Today, on this programme, you will hear gospel, and rhythm and blues, and jazz. All those are just labels. We know that music is music. All of our people got a soul. Our experience determines the texture, the pace and the sound of our soul. We say that we may be in the slum, but the slum is not in us. We may be in the prison, but the prison is not in us. In Watts, we have shifted from "Burn baby, burn" to "Learn baby, learn"…That is why we gather today to celebrate our homecoming and our sense of somebody-ness.'
[*There followed a massed call-and-response version of Jackson's poem I Am – Somebody*]

*Jesse Jackson:'Music is music,' he reckoned*

# 'We're having a great time in Helsinki'
## A five-part masterclass in the art of 'onstage banter'

**Blaze Bayley, Wolfsbane**

'Oh, you're so special tonight. You're so gloriously sexy tonight. You're so fantastic, you're so incredible, you're so sexy, you're so fucking MAD tonight *[loud cheers]*. But I can see one or two faces just over there. Maybe you're not quite into it. Maybe you haven't drunk enough yet. Maybe you're not quite feeling the music yet. Turn up the fucking sound Shirt *[Wolfsbane soundman]*, let's get these people going! Because I tell you, if you're not putting your fist in the air before we go off this stage, I'm coming out there and I'm going to fucking KILL you fuckers!'

*The Marquee, London, 20 February 1993 (A year later, Bayley became Bruce Dickinson's temporary replacement in Iron Maiden)*

**Joe Strummer, The Clash**

'Now it's time for audience participation, right? I want you all to tell me what exactly you're doing here. *[Two voices shout 'Rock'n'roll']* Alright – two for rock'n'roll. What's the rest of you doing here? *[Shout from one man of 'Waiting for the next band to come on!']* Oh yeah. Well, listen: I don't know what size you are round the waist, but I guess it's in advance of 36, alright? So if you want to carry your corpulent body up to the bar and stuff it with a few more barrels of whatever you fancy, then go ahead, right? Anybody else got some decent suggestions?...[More responses, inc. 'Get on with it!']* Get on with what, you big TWIT? Haven't you got any brains at all?'

*The Roundhouse, London, 23 September 1976*

**David Lee Roth, Van Halen**

'HELLO CALIFORNIA! Well, hello Glen Helen Regional Park! Oh, man – I've got to make an announcement right here. Can you hear me out there? *[Audience member fires a water pistol]* Hey man, don't be squirting water

*Blaze Bayley: 'You're so gloriously sexy tonight'*

at me – I'm gonna fuck your girlfriend, pal! Let's rock'n'roll, yeaaargh! This is the time of the evening when the band gets to have a drink right here *[four-foot tall drinks waiter appears]* Is everybody having a good time so far, right here? *[Roth takes slug from a Jack Daniel's bottle]* I wanna take this time to say that this is real whiskey here. The only people who put iced tea in Jack Daniel's bottles is THE CLASH, baby!'

*The US Festival, Glen Helen Regional Park, near San Bernadino, 29 May 1983 (The Clash had headlined the previous night)*

**Guy Picciotto, Fugazi**

'*[Following an outbreak of violent audience 'dancing']* You know, I saw you two guys earlier at the Good Humor *[US ice cream]* truck, and you were eating your ice cream like little boys, and I thought, Those guys aren't so tough! They're eating ice cream. I saw you eating ice cream, pal. Don't you deny it: you were eating an ice cream cone. Oh, you're bad now…but you were eating an ice cream cone, and I SAW you…That's the shit you can't hide, you know. Everybody knows it – the whole place knows it. Ice-cream-eating motherfucker, that's what you are.'

*Fort Reno Park, Washington DC, 9 August 1993*

**Paul Stanley, Kiss**

'Are you having a good time? *[Huge cheers]* Man, that makes it all worthwhile. Our next stop, after we leave your beautiful city…we will be going to…Stockholm *[boos]*. We're having a great time tonight with all you people, but tomorrow we leave for Stockholm *[boos]*… Stockholm *[boos]*…Stockholm *[boos]*. We're having a great time tonight in Helsinki! *[Huge cheers]* But we tomorrow we have to go to Stockholm *[boos]*. But we're having a great time in HELSINKI!'

*Hartwall Areena, Helsinki, 28 May 1998*

# AND AFTER THE SHOW...
The great rock hotels of New York, London, Paris, Munich (and Flint, Michigan)

## NEW YORK

### ☞ Hotel Chelsea
222 W 23rd St, NY 10011
Aka the Chelsea Hotel. Legendary bohemian residence in Manhattan, opened in 1884 as an apartment co-operative, relaunched as a hotel in 1905, and used by both stop-off visitors and long-term residents. As well as associations with Jack Kerouac, Leonard Cohen, Sid Vicious et al, forever linked with Bob Dylan, partly thanks to a reference in Sara from Blonde On Blonde. For an illustrative flavour, try a description of Dylan circa 1966 from the oft-overlooked biography by US writer Marc Spitz. According to one witness, his room 'looked like it was in a state of perpetual disarray'. Spitz goes on: 'In the middle of this scene lay a comatose Dylan dressed in black-and-white striped pyjama bottoms', and 'Brian Jones wandered in along with a willowy nymphette attired in an outrageously revealing body stocking'. Says his source: 'I took one look at this and flashed on ancient Rome at the time of Caligula.'
**Price of a room at time of writing:** *$269 (£190), including your own kitchen*

*Hotel Chelsea: legendary and bohemian*

### ☞ Gramercy Park Hotel
2 Lexington Ave, NY 10010
Fairly legendary place, opened in 1925. Around four decades later, it became a byword for the more bohemian (and cheap) end of Manhattan's rock accommodation. Top anecdote: in the early 1980s, British art-rockers XTC were billeted here, and frontman Andy Partridge received word that Captain Beefheart was also around. They failed to make contact, though bass player Colin Moulding saw the Captain the next morning, 'buying porn from the little concession stand in the hotel'. Says Partridge: 'I quite liked that. It's good to know he has earthly needs.' Since a 2003 redevelopment by the upscale Ian Schrager group, a positive swank-house.
**PORATOW:** *Doubles start at $495 (£355)*

### ☞ The Iroquois
49 West 44th St, NY 10036
During their 17-show residency at Times Square's Bonds International Casino in May-June 1981, The Clash stayed at the Gramercy Park – but for the recording of Combat Rock the same year, they stayed at this Midtown hotel, named after the NY-based confederacy of five Native American tribes. Told that James Dean had been resident for two years 'somewhere on the top two floors', Joe Strummer changed rooms every couple of days in an attempt to breathe Dean-haunted air. Also where Strummer wrote the lengthy lyric for The Clash classic Straight To Hell. And *quel surprise*: in the late 1990s, radically redeveloped.
**PORATOW:** *Doubles start at $339 (£243)*

## LONDON

### ☞ The Columbia
95-99 Lancaster Gate, W2 3NS
Bills itself as 'a family hotel in London', which is one way of looking at it. According to legend, use by Julian Cope-led band The Teardrop Explodes circa 1983 began its long association with the more cash-strapped end of rock; during the Britpop period, a standard 3am scene involved the likes of the Boo

Radleys, Shed Seven, five roadies, a generic US metal band, and three music journalists. Note also this archetypally Columbia-esque tale from Strokes guitarist Albert Hammond Jr, dating from 2001, and involving a jealous band of fellow indie-rockers: 'We were at the Columbia Hotel, all drinking and partying… I decided to walk on the end of the couches, going over everyone's heads, and I went over the last guy – the singer – and he fucking grabbed me in the nuts…it was the I-want-to-hurt-you squeeze.' Such is the stuff of rock dreams.
**PORATOW:** *Doubles are £89.00*

### ☙ Portobello Hotel
22 Stanley Gardens, W11 2NG
Sickeningly 'exclusive' and affectedly discreet establishment favoured by U2, Mick Jagger, George Michael et al; Tina Turner famously rated it so highly she bought the house next door. Damon Albarn worked here as a barman in 1988. 'One night Bono was rude to me and I've never really forgiven him,' he later reflected. 'The Edge, on the other hand, was always really polite.' This rings true, for some reason.
**PORATOW:** *Doubles from £200*

### ☙ The Sanderson
50 Berners St, W1T 3NG
In the small hours of 23 August 2007, the scene of infamous, grim, blood-splattered scenes involving Amy Winehouse and her lovely hubby Blake Fielder-Civil, which colonised that weekend's red-top papers (quoted in the Daily Mirror, she said: 'I was cutting myself after he found me in our room about to do drugs with a call girl'). Said one hotel employee: 'They had to get an outside firm to clean blood off the walls, and then there was a hefty paint job.'
**PORATOW:** *Doubles from £205*

# PARIS

### ☙ Hotel Royal Monceau
37 Avenue Hoche, 75008
*Très* posh flop-house famed for such wealthy clients as Robert De Niro, Britney Spears and Michael Jackson. More notably, the location for the video that accompanied Madonna's 1990 single Justify My Love, done by jet-set photographer and director Jean-Baptiste

Mondino and co-starring her then-squeeze and model/actor/whatever Tony Ward, also a star of her less-than-dignified Sex book. On that basis, you'd be forgiven for expecting somewhere bulging with masked sex parties and libidinous-but-confused women tiptoeing around the corridors in stockings and suspenders. Apparently, it's not actually like that.
**PORATOW:** *After two years of redevelopment, re-opening in 2010. Circa 2008, the most low-end double room was €460 (£426); the 'Royal Suite' was €7000 (£6485). Oooh.*

### ☙ George V
31 Avenue George V, 75008
Unbelievably raffish place where The Beatles stayed during a tiresome three-week Parisian residency in early 1964. On 17 January they learned that I Want To Hold Your Hand was No 1 in the USA, and understandably tumbled into all-night celebrations – during which the usually-decorous Brian Epstein was happily photographed with a chamberpot on his head. According to one onlooker: 'The Beatles couldn't even speak – not even John Lennon. They just sat on the floor like kittens at Brian's feet.'
**PORATOW:** *'Moderate' doubles are €730 (£672!)*

# . MUNICH

### ☙ Bayerischer Hof
Promenadeplatz 2-6, 80333
On 1 December 2002, an Oasis European tour reached Munich, and the band and their entourage reclined in this hotel's Bavarian splendour. Cue a sudden dispute involving Liam Gallagher, the disturbance of a party of five alleged Italian gangsters, the loss of Liam's front teeth, and allegations that he attacked a member of the *Polizei* with 'full force' (his elder brother was elsewhere). He was subsequently fined around £40,000 and, having cancelled three shows, the band lost a small fortune in ticket sales. Noel Gallagher later claimed they were also forced to briefly spend time in hiding, lest the mobsters should be in the mood for horses' heads, sleeping with fishes etc.
**PORATOW:** *A 'standard double' is a cool €391 (£359)*

# LOS ANGELES

## ⚷ Chateau Marmont

8212 Sunset Blvd, CA 90046

Where John Belushi breathed his last, the likes
of Gram Parsons, Graham Nash and the Red
Hot Chili Peppers' John Frusciante spent time
in residence, and Led Zeppelin were billeted
for their first few stays in LA. The usual
debauchery ensued, though corroboration of
the tale involving some of the band riding
motorbikes through the foyer remains elusive.
Stories of grim scenes with female camp-
followers, however, do not. On a slightly nicer
note, Lily Allen stayed here in June 2008 while
on a songwriting holiday. 'I've never stayed in
the room that I'm in before,' she blogged, 'but
rumour has it John Belushi died in here.'

**PORATOW:** *Doubles from $370 (£265)*

## ⚷ Continental Hyatt House

8401 Sunset Blvd, CA 90069

Now the 'Andaz West Hollywood'. Led Zep's
second Californian home-from-home: a far
less chic option than the Marmont, but even
more etched into the group's myth thanks
to their regular booking of up to six of its
floors, and its rebranding as the 'Riot House'.
In 1975, Robert Plant posed for a picture on
his balcony, looked out on West Hollywood
and allegedly exclaimed – perhaps not un-
plonkerishly – 'I am a golden God!' Also: in
1972, Keith Richards and Rolling Stones sax
player Bobby Keys threw a TV out of the
window of Room 1015 (included in the never-
released tour-movie Cocksucker Blues); and in
1981, the end-of-tour-party scene from This Is
Spinal Tap was filmed by the rooftop pool.

**PORATOW:** *Doubles from $345 (£243)*

## ⚷ Sunset Marquis

1200 Alta Loma Rd, CA 90069

A not-dissimilar hidey-hole to the Marmont,
opened in 1963, which claims to offer
sanctuary to those 'in need of rest, relaxation
and, sometimes, a hell of a good time'. On
the latter score, in May 1996 Depeche Mode
singer Dave Gahan OD'd on cocaine and
heroin here, and his heart stopped beating
for two minutes. Which is, perhaps, a bit too
much of a 'good time'. NB: on a slightly less
smackular note, also a favourite of Morrissey.

**PORATOW:** *Doubles start at $250 (£180)*

## ⚷ Le Parc Suites

733 N West Knoll Dr, CA 90069

Having been ejected from Black Sabbath in
1979, Ozzy Osbourne spent three months
here. It sells itself via claims of a mixture of
'sophistication' and 'chic', but Ozzy did little
more than eat pizza, drink, and snort the
powdered pick-me-up the man himself is said
to call 'krell'.

**PORATOW:** *Doubles from $239 (£170)*

# JOSHUA TREE, CALIFORNIA

## ⚷ Joshua Tree Inn

61259 Twentynine Palms Highway, CA 92252

Just over two hours from LA, in the midst
of the eerie beauty of the Californian desert,
and a de facto shrine to country-rock
monarch Gram Parsons, who died here on
19 September 1973. Thanks to a morphine
OD, he expired in Room 8, which country-
rock ghost-seekers can specially request.
Nearby is Cap Rock, the geological feature
in whose shadow Parsons' friend/fixer/roadie
Phil Kaufman drunkenly burned his corpse, a
supposed honouring of GP's wishes.

**PORATOW:** *Room 8 is $105 (£74) a night*

# FLINT, MICHIGAN

## ⚷ Days Inn

2207 West Bristol Rd, MI 48507

A former Holiday Inn, and the location
for Keith Moon's 21st birthday party, on
23 August 1967. Like perfect hosts, the
management put a special 'Happy birthday
Keith' message on their roadside sign, and
allowed him use of a banqueting hall – where
he and The Who jugged it up with their
touring partners Hermans Hermits and
long-lost psychedelicists the Blues Magoos.
The resulting scenes included the obligatory
cake-fight, Moon's 'debagging', and a drunken
dash away from the carnage that resulted in
him smashing one of his front teeth. Later,
guests let fire extinguishers off on scores of
parked cars, ruining their paintwork, a piano
was smashed to bits, and endless debris was
chucked into the swimming pool. Total bill:
according to legend, some $24,000, though
other accounts put it closer to $5000.

**PORATOW:** *Doubles from $58 (£40). But
don't you dare break anything*

# CLEVELAND, OHIO

## 🔑 Comfort Inn

1800 Euclid Avenue, OH 44115
Once the gloriously-named Swingos Celebrity
Inn, an iconic Cleveland hotel that lasted
from 1970 until the mid '80s. It took its name
from its owner, Jim Swingos, though it was a
perfect byword for on-tour hedonism. Cameron
Crowe paid tribute in the 2000 movie Almost
Famous: one line cites it as 'the greatest hotel
in America'. Within walking distance of the
Rock'n'Roll Hall Of Fame, for what that's worth.
**PORATOW:** *Doubles from $129.99 (£79)*

# SEATTLE

## 🔑 The Edgewater

2411 Alaskan Way, Pier 67, WA 98121
So close to the Puget Sound that it used to let
guests fish from their balconies, and infamous
for the stomach-churning 1969 'shark episode'
(actually a red snapper) starring Led Zeppelin
tour manager Richard Coles, a woman named
Jackie, one member of the long-lost Vanilla
Fudge and the late John Bonham (if you're
that bothered, Google it). Led
Zep were banned in 1973 after
leaving around 30 dead mudsharks
all over the hotel and chucking no
end of stuff in the sea. Which was
considerate of them.
**PORATOW:** *Doubles start at $199*

# BERLIN

## 🔑 Askanischer Hof

Kurfürstendamm 53, 10707
Seventeen-room boho joint
occasionally favoured by such
high-end groovers as Tilda Swinton
and David Bowie. The latter spent
time here in 1982; should you
want to sample the vibes, you'll
need to bed down in Room 24.
**PORATOW:** *Doubles from
€117 (£107)*

## 🔑 Hotel Ellington

Nürnberger Straße 50-55, 10789
Only a hotel since 2007, but
associated with Bowie's Berlin
period thanks to the same building's

hosting of a '70s club called Dschungel (trans:
'Jungle'), a painfully chic answer to Studio 54,
famed for a pack of female bouncers who once
turned away Sylvester Stallone ('We don't want
any Rambos in here!' they allegedly sneered).
Its prime-period clientele included Bowie, his
Berlin-era shadow Iggy Pop – and, a little later,
that other adoptive Berliner Nick Cave.
**PORATOW:** *Doubles from €138 (£127)*

# MARRAKECH

## 🔑 La Mamounia

Avenue Bab Jdid, 40000 Marrakech
The backdrop to Mick Jagger, Keith Richards
and Brian Jones's legendary Moroccan trip in
February 1967, preceded by Keith's copping-off
with Brian's then-girlfriend Anita Pallenberg.
Once he arrived, Brian beat up Anita when
she refused a foursome with two Moroccan
prostitutes, whereupon Keith 'just threw her
in the back of the car and split'. Mick Jagger's
most oft-quoted observation was, 'It's getting
fuckin' heavy.' No kidding.
**PORATOW:** *Closed until 2009; circa 2008,
doubles from 3000 Moroccan Dirhams (£250)*

*The Sunset Marquis: Dave Gahan 'checked out'. Nearly*

# Chapter 3

# THE KIT

T here are innumerable songs about cars, girls, love, death and war, but relatively few songwriters have ever sought to really celebrate the actual equipment with which the music is made. You can understand why: better by far to be singing about the stuff of true romance and drama than the Fender Stratocaster, or the correct gauge of Ernie Ball strings (if this latter reference makes no sense, be grateful – or Google it).

So, anyone seeking hymns to what this chapter calls 'The Kit' has long had to make the most of small musical crumbs. Among several, three songs particularly spring to mind: Mott The Hoople's All The Way From Memphis (1973), in which the protagonist mislays his 'six string razor', only to be reunited with it in Oriole, Kentucky; Teenage Riot by the New York alt-rockers Sonic Youth (1988), which contains a brief mention of the high-volume icon known as the Marshall stack; and Summer Of '69 by good old Bryan Adams (1985), a portrait of the artist as a young herbert with his first guitar, which he played 'till my fingers bled'.

For now, though, let's forget about songs and go straight to the heart of the matter: the varied machinery on which nearly 60 years' worth of rock has been made. Strange to think, perhaps, that the Fender Telecaster guitar was introduced in 1950, and arguably still represents the very acme of cool. Stranger still, maybe, that the old-fashioned drum kit is still with us, long pulled back from the gigantic excesses of the 1970s, and once again based around a relatively small handful of bits. There again, should you want to ditch all this and look ahead, the keyboards keep coming, and the story of the drum machine stretches from its early use on Sly And The Family Stone's There's A Riot Goin' On (1971), on into the indefinite future.

For a certain kind of person, long conversations about equipment represent nothing but joy. They spend hours in music shops, and pore over instrument catalogues in the way others stare at pornography. This, it has to be said, is kind of understandable – and once you've got the bug, equipment-world is dependably great. This writer, I should perhaps confess, goes a bit funny at the mention of his Vox AC30 amplifier and reissue Fender with pink fur-lined case, but enough of that already.

Let no one think that the story of wires, wood and speakers can somehow be separated from that of the music itself. What would (I Can't Get No) Satisfaction be without that buzzing headache of an intro, played by Keith Richards through one of the first distortion boxes? Without the chorus unit, The Pretenders, The Smiths and The Police would have sounded completely different – indeed, the 1980s would have been that bit less enjoyable. Other examples pile up. No Marshall amps, no Heavy Metal. No affordable synthesisers, no Human League. And no wah-wah pedal, no progressive rock – if Yes guitarist Steve Howe is to be believed.

'I remember when wah-wah pedals came out and there was this feeling among us that you had to have one immediately,' he said in 2008. 'I bought one within a week – and there was one point where Hank Marvin [of The Shadows] was in the same studio with us and was fascinated. He said, "Wow, you've got a wah-wah, amazing", and that's one of the points that I realised that we were the new breed. We were leaving behind the music of the past.' Cheers then, Mr Wah – it is you who is ultimately responsible for the horror that was 1973's Tales From Topographic Oceans, but we'll have to let it pass.

What follows are glimpses of a world of which too many people remain unaware. There is stuff about the guitars made by such firms as Fender, Gibson and Rickenbacker, as well as something called the Burns Flyte, meant to approximate the look of a Concorde aeroplane. The history of the electronic, keyboard-centric end of the story is partly traced through an under-appreciated BBC employee called Delia Derbyshire. And thanks to the example set by one Clyde Stubblefield, it is incontestably proved that the smaller the drum-kit, the greater the long-term influence.

Anyway, I just thought of another song that references equipment: Youth Of Today, a No 13 hit in 1982 for the Birmingham reggae group Musical Youth. The passage in question was sung by 12-year-old Michael Grant: 'I went downtown, to buy a keyboard/The price of the board made me shout out, Lord.' Fair play: now, as then, these things can be expensive. And at the risk of sounding Neanderthal, guitars are still cheaper and…just better, really. But anyway, to business…

# CLASSIC FENDER GUITARS

Back, to start with, to 1938, Fullerton, California, and Leo Fender (1909-1991), the owner of Fender's Radio Service, which saw to electrical repairs. Having started to make electric lap-steel (or 'Hawaiian') guitars, Fender aimed at creating a solid-body electric guitar – and in 1949, he began work on the guitar that was first called the Esquire, then the Broadcaster, and eventually the Telecaster. From there, he was off: genius marketing popularised the Fender brand, and the Telecaster was followed by a run of classic guitars and basses (as well as amps and keyboards).

In 1965, Fender's firm was sold to the Columbia Broadcasting System – aka CBS – for $13 million, and Fender aficionados started discriminating between pre- and post-CBS guitars – a distinction that was a little overdone, though the quality of Fenders produced in the 1970s was variable (tellingly, Fender himself left the company in 1979). In 1985, a management buy-out took the company out of CBS's hands, and it's been independent ever since. Their sales blurbs have long used the slogan 'the sounds that create legends'. And to be fair, they have a point…

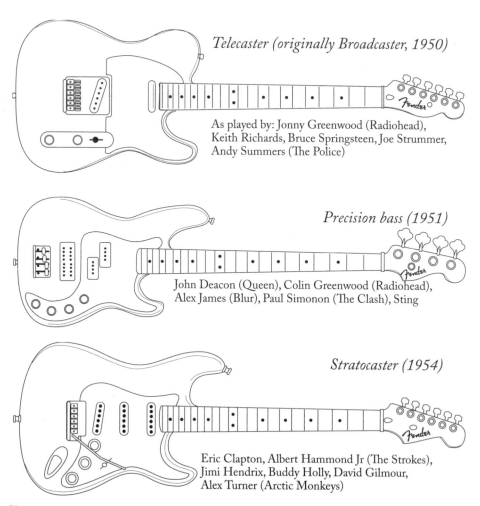

*Telecaster (originally Broadcaster, 1950)*

As played by: Jonny Greenwood (Radiohead), Keith Richards, Bruce Springsteen, Joe Strummer, Andy Summers (The Police)

*Precision bass (1951)*

John Deacon (Queen), Colin Greenwood (Radiohead), Alex James (Blur), Paul Simonon (The Clash), Sting

*Stratocaster (1954)*

Eric Clapton, Albert Hammond Jr (The Strokes), Jimi Hendrix, Buddy Holly, David Gilmour, Alex Turner (Arctic Monkeys)

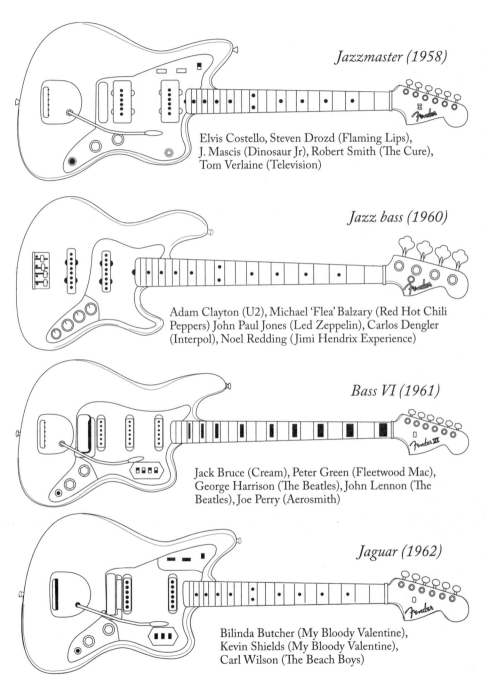

*Jazzmaster (1958)*

Elvis Costello, Steven Drozd (Flaming Lips),
J. Mascis (Dinosaur Jr), Robert Smith (The Cure),
Tom Verlaine (Television)

*Jazz bass (1960)*

Adam Clayton (U2), Michael 'Flea' Balzary (Red Hot Chili
Peppers) John Paul Jones (Led Zeppelin), Carlos Dengler
(Interpol), Noel Redding (Jimi Hendrix Experience)

*Bass VI (1961)*

Jack Bruce (Cream), Peter Green (Fleetwood Mac),
George Harrison (The Beatles), John Lennon (The
Beatles), Joe Perry (Aerosmith)

*Jaguar (1962)*

Bilinda Butcher (My Bloody Valentine),
Kevin Shields (My Bloody Valentine),
Carl Wilson (The Beach Boys)

59

# A VERY BRITISH AMP

## From World War II to Live Aid: the story of the Vox AC30

In July 1962, Beatles manager **Brian Epstein** paid a visit to Jennings' music shop on Charing Cross Road in central London, an offshoot of Jennings Musical Industries, who were also the manufacturers of Vox amplifiers. He was after new kit for the group he looked after: four Liverpudlians, newly back from Germany and freshly signed to the Parlophone label, but whose kit was 'pretty clapped out'. Epstein had in mind a deal whereby the amps would come for free, in return for lots of promotion – which doubtless sounded reasonable enough, but there was one problem: outside the environs of Liverpool and Hamburg, no one much had heard of **The Beatles**.

The shop's manager duly put in a call to his boss, **Tom Jennings**, who seemed unimpressed. 'What does he think we are,' he barked back, 'a fucking philanthropic society?' Somehow, however, a deal was done: Epstein promised that for as long as he was in charge, The Beatles would never use anything but Vox amps (an agreement they stuck to), and he walked away with two AC30 amps, finished in a very fetching beige. They retailed for around £105; just over £1300 in modern money.

The AC30 – the 'AC' bit denotes 'Amplifier combined with speaker'; the '30' part refers to its modest wattage – was the next step on from the AC15, invented in January 1958, and favoured by those early British rock gods **The**

Shadows, as well as **Bert Weedon**, the besuited, London-born guitarist who promised millions of young Britons that they could 'play in a day', and the gloriously-named **Vic Flick**, who played the lead guitar part on the James Bond Theme.

After the AC30 arrived in late 1958, its bright, brassy tone could be heard on one of British rock music's first certifiable classics: The Shadows' **Apache,** which reached number one in the summer of 1960.

The Vox brand, also seen on guitars, basses and organs, was pioneered by Jennings and his chief engineer **Dick Denney**, who met during World War II at the Vickers munitions plant in Dartford, Kent. With various modifications, the AC30 was a mainstay of British rock music prior to the jump in volume represented by the decisive arrival of the Marshall stack, and used not just by The Beatles, but just about every notable name of the early-to-mid-'60s: **The Rolling Stones' Brian Jones** and **Keith Richards, The Yardbirds, The Hollies, The Animals, The Kinks** et al. Having been nudged aside, it returned thanks to the arrival of punk rock and the back-to-the-roots outlook it spawned – used (and advertised) by **Paul Weller** in his **Jam** period, U2's Dave 'The Edge' Evans, **R.E.M.**'s **Peter Buck** and, eventually, such modern musicians as **Noel Gallagher** and **Radiohead**'s **Thom Yorke** and **Jonny Greenwood**, who used AC30s for their breakthrough hit Creep.

The AC30's most loyal champion is Queen's virtuoso and astronomy expert **Brian May**, who habitually does his stuff in front of masses of AC30s (have a look, for example, at footage of their dizzying turn at Live Aid). In 2006, Vox announced the launch of the AC30BM, custom-made to Brian's specifications, and launched on a wave of truly thrilling hype.

'As long as there has been Brian May playing guitar there has always been a wall of Vox AC30s standing proudly behind him,' went the promotional blurb. 'Between Brian's unique style and the AC30's princely tone, there has always been a "kind of magic" that has wooed audiences worldwide for more than 30 years.' You can't argue with that, can you?

*The Vox AC30: 'princely tone' not pictured*

# CLASSIC RICKENBACKER GUITARS

Hats off to Adolph Rickenbacker, the Swiss-born US guitar pioneer who put the first electric guitar into production in 1932. That guitar, however, was a Hawaiian-style 'lap-steel' model, shaped like a frying pan, and in 1946 he sold his business to one Francis Cary Hall, who eventually commissioned a few guitars that became accredited icons, thanks chiefly to The Beatles. John Lennon bought his 'short arm' 325 in 1960, George Harrison was given a 12-string Rickenbacker 360 in February 1964 (to hear it, have a listen to the fade-out from A Hard Day's Night) and Paul McCartney started using a 4001S bass in the studio in 1965. One final thing for anoraks: the 360 initially looked just like the 330, but by the end of 1964 it had been refined into something slightly different. Fans of that version include The Byrds' Roger McGuinn and R.E.M.'s Peter Buck.

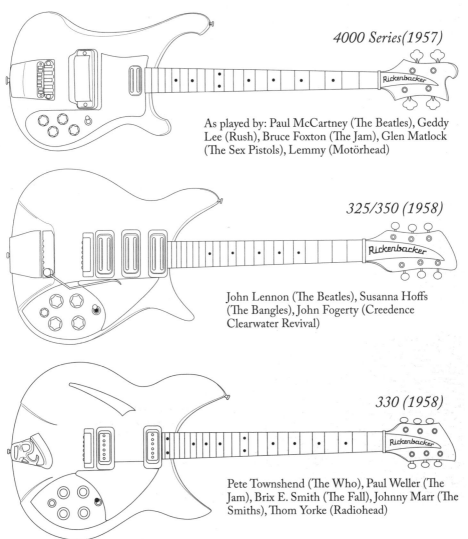

### 4000 Series(1957)

As played by: Paul McCartney (The Beatles), Geddy Lee (Rush), Bruce Foxton (The Jam), Glen Matlock (The Sex Pistols), Lemmy (Motörhead)

### 325/350 (1958)

John Lennon (The Beatles), Susanna Hoffs (The Bangles), John Fogerty (Creedence Clearwater Revival)

### 330 (1958)

Pete Townshend (The Who), Paul Weller (The Jam), Brix E. Smith (The Fall), Johnny Marr (The Smiths), Thom Yorke (Radiohead)

# RELIGIOUS CYMBAL-ISM

The drum kits (including exhaustive specifications) of five percussive gods

## John Bonham

Led Zeppelin *c.1976*

The kit Bonham (1948-1980) used for 1976's Presence LP – 'There ain't a drummer alive with John Bonham's pace, time or shoulders,' said the NME review – and the basis of his set-up for their gigs between 1977 and 1980.

### Ludwig Drums
6½ x 14″ Snare
12 x 15″ Tom-Tom
16 x 16″ Floor Tom
18 x 16″ Floor Tom
29″ Timpani
30″ Timpani
26″ Bass Drum

### Paiste Cymbals
Ching Ring
15″ Sound Edge Hi-Hat
18″ Medium Crash
20″ Medium Crash
24″ Medium Ride
36″ Gong

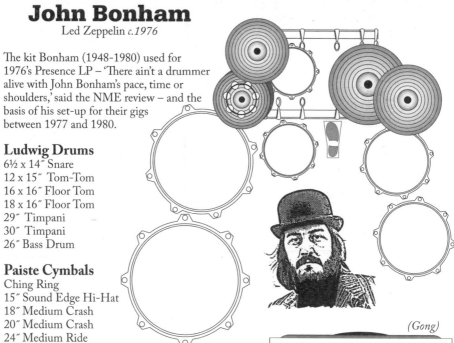

*(Gong)*

## Ginger Baker

Cream *c.1968*

### Ludwig Drums
1940s 5 x 14″ Snare
8 x 12″ Tom-Tom
9 x 13″ Tom-Tom
14 x 14″ Floor Tom
16 x 16″ Floor Tom
Two 22″ Bass Drums

### Zildjian Cymbals
8″ Splash
15″ Hi-Hat
16″ Medium Crash
17″ Med/Thin Crash
18″ Med/Thin Crash
19″ Medium Ride
22″ Medium Ride

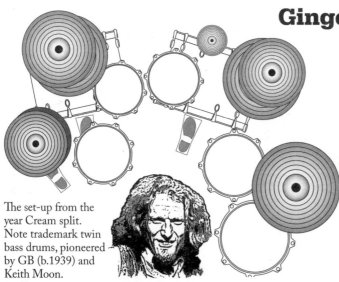

The set-up from the year Cream split. Note trademark twin bass drums, pioneered by GB (b.1939) and Keith Moon.

# Sheila E.
Prince *c.1989*

## Yamaha Drums
8 x 8″ Tom-Tom
Brass Piccolo Snare
10 x 10″ Tom-Tom
10 x 12″ Tom-Tom
13 x 13″ Tom-Tom
14 x 14″ Tom-Tom
14 x 15″ Tom-Tom
16 x 16″ Floor Tom
16 x 18″ Floor Tom
Two 22″ Bass Drums

## Paiste Cymbals
8″ Splash
13″ Hi-Hat
16″ Crash
16″ Fast Crash
17″ Crash
18″ Crash
18″ China
20″ Ride
20″ China

The kit used by the woman otherwise known as Sheila Escovedo (b.1957) on Prince's Lovesexy tour between July 1988 and February 1989. After suffering a collapsed lung, she left his band; her first post-Prince solo album was called – no, really – Sex Cymbal.

# Clyde Stubblefield
James Brown Orchestra/The JBs *c.1969*

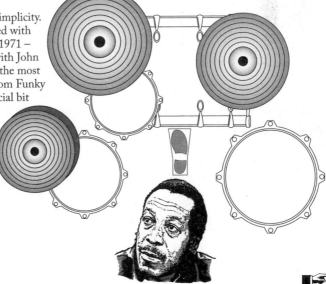

A lesson in the beauty of simplicity. Stubblefield (b.1943) played with Brown between 1965 and 1971 – both solo and in tandem with John 'Jabo' Starks – and created the most sampled beat in history: from Funky Drummer (1969 – the crucial bit starts at 5:38). 'I consider myself a master chef,' he later reflected.

## Ludwig Drums
5 x 14″ Snare
9 x 13″ Tom-Tom
16 x 16″ Floor Tom
22″ Bass Drum

## Zildjian Cymbals
14″ Hi-Hat
18″ Crash
20″ Ride

# Keith Moon

The Who *c.1975*

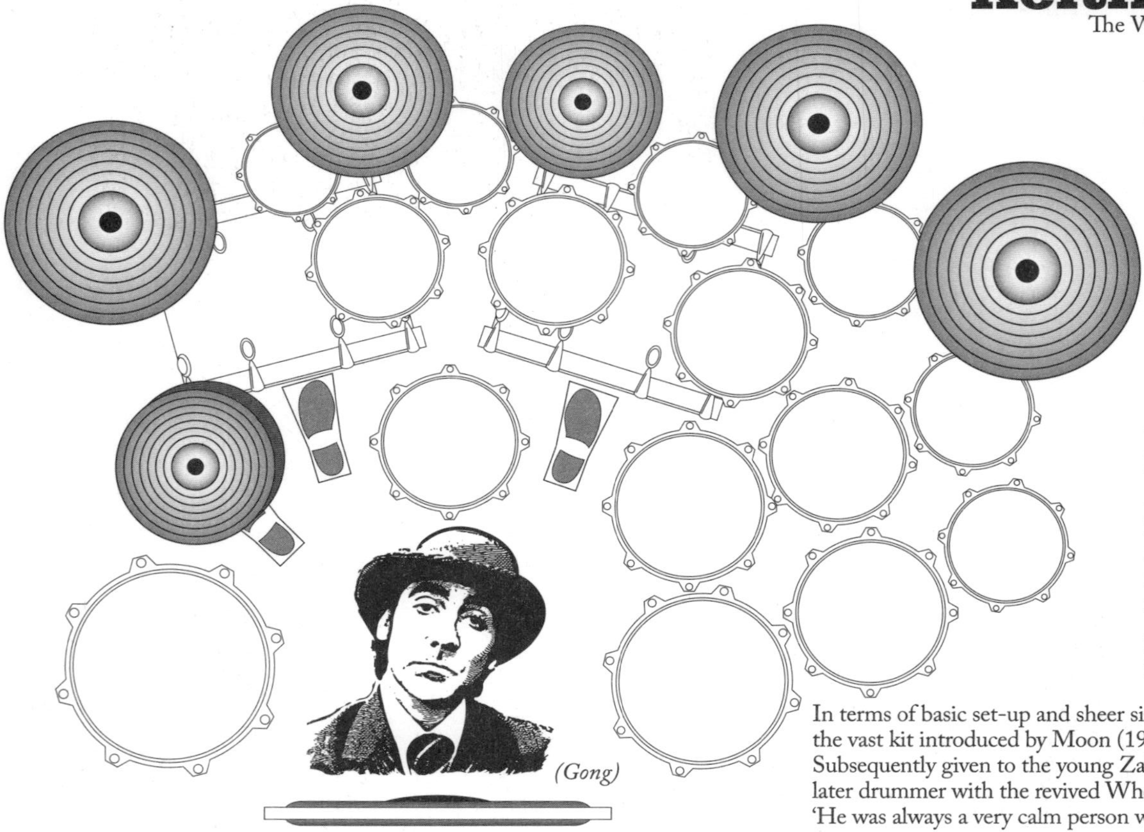

## Premier Drums

14 x 5½″ Snare
Two Timbales
10″ Single-headed Tom
12″ Single-headed Tom
13″ Single-headed Tom
14″ Single-headed Tom
Two 15″ Single-headed
Toms
12″ Mounted Tom
13″ Mounted Tom
14″ Mounted Tom
16 x 18″ Floor Tom
18″ Floor Tom
Two 22″ Bass Drums
Premier 22½″ Timpani

## Paiste Cymbals

14″ Hi-Hat
14″ Splash
18″ Crash
Two 20″ Crash
22″ Ride
36″ Gong

In terms of basic set-up and sheer size, a continuation of the vast kit introduced by Moon (1940-1978) in May 1974. Subsequently given to the young Zak Starkey (son of Ringo, later drummer with the revived Who and Oasis), who recalled: 'He was always a very calm person when he was with me.'

*(Gong)*

# 'I WILL SUPPLY THIS MAN WITH THE WEAPON HE REQUIRES'

## The history of the Marshall amp

It's not the most glamorous place to start: a 1992 song by 'Andy Scott's Sweet', an incarnation of '70s glam-rockers **The Sweet** led by a guitar player from Wrexham. Still, the long-forgotten tune they cleverly titled **Marshall Stack** nailed the essential magic of the eight-speaker, twin-cabinet piece of kit that still stands as a byword for long hair, unnecessary volume and gurning during guitar solos. From the top, then: 'Well he's six feet tall/And he's three feet wide/And when he's turned up loud/You'd better step aside.' Yeah!

The story of the Marshall amp is also the tale of **Jim Marshall**, born in July 1923, and raised in Southall, West London. A sometime jazz drummer and teacher – among his pupils was future Jimi Hendrix compadre **Mitch Mitchell** – Marshall began building amps in 1960, using his garage as a workshop. He soon opened a music shop in Hanwell, near Heathrow Airport, and attracted a clientele that included **Pete Townshend**: one of the musicians whose criticisms of existing amps and speakers – 'too clean', they apparently reckoned – gave Marshall and his staff the smart idea of putting four 12-inch speakers in a single cabinet.

In 1965, desperate to be heard above **Keith Moon**, Townshend and Who bassist **John Entwistle** were responsible for prompting the invention of the Marshall stack: a single amplifier wired to two 4 x 12 speaker cabinets, with an output of 100 watts – these days the standard requirement of any jobbing guitarist but back then the stuff of borderline recklessness. As Townshend later recalled, 'Jim Marshall's eyes sort of lit up and he said, "I will supply this man with the weapon he requires."'

Among the musicians who followed The Who's lead were **Cream**, **The Small Faces** and **Hendrix** – and the latter enthusiastically pioneered another important development, 'daisy chaining' four speaker stacks together, and thus decisively associating the Marshall logo with truly skull-crushing volume.

By the late 1970s, guitarists were demanding the kind of sharp, squealing sound

synonymous with what was soon known as Heavy Metal, and Marshall introduced a new kind of amp: the so-called 'MV' (or Master Volume) series, later known as the JCM 800 line, and beloved of Ozzy Osbourne sidekicks **Randy Rhoads** and **Zakk Wylde**, and – eventually – Saul 'Slash' Hudson of **Guns N' Roses**. In the meantime, musicians fond of loud volume and showing off had enshrined a true icon: the wall of Marshall speakers, a trademark of everyone from **Metallica** to **Status Quo**. The classical-metal fusioneer **Yngwie Malmstein** uses 27, while **Kerry King** and **Jeff Hanneman** of thrash-metal trailblazers **Slayer** are in the habit of playing through as many as 58 – though as any seasoned roadie will tell you, the bigger the Marshall wall, the greater the possibility of 'dummy stacks'.

While we're here, a quick word about the godlike **Nigel Tufnel**, fictional guitarist – played by **Christopher Guest** – whose Marshall amp that went 'up to 11' in This Is Spinal Tap gave rise not just to the phrase 'one louder', but one of the company's best ever inventions. In 1990, Marshall launched a new version of their JCM 900 amp, whose volume control reached 20. As Guest/ Tufnel said at the time, 'That's nine louder, innit?'

*The Marshall stack – not, just to be clear, a 'dummy'*

# CLASSIC GIBSON GUITARS

For this one, we go way back: to the birth of Orville H. Gibson (1856-1918) who co-founded the Gibson Mandolin-Guitar Manufacturing Company in Kalamazoo, Michigan in 1902. Gibson made its first electric guitars in the mid-1930s, but the rock part of this story decisively began in 1951, when Gibson asked the singer/inventor Les Paul to put his name to a new solid-bodied electric guitar. In the mid-1940s, Gibson's owners the Chicago Musical Instrument Company (who'd bought the company in 1944) had looked at Paul's prototype for the same idea and called him 'the guy with the broomstick' – but now they needed his help. In return for a royalty, the Gibson Les Paul was born, and thus commenced a 50-plus-year story whose most recent innovation is a line of 'Robot Guitars', which tune themselves. But that, we're saying, is cheating.

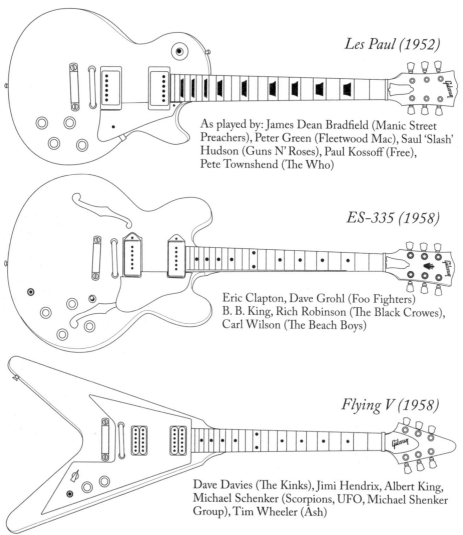

## Les Paul (1952)

As played by: James Dean Bradfield (Manic Street Preachers), Peter Green (Fleetwood Mac), Saul 'Slash' Hudson (Guns N' Roses), Paul Kossoff (Free), Pete Townshend (The Who)

## ES-335 (1958)

Eric Clapton, Dave Grohl (Foo Fighters) B. B. King, Rich Robinson (The Black Crowes), Carl Wilson (The Beach Boys)

## Flying V (1958)

Dave Davies (The Kinks), Jimi Hendrix, Albert King, Michael Schenker (Scorpions, UFO, Michael Shenker Group), Tim Wheeler (Ash)

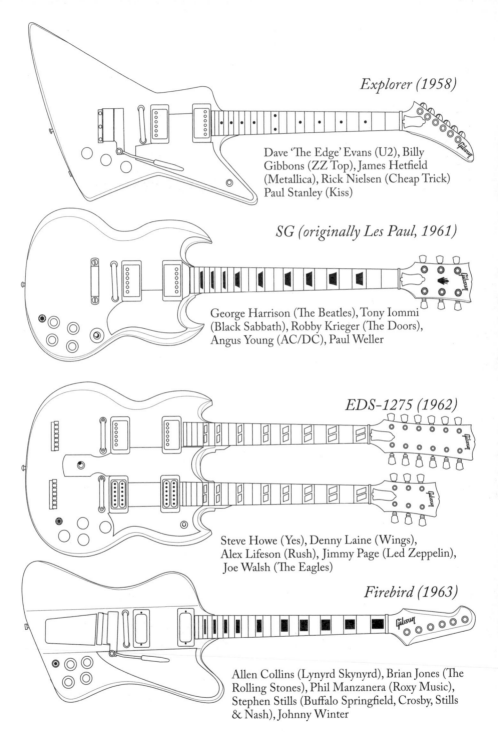

*Explorer (1958)*

Dave 'The Edge' Evans (U2), Billy Gibbons (ZZ Top), James Hetfield (Metallica), Rick Nielsen (Cheap Trick) Paul Stanley (Kiss)

*SG (originally Les Paul, 1961)*

George Harrison (The Beatles), Tony Iommi (Black Sabbath), Robby Krieger (The Doors), Angus Young (AC/DC), Paul Weller

*EDS-1275 (1962)*

Steve Howe (Yes), Denny Laine (Wings), Alex Lifeson (Rush), Jimmy Page (Led Zeppelin), Joe Walsh (The Eagles)

*Firebird (1963)*

Allen Collins (Lynyrd Skynyrd), Brian Jones (The Rolling Stones), Phil Manzanera (Roxy Music), Stephen Stills (Buffalo Springfield, Crosby, Stills & Nash), Johnny Winter

# 'MAN, THAT LITTLE THING REALLY BOOGIES!'

## From Carlos Santana to Limp Bizkit: the history of San Francisco's Mesa Boogie amps

Rather unpromisingly, it all started in a San Francisco shop called Prune Music, where a young repairman called Randall Smith fixed amps belonging to such renowned local musicians as **Big Brother And The Holding Company**, **The Grateful Dead** and **Country Joe And The Fish**.

In 1969, partly as a joke, Smith did some unexpected work on a small Fender combo (that is, both amp and speaker in one unit) belonging to the latter group's guitarist **Barry Melton**, and 'hot-rodded' it with a new speaker and transformers so it blared out a much louder noise than anyone would expect. According to legend, the new amp was tested in the front of Prune Music by a passing **Carlos Santana**, who marvelled at its distortion-soaked, super-sustaining tone. It sounds like something from a film, but it's reportedly true: a crowd gathered outside the shop to hear Santana wailing away, whereupon the guitarist said, 'Man, that little thing really boogies!', and Randall Smith got his big idea.

He duly left Prune Music and launched a new company (Mesa is a suburb of Phoenix, Arizona, though the name seems to have been chosen at random). Seizing on Smith's 'hot-rodding' trick, its first big product was the so-called Mark I, which produced the overheated sound forever associated with Santana and quickly known as 'Boogie lead'. For an instant understanding, go straight to Santana's 1970 album Abraxas – or, if you want to hear something a little different, the self-titled first album by those LA indie-rock ironists **Weezer** (1994), which singer-guitarist and amp expert **Rivers Cuomo** ensured was drenched in the Mark I's fuzzed-up sound.

In the wake of the Mark I came a whole Mark series – the Mark II, the Mark IIA, the Mark IIB, on in turn to the Mark IV – and by 1983 Mesa's list of musicians who used their stuff extended into the distance, and included **Keith Richards**, **Frank Zappa**, **Prince**, **Pete Townshend**, **Mick Ronson**, **Black Sabbath**, **Supertramp**, **The Clash** and, for some reason, **Barry Manilow**. Santana, however, remained the company's poster-boy, starring in a run of somewhat Spinal Tap-esque adverts. 'It has to do with his ear, his heart, his touch,' read one of the best (or, looked at another way, worst). 'We say thanks…for breathing fire through our amps.' That's right!

In 1989, there came another watershed invention. 'We yearned for more in our mosh,' says the company's promotional blurb. 'In the early dawn of the goatee and tattoo era we longed to create another classic.' Such was the thinking behind – and it's not the sexiest name, but anyway – the Dual and Triple Rectifier series of amps, whose crunchy tone was eventually taken up by Nu Metal bands such as **Korn**, **Linkin Park** and **Limp Bizkit**, as well as the **Foo Fighters**' Dave Grohl.

Incidentally, if you want to experience the Mesa magic while not annoying your neighbours, there is the F-30, a compact unit hyped up as only Mesa know how. It's apparently a 'shocking tone monster' that can produce 'one of the most hellacious crunch sounds around' and 'a spankin' attitude only these nine-pin power punks can deliver'. Once again: that's right!

*The Mesa Boogie F-30: it's a 'shocking tone monster', apparently*

# Knives out!

## The blade/rock interface, starring Keith Emerson and Johnny Marr

'Jimi Hendrix played the guitar behind his back,' Keith Emerson once reflected. 'I took to riding the L100 [Hammond organ] like a bucking bronco. I'd play Bach's Toccata And Fugue from behind the keyboard. I'd hold down chords with knives during our version of Dave Brubeck's Rondo.' Emerson was the organ player in The Nice, the '60s British quartet who played a key role in inventing progressive rock. At the peak of their mind-numbingly extended version of the aforementioned jazz classic, he would pull knives from his belt and jam them into the keyboard, sustaining a screeching organ chord while he flamboyantly abused his instrument.

With progressive monarchs Emerson, Lake & Palmer, the blade-based tomfoolery continued, though these days he's more sensible. 'I don't stick knives in the keyboards any more,' he said in 2008. 'The roadies would get fed up replacing them.'

In Emerson's account, it was a roadie who originally supplied him with the requisite hardware: future Motörhead singer/bassist Ian 'Lemmy' Kilmister, who supposedly gave him two Hitlerjugend knives from his burgeoning collection of Nazi artefacts. The latter, however, is having none of it. 'It's not true,' said Lemmy in 2006. 'I don't know where he got that from.'

And so to Johnny Marr, and The Smiths' Stop Me If You've Heard This One Before (1987), in which the intro is punctuated by strangely metallic power-chords. 'I'd take this really loud Telecaster of mine, lay it on top of a Fender Twin Reverb with the vibrato on, and tune it to an open chord. Then I'd drop a knife with a metal handle on it, hitting random strings,' Marr later said. Smiths fans with sensitive hearing may be able to make out the same effect in This Charming Man (1983), though Marr says it's 'buried beneath about 15 tracks of guitar'.

# 'Have you tried bowing the guitar?'

## The story of Jimmy Page's best trick

Jimmy Page was inspired to take a violin bow to his guitar by David McCallum, a classically-trained violinist whose identically-named actor son starred in The Man From U.N.C.L.E. 'He said to me one day, "Have you ever tried bowing the guitar?"' Page later recalled. 'I tried it, and I realised there was something in it.'

The eureka moment happened in the mid-'60s, when Page was a session musician, and another guitarist was already using the technique: Eddie Phillips of mod-psychedelia fusioneers The Creation, who claimed to have first tried it in 1963. Page went public with the bow in August 1966 in San Francisco where, having joined The Yardbirds to play bass, he deputised on lead guitar for an illness-stricken Jeff Beck (and thereby briefly became the band's co-lead guitarist once Beck had returned). Having formed Led Zeppelin, he used the trick sparingly: on Dazed And Confused and How Many Times from their self-titled debut album (1969), and In The Light from Physical Graffiti (1975), on which it was used with an acoustic guitar.

To see Page and his bow in full flight, have a look at the Led Zep concert film The Song Remains The Same. 'On that album, I think some of the bowed melodic lines are pretty incredible,' he said in 1993. 'I remember being really surprised with it when I heard it played back. I thought, "Boy, that really was an innovation that meant something."'

*Jimmy Page: bow fiddly*

69

# I LIKE TO MOOG IT, MOOG IT

## A 30-year history of the synthesiser, 1957-87

**1957** In the USA, the RCA corporation comes up with the Mark II Sound Synthesiser, a big leap on from Mark I, revealed in 1955. It has one brilliant feature: a sequencer, meaning it can be programmed with patterns of notes that no mere human could possibly pull off.

**1963** Under the auspices of the BBC Radiophonic Workshop, the oft-overlooked **Delia Derbyshire** creates a proto-synthpop masterpiece: the Dr Who theme (written by one Ron Grainer), whose sounds are created via painstakingly-made tape effects.

**1964** New York native **Robert Moog** (you actually pronounce it 'Moag') unveils the first keyboard-based synthesiser, called the Moog Modular, at that year's Audio Engineering Society Convention in Manhattan. He takes orders straight away.

**1967** The first Moog synthesiser – the 900 – goes into production, and is shown off to curious musicians at the Monterey Pop festival, near San Francisco. The same year, it features on **The Doors'** LP Strange Days and Pisces, Aquarius, Capricorn & Jones Ltd. by **The Monkees**. Its huge dimensions and tangled wires suggested a scaled-down telephone exchange.

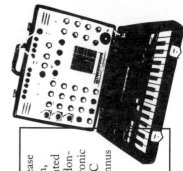

**1971** The pleasingly portable MiniMoog (*pictured*) goes into production. Among its first users: prog keyboard titans **Keith Emerson** and **Rick Wakeman**.

**March 1972 Stevie Wonder** releases Music Of My Mind, made with two electronic music pioneers and Moog experts called **Bob Margouleff** and **Malcolm Cecil**, who make synth-centred records under the name **Tonto's Expanding Headband**.

**March 1973 Pink Floyd** release The Dark Side Of The Moon, which uses two freshly-invented synths produced by the London-based company EMS (Electronic Music Studios), run by a BBC Radiophonic Workshop alumnus called **Peter Zinovieff**: the VCS3 (it stands for Voltage Controlled Synthesiser) and the Synthi A (*pictured*).

**October 1973 Kraftwerk** release the album Ralf und Florian, marking their first decisive use of synthesisers, which will really burst to the fore on the following year's LP Autobahn. Among their favoured machinery are a MiniMoog and an EMS Synthi AKS, as well as kit they've knocked up themselves.

**1978** The Japanese firm Roland introduce the polyphonic Jupiter 4. To hear its glories, have a listen to I Dream Of Wires by **Gary Numan**, or – in 'arpeggiator' mode – **Duran Duran**'s Rio.

**1981** The obligatory mention for Basildon synth pop troupe **Depeche Mode**. In April their first single Dreaming Of Me peaks at No 57, but by September they're in the Top 10 with Just Can't Get Enough. Among their kit: the just-introduced Moog Source.

**1983** A real game changer. Yamaha introduce the DX7, a new digital synthesiser that arguably defines the essential sound of the 1980s – as heard on **Harold Faltermeyer**'s gnaw-your-arm-off 1985 UK hit Axel F, taken from the soundtrack of Beverly Hills Cop.

**1976** Korg unveil a monophonic synth called the 770 *(pictured)*, subsequently bought by **Simple Minds** and the early **Human League**.

**1979** The Australian company Fairlight demonstrate the first CMI (Computer Musical Instrument), a ground-breaking polyphonic sampling synth. **Kate Bush**'s 1980 album Never For Ever is among the first LPs on which it can be heard; producer **Trevor Horn** is duly bowled over and famously uses it on **Frankie Goes To Hollywood**'s 1983 No 1 single Relax.

**1982** Roland introduce the Juno 60, a polyphonic keyboard much beloved of the **Eurythmics. A Flock Of Seagulls** are also quite partial.

**1987** Novel use of the Roland TB-303 *(pictured right)*, a bassline-generating unit, defines the first stirrings of Acid House: it produces the 'squelch' sound at the heart of such trailblazing tunes as Acid Tracks by the Chicago-based **Phuture**. Soon enough, electronic dance music threatens to eat the world, and the story is complete. Kind of.

# Delay, distortion, fuzz and 'flange'
Rock's answer to submarine science: effects pedals and the guitarists who've used them

## Fuzz
Among the first mass-marketed effects pedals was the Fuzz-tone, manufactured by Gibson guitars offshoot Maestro circa 1964. 'Guttural, mellow, raucous, tender, raw – the "fuzz" effect,' raved the adverts, and the world was decisively turned on by Keith Richards' use of it on (I Can't Get No) Satisfaction in 1965. Note also the Dallas-Arbiter Fuzz Face, invented in the UK, introduced in 1966, and much loved by that great effects king Jimi Hendrix (much more of whom below).

*The Fuzz Face*

## Univibe
Introduced in 1968 by the Univox company, aimed at replicating the revolving-speaker sound beloved of psychedelicists, and housed in a big old sheet-metal box. Those in the know refer to its sound as a 'pulsating swirl': for evidence, listen to **Jimi Hendrix**'s Machine Gun (1970) and out-there reading of The Star Spangled Banner (1969). Guitar-shop regulars take note: the same essential sound is delivered by any number of phaser (or phase-shifter) units.

## Flanger

Amazing rock fact: the name of this effect is traceable to **John Lennon** asking Beatles producer **George Martin** how he achieved the trippy effect on his vocals that came from an effect simply known as Automatic Double Tracking. 'It's very simple,' Martin replied. 'We take the original image and we split it through a double-bifurcated sploshing flange with double negative feedback.' Ergo the phaser-like flanger, whereby the sound of a guitar – or anything else – moves in and out of sync with itself, creating a queasy kind of sonic wobble. To instantly understand, have a listen to **The Clash**'s Lost In The Supermarket (1979), and a **Mick Jones** guitar part done on an MXR Flanger, introduced in 1977.

*George Martin*

## Chorus
A chip off the flanging block, whose lush, aquatic tone defined the prevailing guitar sound of the early to mid 1980s. The first proper example was the Boss CE-1 Chorus Ensemble, introduced in 1976, and showcased by **Andy Summers** on such **Police** hits as Message In A Bottle (1979). Chorus was/is also much beloved of such guitarists as The Pretenders' **James Honeyman-Scott**, The Cult's **Billy Duffy**, The Cure's **Robert Smith**, and The Smiths' **Johnny Marr**. **Kurt Cobain** was also partial, as proved by, say, Nirvana's Come As You Are (1991).

## Wah-wah
This one's all about a 'sweepable peaking filter', though non-scientists might like to think of it as a way of loading a guitar sound with either treble or bass, using a foot pedal (which is not quite right, but almost there). Whatever, the Clyde McCoy Wah-Wah (1966), Vox Wah (1967) and Cry Baby (1968) quickly became truly iconic – by way of a reminder, listen to **Hendrix**'s Voodoo Child (Slight Return) (1968), **Isaac Hayes**' Theme From Shaft (1971), or **The Stone Roses**' Fools' Gold (1989). Oh, and one other thing: **The Band**'s Up On Cripple Creek (1969) was the first recorded example of a keyboard being stuck through a wah-wah unit.

## Octave divider
**Hendrix** strikes again. In 1967, his effects guru Roger Mayer – who, somewhat fascinatingly, started out doing secret work on the science of submarine warfare for the British navy – came up with the Octavia, a device that could treat his guitar signal to add a note an octave up, a trick

you can hear on the solos in Purple Haze (1967). Copycat pedals soon followed, and though the effect eventually fell out of fashion, it was revived by **Jack White**: it's an octave-divider that makes his guitar sound like a bass on **The White Stripes**' Seven Nation Army (2003).

## Overdrive/Distortion

Essentially, two ways of making even the most bog-standard guitar-and-amp set-ups approximate the sound of an overheating speaker being taken to within an inch of its life by a sonic lunatic (or something). The old-school king of the first kind of device was the Ibanez TS-808 Tube Screamer, introduced in 1979, and favoured by the Texan blues-rock god **Stevie Ray Vaughan**. The second is exemplified by the thrillingly simple Turbo RAT pedal (1989), invented in Kalamazoo, Michigan, and favoured by the likes of the Pixies' **Frank Black** and ex-Blur fella **Graham Coxon** (as well as bassist **Alex James**, who put his bass through one on 1997's Song 2).

## Delay

Before the late 1970s, guitarists who fancied using echo relied on bulky inventions like the Maestro Echoplex, forever associated with the British folk-rock virtuoso **John Martyn**. Around the turn of the decade, however, there came a new breed of analogue delay pedals, quickly followed by digital devices – and thus was born the trademark sound of U2's Dave **'The Edge'** Evans, minted on The Unforgettable Fire (1984). Aspiring U2 tribute bands and people who want to torture their neighbours with multiple renditions of Where The Streets Have No Name should take note: his secret was the Korg SDD-3000, introduced in 1982.

## Talk Box

Not nice at all. You know it when you hear it: via a plastic tube, the guitar cross-fertilised with a human voice, to make it sound a bit like a monster from Dr Who. The definitive device was the Heil Talk Box, the work of a renowned US sound engineer named Peter Heil, who donated one of the first to soft-rock figurehead **Peter Frampton**. It was thus used on Frampton Comes Alive (1976) and, thanks to Frampton's influence, **Bon Jovi**'s Living On A Prayer (1986). Hell awaits, we're saying.

*Bob Heil's Talk Box*

# Putting it all together the Jimi Hendrix way

The virtuoso's onstage set-up, circa 1969: four pedals, one guitar, and three stacks

*a Fender Stratocaster, b Univox Univibe, c Univibe foot controller, d Vox Wah, e Roger Mayer Octavia, f Dallas-Arbiter Fuzz Face, g Marshall stacks*

# THE UNUSUAL SUSPECTS

Your Stratocasters and Les Pauls might look good, but some people will always want to step outside the world of Fenders, Gibsons and Rickenbackers, and put an accent on the guitar as an oddly-contoured, possibly futuristic statement of individuality. It's been a gambit favoured by no end of guitarists, from Bo Diddley through Brian Jones and on in turn to scores of Heavy Metallers. Oh, and one other thing: some allegedly 'classic' models were simply too ugly to print. Here, one thinks of the very '80s-esque Steinberger line of guitars and basses, essentially headless necks clamped to small black boxes, enthusiastically taken up by the likes of Genesis's Mike Rutherford, Curt Smith out of Tears For Fears and David Bowie circa Tin Machine. They have not endured, and we do not want to encourage a comeback.

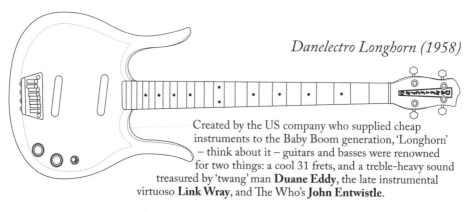

## *Danelectro Longhorn (1958)*

Created by the US company who supplied cheap instruments to the Baby Boom generation, 'Longhorn' – think about it – guitars and basses were renowned for two things: a cool 31 frets, and a treble-heavy sound treasured by 'twang' man **Duane Eddy**, the late instrumental virtuoso **Link Wray**, and The Who's **John Entwistle**.

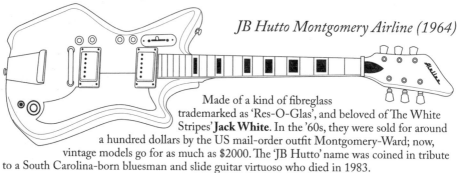

## *JB Hutto Montgomery Airline (1964)*

Made of a kind of fibreglass trademarked as 'Res-O-Glas', and beloved of The White Stripes' **Jack White**. In the '60s, they were sold for around a hundred dollars by the US mail-order outfit Montgomery-Ward; now, vintage models go for as much as $2000. The 'JB Hutto' name was coined in tribute to a South Carolina-born bluesman and slide guitar virtuoso who died in 1983.

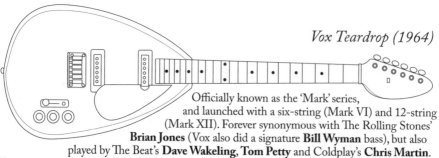

## *Vox Teardrop (1964)*

Officially known as the 'Mark' series, and launched with a six-string (Mark VI) and 12-string (Mark XII). Forever synonymous with The Rolling Stones' **Brian Jones** (Vox also did a signature **Bill Wyman** bass), but also played by The Beat's **Dave Wakeling**, **Tom Petty** and Coldplay's **Chris Martin**.

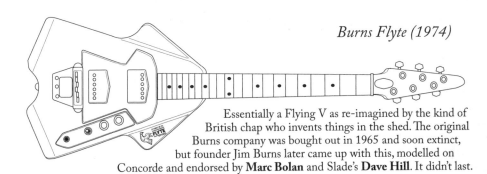

*Burns Flyte (1974)*

Essentially a Flying V as re-imagined by the kind of
British chap who invents things in the shed. The original
Burns company was bought out in 1965 and soon extinct,
but founder Jim Burns later came up with this, modelled on
Concorde and endorsed by **Marc Bolan** and Slade's **Dave Hill**. It didn't last.

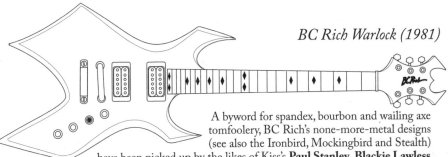

*BC Rich Warlock (1981)*

A byword for spandex, bourbon and wailing axe
tomfoolery, BC Rich's none-more-metal designs
(see also the Ironbird, Mockingbird and Stealth)
have been picked up by the likes of Kiss's **Paul Stanley**, **Blackie Lawless**
from W.A.S.P and Mötley Crüe's **Nikki Sixx**. We like the Warlock best, thanks to 1)a proud
endorsement from Slayer's **Kerry King**, 2)adverts featuring a skull in a wig, and 3)the name.

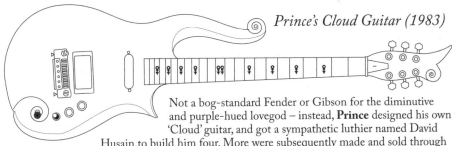

*Prince's Cloud Guitar (1983)*

Not a bog-standard Fender or Gibson for the diminutive
and purple-hued lovegod – instead, **Prince** designed his own
'Cloud' guitar, and got a sympathetic luthier named David
Husain to build him four. More were subsequently made and sold through
Prince's two shops in Minneapolis and London, before the guitar firm Schecter produced
replicas. They're very small, apparently.

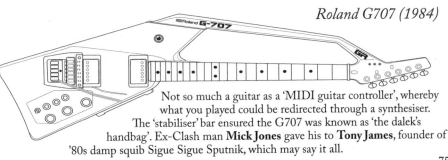

*Roland G707 (1984)*

Not so much a guitar as a 'MIDI guitar controller', whereby
what you played could be redirected through a synthesiser.
The 'stabiliser' bar ensured the G707 was known as 'the dalek's
handbag'. Ex-Clash man **Mick Jones** gave his to **Tony James**, founder of
'80s damp squib Sigue Sigue Sputnik, which may say it all.

# Chapter 4

# THE MUSIC AND LYRICS

I n 1967, The Byrds – who were obviously feeling rather jaded – released a single called So You Want To Be A Rock'n'Roll Star, one of countless items in the canon that casts a sceptical eye over the mess of ambition, chicanery and profit-and-loss that lies behind the average musical career. By way of a bit of backhanded musical advice, its second line found its authors advising anyone who was interested to first buy an electric guitar, and then 'take some time and learn how to play'.

As the various musical feats pulled off by that group prove, there's something to that advice but, then again, perhaps not. To change the course of music history, you do not always have to know an E6 from a Cmajor7 and have a drummer who can do a bit more than the basics. Indeed, there's a case to be made for the idea that rock'n'roll's whole point was to make the rudiments of music so simple that anyone could join in, thus increasing the chances of some great super-democratic teenage riot (kind of thing). If you listen to The Kingsmen's watershed hit version of the rock standard Louie Louie, released in 1963 (more of which follows), that sounds like its basic message, as with most of the primitively thrilling 'garage' and punk music that followed it.

For better or worse, the same idea has long defined the world of indie-rock, as was once proved when a journalist from a British music magazine asked that week's toilet-circuit hopefuls about their attitude to matters of technical proficiency. Was it, he wondered, basically a matter of, 'Pick up a guitar, plug it in, hit it'? 'Yeah,' said his interviewee. 'That's pretty much how I got started.' The group in question, in case anyone was wondering, were called Huggy Bear: they were no geniuses, but if you listen to a thrilling 1993 single called Her Jazz, you'll understand how potent cheap and clumsy music can be.

There are two items in this chapter that make the point even more explicit. One is called 'Play the guitar in an hour', and it sets out how you might be able to do exactly that, by following the lead set by such noble minimalists as Bonehead out of Oasis, Spiritualized's Jason Pierce and Status Quo. There's also a brief tutorial titled 'Play the bass in half an hour', which essentially says that though there might be more satisfactory ways of providing rock's 'bottom end', thrumming along with very little dexterity at all will easily get you by. And the drums? It might take a day or two to get your feet and hands properly co-ordinated while understanding that good drumming is – according to Blur's Dave Rowntree, anyway – a matter of 'playing the gaps not the music', but the same point often applies, and simplicity is too often underrated. This is obviously not the whole story, and being able to play in an interesting and varied way has its uses, but it's surely worth bearing in mind. If you don't, you may end up playing what was once known as 'progressive' rock, and you really wouldn't want that to happen.

But what about the words? This is a bit harder, if only because yelping the first thing that comes into your head may well may lead you to instantly fall flat, so there's a strong argument for at least a limited grasp of metre, rhyme and having something interesting to say. There again, to make things even more complicated, no end of people have achieved great success by singing borderline nonsense. This can be a good thing, as proved by such early rock classics as Tutti Frutti and Be-Bop A Lula. But it can also be thoroughly bad, which you may know if you own any number of records: even U2 fans, for example, will concede that a song called Elevation, replete with inexplicable stuff about a mole 'digging in a hole' and one line that rhymes 'guitar' with 'cigar', is not exactly their greatest achievement.

In that context, all we can do is offer some advice. You may want to pay tribute to Ian Dury And The Blockheads by picking up a guitar, hitting it, and then writing an elegant short story about stealing pornographic magazines in Romford. You could also follow the lead set by that great modern poet Thom Yorke, and base your oeuvre around such reference points as cars, plane crashes, worms and dirt. Or maybe you'd like to emulate the Manic Street Preachers, and make mention in your music of such varied figures as Lenin, the cricketer Matthew Maynard, Madonna, Jack Lemmon and good old Pol Pot.

Back to The Byrds. Having dispensed its wisdom about guitars and learning to play them, So You Want To Be A Rock'n'Roll Star also underlines the importance of having your 'hair combed right' and ensuring 'your pants fit tight', which is what the chapter after this one is all about. In the meantime, as a certain kind of DJ used to say, cue the music…

# GENRES? I'M ONLY DANCING!*

**Beyond punk, prog and Britpop – the musical sub-divisions time forgot. Mostly…**

## Alt-country

*c.1995* aka 'Americana'. Genre named after internet newsgroup, with pedigree dating back to 1990 and the first album by Illinois band Uncle Tupelo. Proudly tapping back into influence of such country pioneers as The Carter Family, Hank Williams et al, along with trailblazing country-rocker Gram Parsons, new crop of bands attempted to avenge bland-out personified by Garth Brooks and get back to country music's more gritty aspects. As with basic idea, scene's journal No Depression (est. 1995) still with us.
**Bands/Artists**: Uncle Tupelo, The Handsome Family, Bonnie 'Prince' Billy

*Alt-country couple The Handsome Family*

## Anarcho-punk

*c.1979* Ideologically-hardened outgrowth of initial punk upsurge that angrily emphasised politics of pacifism, feminism, animal rights and – of course – anarchism. Idea's most prominent flagbearers were East London collective Crass, though plenty of bands popularised similar mixture of fury, army surplus apparel and oft-graffitied 'anarchy' symbol (it looks like this Ⓐ).
**Bands**: Crass, Flux Of Pink Indians, Conflict

## Anti-folk

*c.1985* Pioneered in response to well-established New York folk scene, and centred on after-hours Lower East Side club called The Fort. Denoted non-electric music with distinct punk aspect, and frequent emphasis on political consciousness – most successful standard-bearer was the early Beck, though idea still evident in music of occasional acoustic-based iconoclasts.
**Artists**: Beck, Adam Green, Hamell On Trial

## Big beat

*c.1998* Genre crystallised by opening of Big Beat Boutique club night at Brighton's Concorde venue in 1996. Basic idea: pulling dance music away from 1)increasingly moronic aesthetics of house music, and 2)clubland elitism, via injection of rock-esque beats and samples. Scene dominated by South Coast label Skint. Faded by 2001-ish, but music still sounds great when you're drunk.
**Artists**: Fatboy Slim, The Chemical Brothers, Bentley Rhythm Ace

## Cowpunk

*c.1983* Genre-name applied to two very different ideas: American attempt to fuse punk approach with countrified touches, centred on Southern California, and London-centred scene, seen as rebellion against New Romantics, that had more in common with skiffle and leant towards folk-punk fusion pioneered by The Pogues. First weathered much better, though both long dead.
**US bands**: The Beat Farmers, The Blasters
**UK bands**: The Boothill Foot Tappers, Shillelagh Sisters

## Electroclash

*c.2001* Superficially exciting movement-cum-scene whose triple centres were Berlin, New York (term was invented by local DJ Larry Tee), and East London. Harked back to NY of early '80s, with arty-farty aspect redolent of scene around Andy Warhol, pronounced early hip hop influence, and much use of old-school analogue equipment. By 2003, but a memory.
**Bands/artists**: Peaches, Fischerspooner, Chicks On Speed

*Lame pun refers to 1972 song by glam-rocker David Bowie, covered in 1980 by rockabilly revivalists the Polecats*

**Folktronica**
*c.2001* Generic development traceable to fondness of dance music devotees for returning home post-club and listening to such folk-ish icons as John Martyn, Nick Drake et al. Basic idea combines dance-esque technology and repetition with soothing, pastoral feel. Annual Welsh Green Man festival is essentially gathering of Folktronica tribe.
**Bands/artists**: Four Tet, Adem, Tunng

**Fraggle**
*c.1991* Name for alternative rock bands, some of whom basically represented younger end of 'Grebo' genre, reputedly coined by band-booker at indie venue Harlow Square in recognition of similarity between scruffily-attired groups/fans and characters from Muppets spin-off TV show Fraggle Rock.
**Bands**: Ned's Atomic Dustbin, Senseless Things, Mega City Four

**Freakbeat**
*c.1983* Retrospectively invented – by owner of '60s-fixated record label Bam Caruso – to describe groups who combined pop-oriented, often mod-aligned 'beat' music with first stirrings of psychedelia. Music

*Julian Hewings, aka 'Hooligan', of New Wave Of New Wavers These Animal Men*

tended to combine primitive effects with loud volume, and took lead from The Who. Often interchangeable with 'psych', and much beloved of kind of people who wear crushed velvet and live in Brighton.
**Bands**: The Creation, John's Children, The Move

**Grebo**
*c.1987* Colloquial term coined in West Midlands, used to describe crop of local(ish) groups united by garish, somewhat Mad Max-esque fashion sense (e.g. dreadlocks, Doc Martens, big shorts), ragged rock with occasional dance influence, and curry-down-your-front excess.
**Bands**: Pop Will Eat Itself, Gaye Bykers On Acid, Crazyhead

**Landfill Indie**
*c.2008* Concept first coined in The Word magazine to malign tendency of modern British 'alternative' bands to crowd around depressingly ordinary musical blueprint fit only for rubbish-dump: chundering guitars, big choruses, zero sense of adventure, though millions of record buyers remain inexplicably enthusiastic. Use of word 'The' in band names apparently obligatory.
**Bands**: The Pigeon Detectives, The Fratellis, The Wombats

**Mash-up**
*c.2001* aka 'Bastard pop': briefly fashionable deluge of records that spliced together unlikely songs into new hybrid forms. Results included superficially impressive fusions of Christina Aguilera's Genie In A Bottle with The Strokes' Hard To Explain, and Gary Numan's Cars and Adina Howard's 1995 US hit Freak Like Me, subsequently adopted by the Sugababes.
**Artists**: Too Many DJs, Girls On Top, Freelance Hellraiser

**New Wave Of New Wave**
*c.1993* Somewhat humorous term coined by NME journalists to rope together punk-influenced, implicitly anti-grunge bands with pronounced sense of Britishness – and, very often, fondness for amphetamine sulphate. Best of crop were subsequently tarred with 'Britpop' brush, rest fast-tracked to obscurity.
**Bands**: S\*M\*A\*S\*H, These Animal Men, Elastica (kind of)

## No Wave
*c.1977* Symbolised rejection of so-called
New Wave and US punk's more retro-rock
elements by loose-knit milieu focused on New
York's Lower East Side, and people aiming
to create music with precious little influence/
precedent. Ex-Roxy Music bod Brian Eno was
enthusiastic, and produced multi-artist album
No New York.
**Bands**: Suicide, Teenage Jesus And The Jerks,
Contortions

## Noelrock
*c.1996* At peak of Oasis's pre-eminence in UK,
NME invented rum-sounding genre, based
on Noel Gallagher's approval of clutch of
guitar bands. 'If the most successful songwriter
of his generation champions a group,' said
not-fawning-at-all article, 'then said group are
guaranteed more kudos and, quite possibly,
more sales.' Ergo wave of meat-and-potatoes
rock with revivalist aspect that arguably
represented fag-end of Britpop, though
millions of sales were briefly racked up by
bands who favoured '60s influences and often
laddish disposition.
**Bands**: Cast, Ocean Colour Scene, Kula Shaker

## Oi!
*c.1980* Term introduced to culture by then-
music journalist Garry Bushell. Described
avowedly working-class bands, essentially
set on reclaiming spirit of punk from more
arty-farty outfits and proudly maintaining
social-realist outlook and pared-down music
pioneered by, say, Sham 69 – an idea quickly
appropriated by neo-Nazi elements. Thus, these
days not a term one hears much.
**Bands**: Cockney Rejects, Angelic Upstarts,
The 4 Skins

## Post-rock
*c.1996* Initially coined by music writer Simon
Reynolds in 1994 review of East London outfit
Bark Psychosis, nailed as musical blueprint by
Kentucky-based indie band Slint, and briefly
ubiquitous between 1996 and 1997. Essential
idea: rock stripped of song structures and
rendered experimental, but without prog-rock
indulgence (or, reductively speaking, intros that
go on forever).
**Bands**: Slint, Tortoise, Godspeed You! Black
Emperor

## Psychobilly
*c.1982* Word first used in 1976 Johnny Cash
hit One Piece At A Time, and subsequently
pilfered by The Cramps. Thanks partly to their
example, decisively took off as a genre in the
UK, thanks to mixture of punk and rock'n'roll
revivalism, and the crucial Klub Foot club
night, held at the Clarendon in Hammersmith,
West London. For quick undertanding of scene
and its '50s roots, go to deeply entertaining
compilation Rockabilly Psychosis And The
Garage Disease (1984).
**Bands**: Meteors, Guana Batz, The Sting-Rays,
Demented Are Go

## Riot Grrrl
*c.1992* Long-overdue rebellion against male-
dominated mores of rock that took name from
fanzine co-authored by musicians based around
Washington DC, and quickly spread to the UK,
bringing occasional female-only gigs and idea
that musical technique was overrated. Cause
was briefly taken up by weekly music press, but
fizzled out fast; most enduring song remains
Bikini Kill's 1993 track Rebel Girl.
**Bands**: Bikini Kill, Bratmobile, Huggy Bear

## Shambling
*c.1986* First used to describe long-lost
Yorkshire-based band Bogshed (originally
called The Amazing Roy North Penis Band in
tribute to sometime host of BBC1's Basil Brush
show) by John Peel, and subsequently extended
to variety of UK indie-rockers who, put simply,
could often barely play. De rigueur sartorial
style emphasised infantilist aspect, e.g. crap
sandals, hair-slides, half-mast trousers.
**Bands**: Bogshed, Talulah Gosh, The Pastels

## Shoegazing
*c.1991* Name given to slew of indie-rock
bands by Food records boss and Blur associate
Andy Ross, to denote habit of 'performing'
while staring at floor – though most bands
thus denoted also shared Thames Valley
origins, influence of My Bloody Valentine
and passionate love of effects pedals. Owing
to somewhat incestuous nature of associated
milieu (built around long-defunct West End
nightclub Syndrome), Melody Maker archly
coined alternative term 'The Scene That
Celebrates Itself'.
**Bands**: Ride, Chapterhouse, Slowdive

# FULL METAL BRACKETS
## The genre that spawned the most sub-genres: Heavy Metal

**New Wave Of British Heavy Metal**
*c.1980* Aka NWOBHM (pronounced 'nuh-wob-um'). Invented by Geoff 'Deaf' Barton, journalist who founded Kerrang! magazine, and based around welcome injection of Metal with no-nonsense, proletarian aspect.
**Bands**: Iron Maiden, Saxon, Def Leppard

**Glam Metal**
*c.1981* Also became known as Hair Metal and Poodle Rock. Pioneered by Finnish band Hanoi Rocks, adopted en masse in LA, and soon huge. In supposed Second Wave, became so 'glam' as to apparently come close to losing any Metal aspect at all.
**Bands**: Mötley Crüe, Poison, Warrant

**Thrash Metal**
*c.1982* May be Metallica's doing, as evidenced by debut album Kill 'Em All. Basic idea: seizing on example set by NWOBHM, avenging Glam bands, and specialising in super-fast songs and misanthropic lyrics.
**Bands**: Metallica, Megadeth, Slayer

**Death Metal**
*c.1984* Sub-genre that blurred into Black and Thrash Metal, but was that bit more brutal. As with some other metal types, often denoted – and still does – interest in putrefaction, suffering, and all that stuff.
**Bands:** Possessed, Death, Deicide

**Black Metal**
*c.1984* Takes name from 1982 album by Geordie metal trio Venom, who spawned imbalanced music – often made by Norwegians – that tended to big up the Devil, hatred etc. Forever associated with very bad stuff thanks to Satanist musician named Varg Vikernes, who burned down churches and murdered the guitarist with Black Metal band Mayhem (he's currently serving a 21-year sentence in prison).
**Bands**: Darkthrone, Mayhem, Celtic Frost

**Viking Metal**
*c.1988* What larks! Popularity of extreme Metal genres in Scandinavia and latent Norse element in heavy rock – witness trailblazing mention of Valhalla in Led Zep's Immigrant Song – led to inevitable fusion of North-European mythology and Black Metal elements.
**Bands**: Bathory, Enslaved, Borknagar

**Rap Metal**
*c.1992-93* An obvious enough idea, encouraged by much sampling of metallic(ish) sources – Led Zep, Aerosmith, AC/DC – by such seminal rap acts as Run DMC and the Beastie Boys. In 1991, idea furthered by Anthrax/Public Enemy collaboration on the latter's Bring The Noise, and sub-genre soon arrived in full effect, forming essential blueprint for Nu Metal.
**Bands**: Rage Against The Machine, Body Count, SX-10

**Nu Metal**
*c.1998* Laid waste by grunge, Metal almost breathed its last – but then came new breed, partly inspired by Rap Metal, who emphasised themes of teenage alienation and created millions-strong international subculture, who wore black 'hoodies', and – *quelle surprise* – despised Nu Metal tag. Still going strong(ish).
**Bands**: Korn, Linkin Park, Deftones

*Venom's Conrad Lant, aka Cronos, 'Rabid Captor of Bestial Malevolence'*

# Teach yourself guitar in an hour

To start, a quick word from **Jason Pierce**, the chief creative force of **Spiritualized**, the art-rock project who released their first work in 1990 and are still with us. 'The first bunch of songs I wrote all used E,' he once said. 'Then I started throwing in an A for some songs, then I started using G because my voice changed, and sometimes I'll add in a D if I think I need to. There aren't any rules, but those four chords cover most of rock'n'roll.'

To take your first steps as a guitarist, you first need to tune your guitar (Google 'guitar tuner', and go from there). Then, give numbers to the digits of your fingering hand as demonstrated in this illustration, which will allow you to understand chord diagrams. After that, steel yourself for a good deal of pain, which can be allayed by regularly dipping your fingers in white spirit. Then bear in mind this story about the ex-Oasis guitarist **Paul 'Bonehead' Arthurs**, retold in the Oasis biography What's The Story?, written by their one-time Head of Security, Ian Robertson.

'After a show in LA in February '95, some guitar fetishist bluffed his way into the dressing room and began to offer his opinions, completely unsought: "Man, all you played was, like, A, C, D or G." Bonehead's reply could only be construed as helpful. "Listen, dickhead, that might well be all I played, but I'm the one playing it, I'm the one in the band, and you paid to see me do it."'

*The key to the crucial chord-code*

## The Jason Pierce/Bonehead chord guide

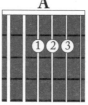

Pierce, Bonehead, and the big five shapes

To rock out in a minimalist style according to the blueprint explained above, here's what you need – and when it comes to some classic songs, even some of this is surplus to requirements. The Velvet Underground's **Heroin**, for example, uses only D and G, with the open D string (third from the bottom) used as an ongoing drone.

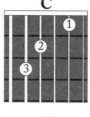

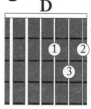

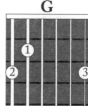

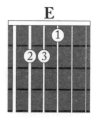

## The three-chord trick

Just about all blues songs and most classic rock'n'roll tunes are built around the classic three-chord progression. In the key of A, you go like this: play A for four bars, then D for two bars, then A again for two bars, then E for one bar, D for one bar, and then back to A. In the key of D, the same pattern runs thus: D-G-D-A-G-D. This thrillingly simple idea will enable you to have a go at any number of songs, from **Hound Dog** and **Blue Suede Shoes**, through Bob Dylan's **Subterranean Homesick Blues**, to Led Zeppelin's **Rock And Roll**.

## The barre chord

In fact, Bonehead's real speciality – as with a lot of guitarists – was the barre chord, a shape you can shift up and down the neck, allowing you to play just about any major-key chord you like (though it'll initially be very painful). Moreover, if you hold down the barre chord shape and then lift off finger number two, you're into minor chords, which opens up a whole new universe. At the seventh fret, for example, you'll get B minor, which fits into the key of D, and another classic chord progression: D-B minor-G-A, which is the basis of The Undertones' **Teenage Kicks.**

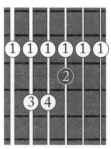

*The barre chord*

*The diagram*

## Rhythm guitar for the lazy

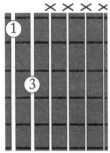

But never mind all that. Using the same anywhere-along-the-neck principle of the barre chord, you can actually play rhythm guitar using just two fingers (numbers 1 and 3, ideally) and a shape that suffices for the chug-chug-chug sound of a lot of punk, hard rock and heavy metal, and – once you've got a distortion pedal – big, evil-sounding riffs, à la **Tony Iommi** from **Black Sabbath** (who was forced into this approach by an industrial accident that removed the ends of fingers 2 and 3). Also, you can copy the same two-fingered shape on to the A and D strings, and the D

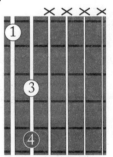

*Iommi shape*

*The key to Quo*

and G strings. With some thought, this thrillingly basic idea will enable you to approximate any number of classics, from Deep Purple's guitar-shop standard **Smoke On The Water** to the Sex Pistols' **God Save The Queen**. Even better, by using finger 4 to alternately fret a note two frets above finger number 3, you'll get into the propulsive 'der-ner-ner' riff that began with **Chuck Berry**, and has defined nearly four decades of music by the legendarily primitive **Status Quo.**

## One last trick: suspended 4th chords

Again, using the same principle as the barre chord, there's an alternate shape for major chords in which you only play the guitar's top four strings, and finger 4 is freed up. You can then use that digit for a note one fret above finger number two, which creates what's known as a suspended fourth (or 'sus4') chord. With about two minutes of experimentation, you'll then quickly unlock the basic riff from **Pinball Wizard** by The Who, The Rolling Stones' **Start Me Up**, Free's **All Right Now** and The Cult's **Love Removal Machine.**

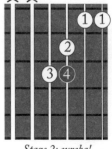

*Stage 1*

*Stage 2: eureka!*

So there you have it: now go and form a band.

# 'PLAY THE GAPS, NOT THE NOTES'

### The Zen-master guide to rock drumming, with Blur's Dave Rowntree

Giving a reasonable impression of competence on the drums is that bit harder than doing so on the guitar or bass, so it's maybe best to take the advice of a true expert: Blur's Dave Rowntree, who has been a drummer since his childhood and, on account of a classical training, knows that extra bit about the rudiments of his trade. What you're about to read is a little bit Zen-master, and therefore gets you to the heart of the delicate balancing act that is keeping time in a rock group.

But first, a point of fundamental importance. 'Playing an instrument is all about practice,' he says. 'What you get out is directly proportional to what you put in. The more you practise, the better you get. Those that are best have practised the most, and those that are the worst are the ones that don't think practice is important.'

And so to the mystical bit. 'There are some muso kind of things that I've discovered over the years,' says Rowntree. 'The fundamental thing about drumming is that you should actually play the gaps, not the notes. To be able to do that, you have to be good enough to let the drums play themselves, while you concentrate on the gaps. That's a kind of virtuoso ability: to imagine something, and

84

let your arms and legs just play it, without you having to think, Ooh, hang on – I put that there and then I hit that there. You should just go, Hmmm, and let the drums play themselves. And, when you get to that point, you can concentrate on the gaps. What you don't play is more important than what you do.'

At this point, he mentions the English jazz drummer Kenny Clare (1929-84), and the American jazz icon Buddy Rich (1917-87). 'You listen to the best jazz guys,' he says, 'and they're very like that. Sometimes, they go all out. But in general they're playing the very minimum they can get away with. Think about those Julian Opie drawings of Blur *[the famously minimalist portraits that adorned their Best Of album, released in 2000]*. It's incredible how few lines you need to get somebody's likeness. It's the same in drumming: it's amazing how little you have to play in order to keep get the rhythm right.'

He also emphasises the importance of being comfortable with your place at the back. 'If you can't resign yourself to where you fit in the music, you probably shouldn't be a drummer. It takes all sorts to be in a band, and you do need somebody who can stand in front of stage in front of a thousand people and go *[puts hands in the air triumphantly]* "Look at me!" I can't do that. To be a drummer who's got that urge… well, because it's a frustrated urge, they tend to play a kind of drums and live a kind of lifestyle that doesn't stand the test of time. The singer gets all the attention. That's the way it's always been in bands. If you can't resign yourself to that early on, you become Keith Moon and die a tragic death.'

To finish, he chews over the perils of the unnecessarily large drum kit – symbolised in this conversation, for one reason and another, by Neil Peart (b.1952) from the Canadian prog-metal trio Rush, whose equipment has long contained drums and cymbals easily exceeding double figures.

'With people of a slightly obsessive nature, I can understand why that happens, because it's easy to just add one more thing. You can imagine Neil Peart probably started off with a five-piece kit and two cymbals, and thought, I'll just get one more cymbal, cos then I add a bit of colour. And then it was, I'll have another drum there too. And before you know it, you've got a kind of…*menagerie.'*

# GREAT SONG ARCHETYPES #1: LOUIE LOUIE

The garage-rock classic Louie Louie was written by the Louisiana-born singer and songwriter **Richard Berry** in 1955, and inspired by a Spanish-language song titled El Loco Cha Cha, originally known as Amarren Al Loco (Tie Up The Crazy Guy), which has much in common with the Cuban folk classic Guantanamera. Berry copied its three-chord, ten-note riff (1-2-3/1-2/1-2-3/1-2) for a song most memorably covered in 1963 by **The Kingsmen**, from Portland, Oregon (and later immortalised in the scene from Quadrophenia in which a dancing Phil Daniels dives into the crowd below). Having reached No 2 in the Billboard Chart, Louie Louie became a standard, and spawned not only scores of covers by the likes of **The Kinks**, **The Beach Boys** and **The Stooges**, but a never-ending array of songs based on its central musical figure. Notable examples include **The Rolling Stones**' Get Off My Cloud (1965), **Lou Reed**'s Vicious (1972), **Boston**'s 1976 soft-rock classic More Than A Feeling, **John Travolta and Olivia Newton-John**'s Summer Nights (from Grease, 1978), and **Julian Cope**'s World Shut Your Mouth (1986). See also **Transvision Vamp**'s 1989 hit Baby I Don't Care, **Nirvana**'s Smells Like Teen Spirit (1991), **Eels**' Mr E's Beautiful Blues (2000), and **R.E.M.**'s 2008 hit Supernatural Superserious. Marking its entry into the rap era, Louie Louie was sampled on the **Ultramagnetic MCs**' Travelling At The Speed Of Thought in 1986. It also re-entered the popular consciousness as the de facto signature tune of John Landis's 1978 movie Animal House.

# GREAT SONG ARCHETYPES #2: THE BO DIDDLEY BEAT

Bo Diddley was born Ellas Otha Bates in McComb, Mississippi, on 30 December 1928. As well as his signature rectangular guitar, his enduring contribution to rock'n'roll is what became known as the Bo Diddley Beat, a percussive, rumba-like figure whose most obvious antecedent can be found in a call-and-response American standard titled Hambone (recorded, for example, in 1952 by the jazz/R&B drummer **Red Saunders**). Exemplified by such Bo Diddley recordings as 1956's Who Do You Love and 1957's Hey Bo Diddley, the beat soon became a regular feature of rock records, as proven by **Buddy Holly**'s Not Fade Away (1957, covered by **The Rolling Stones** in 1964), **Elvis Presley**'s (Marie's The Name) His Latest Flame (1961), and **The Strangelove**'s 1965 single I Want Candy, a hit for **Bow Wow Wow** in 1982.

In the ensuing four decades, the list of songs built on the Bo Diddley Beat has only extended; it includes **The Stooges**' 1969, **David Bowie**'s Panic In Detroit (1973), **Guns N' Roses**' Mr Brownstone (1987), **U2**'s Desire (1988), **George Michael**'s Faith (1988), **Primal Scream**'s Movin' On Up (1991), **Paul Weller**'s Woodcutter's Son (1995), and **The White Stripes**' Screwdriver (1999). Even when the beat is not explicit, plenty of classic songs use it more subtly: witness **The Smiths**' How Soon Is Now (1985), and Hateful, from **The Clash**'s London Calling (1979). Bo Diddley died on 2 June 2008, when Saul **'Slash' Hudson** was quoted thus: 'An entire rhythm is owed to just one guy – and that's pretty rare.'

*Bo Diddley's rectangular guitar*

# THE THOM YORKE LYRIC INDEX

A guide to his interests-cum-obsessions, including both Radiohead songs and his solo stuff: cars, stars, worms, dirt, water and more worms…

## TRANSPORT

*A career-long Yorke obsession, chiefly focused on cars and roads. 'You constantly hear of friends who die in car accidents for no reason,' he said in 1997. 'It fucks with my head completely. The day we have to stop getting in cars will be a very good day.'*

**Cars/Driving**
Stupid Car *1992*
Million Dollar Question *1992*
Punchdrunk Lovesick
Singalong *1994*
Killer Cars *1995*
Airbag *1997*
Subterranean Homesick
Alien *1997*
Let Down *1997*
Fitter Happier *1997*
Morning Bell *2000 & 2001*
Pyramid Song *2001*
Kinetic *2001*
And It Rained All Night
*2006 (solo)*
The Drunkk Machine
*2006 (solo)*
All I Need *2007*

**Ships/Boats**
Optimistic *2000*
Pulk/Pull Revolving
Doors *2001*
Pyramid Song *2001*
There There *2003*

**Motorways/Interstate highways**
Killer Cars *1995*
Maquiladora *1996*
Let Down *1997*

**Trains**
Black Star *1995*
Black Swan *2006 (solo)*

And It Rained All Night
*2006 (solo)*

**Planes**
Ripcord *1993*
The Bends *1995*
Lucky *1997*

**Tanks**
The Bends *1995*
Cuttooth *2001*

## HOME & FAMILY

*Radiohead are hardly devil-may-care rock'n'rollers, which may be why their music is smattered with references to hearth and home – though there again, some of this (e.g. seven references to walls) is a matter of standard-issue existential metaphor.*

**Children/Babies**
Bones *1995*
Fitter Happier *1997*
Climbing Up The Walls *1997*
Kid A *2000*
Idioteque *2000*
Morning Bell *2000 & 2001*
Fog *2001*
I Will *2003*
A Wolf At The Door *2003*

**Walls**
Thinking About You *1992*
Sulk *1995*
Paranoid Android *1997*
Climbing Up The Walls *1997*
The Gloaming *2003*
Cymbal Rush *2006 (solo)*
Jigsaw Falling Into Place *2007*
Bangers + Mash *2007*

**Doors**
Just *1995*

How Can You Be Sure? *1996*
Talk Show Host *1996*
A Wolf At The Door *2003*

**Windows**
Life In A Glass House *2001*
Scatterbrain *2003*
A Wolf At The Door *2003*
Skip Divided *2006 (solo)*

**Gardens/Lawns**
Nice Dream *1995*
No Surprises *1997*
Morning Bell *2000 & 2001*

**Keys/Locks**
Just *1995*
Climbing Up The Walls *1997*
House Of Cards *2007*

**Breakfast**
Myxomatosis *2003*
Gagging Order *2003*

**Fridges**
Karma Police *1997*

## ANIMAL CORNER

*Herein lies a veritable menagerie: quite a lot of birds and, among several other creatures, flies and worms; the latter have been mentioned five times. Which probably says a lot.*

**Birds, chickens, eggs etc.**
Street Spirit (Fade Out) *1995*
Paranoid Android *1997*
Life In A Glass House *2001*
Scatterbrain *2003*
Talk Show Host *1996*

**Dinosaurs**
Optimistic *2000*
Where I End And You
Begin *2003*

**Fish**
Optimistic *2000*
Weird Fishes/Arpeggi *2007*

**Pigs**
Paranoid Android *1997*
Fitter Happier *1997*

**Dogs**
India Rubber *1995*
Knives Out *2001*
Bodysnatchers *2007*
Skip Divided *2006 (solo)*

**Worms**
The Trickster *1994*
You Never Wash Up After
Yourself *1994*
Atoms For Peace *2006 (solo)*
And It Rained All Night
*2006 (solo)*
Weird Fishes/Arpeggi *2007*

**Flies**
Molasses *1995*
Optimistic *2000*
2+2=5 *2003*

# WATER

*Up there with
transport as a
regular Yorke
concern; it all
peaked in 2000–
2001, thanks to
his increasing fear of eco-disaster.
Note, for example, the sleevenotes
that came with Radiohead's Kid
A, headed 'Selected examples of ice
melt around the world'.*

**The Sea**
In Limbo *2000*
Where I End And You
Begin *2003*
Weird Fishes/Arpeggi *2007*

**Rivers/Waterfalls**
How To Disappear
Completely *2000*
Pyramid Song *2001*
I Might Be Wrong *2001*
Like Spinning Plates *2001*

We Suck Young Blood *2003*

**Floods, water in general**
Vegetable *1993*
Dollars And Cents *2001*
Sail To The Moon *2003*

**Lakes**
Lucky *1997*

# RELIGION, THE OCCULT ETC.

*Normal(ish) rock-
lyric fare. NB: the
reference to 'bishop's
robes' in the song
of the same name
is believed to be a
dig at one Michael
St John Parker, the headmaster of
the fee-paying Abingdon School
when all five of Radiohead were
pupils, who was fond of wearing
academic gowns.*

**God**
Sulk *1995*
Paranoid Android *1997*

**The Devil**
Videotape *2003*
I Am A Wicked Child *2003*
Skip Divided *2006 (solo)*

**Bishops/Vicars**
Bishop's Robes *1996*
Bangers + Mash *2007*

**Ghosts**
The Tourist *1997*
You And Whose Army *2001*
Weird Fishes/Arpeggi *2007*
Jetstream *2006 (solo)*

# MISCELLANEOUS

*To finish, a
grab-
bag
of
occasional lyrical
motifs that together
shine more light on
TY's doom-laden*

*worldview. Which is not to
knock him, incidentally: note
that a Radiohead B-side called
The Amazing Sounds Of Orgy
mentioned ,'The day the banks
collapse on us'. In 2001!*

**Dust, dirt, 'the stink',
'the filth'**
The Bends *1995*
Just *1995*
Paranoid Android *1997*
And It Rained All Night
*2006 (solo)*

**Trapdoors**
In Limbo *2000*
Pulk/Pull Revolving Doors
*2001*

**Power cuts**
My Iron Lung *1994*
Scatterbrain *2003*
Analyse *2006 (solo)*

**Knives**
Faithless The Wonder
Boy *1993*
Knives Out *2001*

**Phones/Mobiles/
Answering machines**
Nice Dream *1995*
Idioteque *2000*
A Reminder *1997*
A Wolf At The Door *2003*
A Rat's Nest *2006 (solo)*

*Thom
Yorke: it's
all about
cars and
worms*

# Play the bass in half an hour

**A life-changing tutorial featuring Blur's Alex James, also starring The Clash's Paul Simonon...and Sting**

'I wanted to play a keyboard: they were £600, and basses were £50. It was economics. But I was very lucky. If you're going to play keyboards or guitar, there are quite a lot of technicalities to master. With bass, it's just like having a big black felt-tip marker pen, or a big crayon. It's like a child's toy, really. So you don't have to think about lessons at all. You can worry about your hair.'

So says Blur's **Alex James**, who should know. Unless you aim for the kind of virtuosity one would associate with such players as **Paul McCartney**, **Bootsy Collins** and legendary thumb-god **Mark King** from Level 42, bass can indeed be the instrument not for musicians, but musicians' friends. The basic rudiments are blissfully simple, and there's really not much to worry about in the way of hardware and fancy accessories either. Alex goes on: 'There's an unspoken rule among bass players – that we don't talk shop. We roll our eyes when people start talking about all that. We don't have to worry about pedals or amps or anything. There's only four strings. You can pick it up quite quickly. Ten minutes will do it.'

Moreover, many successful(ish) bass players hold fast to the idea – either the essence of Zen wisdom or a matter of chronic laziness, depending on your point of view – that less is definitely more. U2's **Adam Clayton** is one of rock history's most minimalist bass players, and he knows what this means. In 2009, he said this: 'What I hate is having to change chord. If I can just do one thing on one note, but do it exactly the same, every single time forever...That is happiness for me.' He was apparently making a joke, but there again, listen to a lot of U2 basslines: they're not that far off.

Anyway, by way of getting started, an easy jumping-off point is to follow the lead set by The Clash's **Paul Simonon** in 1976: buy a cheap bass, get some Tipp-ex, and mark most of the notes you'll need on the neck. The basic idea is shown opposite; over time, as with typing, you'll instinctively know where the notes are, so you can rub the markings off. Two other important things: the strings should be tuned to E, A, D and G, and you'll need to think of your four fretting fingers as numbers 1, 2, 3 and 4 (for details, go back to page 82). Oh, and in answer to the eternal fingers or plectrum question, Alex James suggests 'a little bit of both'. And so to business...

*The on-bass notation of Paul Simonon (left): grasp this and, as Alex James (top) says, 'You can worry about your hair'*

88

# If you must, just play the basis of the guitar part

Not that this is really to be encouraged, but in plenty of classic rock music the bass player pretty much sticks to the mind-numbingly simple idea of always playing the 'root' note of the rhythm guitar part. Thus, if it's an E major, you play an E, and if it's an A minor, play A. As to when to hit a note, you have essentially two options: to follow the bass drum and play no more than four notes per bar (for a rough idea, have a listen to the verses of Joe Jackson's 1980 hit **It's Different For Girls**), or thwack out eight notes per bar. The latter is the basic idea behind most songs on The Sex Pistols' **Never Mind The Bollocks**, Oasis's **Definitely Maybe**, and Nirvana's **Smells Like Teen Spirit**. To master most of the latter, just thrum away on F, B♭, G♯ and C♯ – or consult the Simonon ready-reckoner and agree with your guitarist to drop it down to E, B, G and C. Simple!

## Octaves

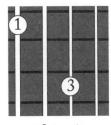

A veritable piece of piss, and an easy one to impress people with ('It can sound very Germanic,' says Alex James). Using your first and third fingers as shown, you can play the same notes on the first and third or second and fourth strings, which will mean they're an octave apart. Such is the secret behind The Knack's 1979 gonzo-rock beauty **My Sharona** (it's in G) and the intro to Jimi Hendrix's **Purple Haze** (in E).

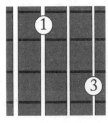

*Octave 1*

*Octave 2*

## The pentatonic minor scale

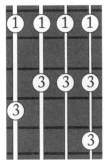

'It's the only one you need,' says Alex. In any key, you should first try five notes: in A, for example, they're A, C, D, E and G. Alex has used it in such Blur songs as **Girls & Boys** and **Song 2** – the latter song's basic bass riff is in the pentatonic minor scale of F, and built from F, E♭, G♯, B♭ and C. The first diagram shows how to play these notes anywhere on the neck, and the second one reveals another trick: if you miss out the second note, you're close to the basic basslines for The Beatles' **Taxman** (it's in D) and The Jam's very similar **Start!** (the same pattern in G, then D).

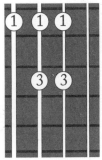

*The scale*

*Taxman/Start! basics*

## The fifth below

Really simple. 'If you've got your finger on any given fret,' says Alex, 'if you take your finger down a string in the same position, you can have a lot of fun. And it'll impress the girls.'

## Sting's bass player joke

As told to Alex James: 'This bloke wants to learn how to play the bass. He goes to the bass teacher, and the bass teacher says, "Right – go, E, E, E, A." He plays it: E, E, E, A. The teacher says, "Practise that, and come back next week for lesson number two." The bloke comes back the next week, and the teacher goes, "Right – go A, A, A, D." He plays it: A, A, A, D. The teacher says, "OK, come back next week, and I'll give you lesson three." The next week, the bloke doesn't turn up. They run into each other a little while later, and the teacher says, "Why didn't you come back?" The bloke says, "I was getting loads of gigs."'

# 'FLY...HIGH...SKY...DRAGONFLY'
## The definitive crap rhyming dictionary

**butterflies/flutterbyes/'everyone lies'** *Genesis, Supper's Ready, 1972* Amazing tripe from their seven-part prog-rock behemoth, also starring Winston Churchill and characters called 'Ikhnaton' and 'Itsacon', and partly performed by Peter Gabriel while dressed up as a giant flower. Punk rock, anybody?

**classic/attic/addict** *Adrian Gurvitz, Classic, 1982* Legendary triple howler by beardy, London-born singer-songwriter. Unforgivable, and so it proved: after the follow-up reached No 61, he was never seen again. NB: in 2007, a correspondent to the Guardian described how song had spawned family game based on collisions of artistic forms/accolades and parts of the house, e.g. 'bodice-ripper'/'backyard shitter'.

**coagulatin'/contemplatin'** *Barry McGuire, Eve Of Destruction, 1965* Cynical stab at cornering 'protest' market by US songwriter P. F. Sloan reached No 1 in the US, but at least did world a favour by embodying one rule: with or without the 'g', there's surely no place for the word 'coagulating' in rock.

**cough/Nabokov** *The Police, Don't Stand So Close To Me, 1980* Ooh! Look at him! He reads books and everything! Couplet in pervy teacher/pupil drama may be low-point of Sting's career. There again, read on...

**cute/'the point is probably moot'** *Rick Springfield, Jessie's Girl, 1981* Garbled meeting of words at heart of US No 1 smash about unrequited love for titular female by Australian-American singer. Clue to Rick's predicament arguably in lyrics, i.e. hot chicks don't go for blokes who say things like 'the point is probably moot'.

**diplomat/laundromat** *Spandau Ballet, Highly Strung, 1984* Worst moment from baffling tribute to character named 'Little Jo': apparently once an international civil servant, now reduced to sitting in launderettes. 'They washed her mind', apparently.

**diplomat/'a Siamese cat'** *Bob Dylan, Like A Rolling Stone, 1965* Early warning about the 'd' word that Spandau's Gary Kemp should have heeded. True to BD's reputation as new Arthur Rimbaud, followed by 'discover that' and 'where it's at'.

**door/'nuclear war'** *Duran Duran, Is There Something I Should Know?, 1983* Very poor crystallisation of woman trouble within faux-poetic lyric from Simon Le Bon, which surely comes close to ruining whole song. A UK No 1, nonetheless.

**famous/'money hangin' out the anus'** *Puff Daddy featuring Mase, Can't Nobody Hold Me Down, 1997* Decisive proof that artist known these days as P. Diddy may be worst rapper ever. Re-imagining money/anus claim as literally true surely brings to mind a very British recommendation: 'You want to get that sorted out.'

**'flew away'/'a tray'** *Procol Harum, A Whiter Shade Of Pale, 1967* Demonstration of pitfalls of very English word 'tray', also used by Morrissey in 1988's Everyday Is Like Sunday, which rhymes requisite day of week with 'a cheap tray'. As with, say, 'kettle' or 'mug tree', never cuts it.

**fly/sky/high/dragonfly** *Lenny Kravitz, Fly Away, 1998* Crown prince of sky-scraping naffery delivers quadruple blooper on his sole UK No 1 to date. As was swiftly pointed out, dragonflies are ill-suited to high/sky-type business; they just kind of hover over water.

**fortune teller/Stella/'finally smell her'** *Red Hot Chili Peppers, The Zephyr Song, 2002* RHCP singer/lyricist Anthony Kiedis is no word-god, as proved by four-way, borderline nonsensical horror from By The Way album. While we're here, a mention also for 1988's trailblazing Love Trilogy, in which he claims his 'love' is both 'death to apartheid rule' and 'the pussy juice'. Great, that.

**'fun tonight'/'Wang Chung tonight'** *Wang Chung, Everybody Have Fun Tonight, 1986* From biggest US hit for British trio, who did mercifully little business at home (name translates in Chinese as 'yellow bell' and refers to – yee-haw – idea of standardised bass pitch in ancient China). In 2004, voted third 'most awesomely bad song ever' by VH1.

**ghost/most/piece of toast** *Des'ree, Life, 1998* Jaw-dropping doggerel from the British soft-soul merchant born Desiree Weeks. Another poll result: in May 2007, voted the worst lyric ever by listeners to the BBC station 6 Music.

**grab it/'silly rabbit'** *Public Enemy, Don't Believe The Hype, 1988* Low moment in irate word-splurge about rap icons' talent for causing controversy; fact that group's in-house japester Flavor Flav says 'rabbit' line is really no defence.

**grumble/apple crumble** *ABC, That Was Then But This Is Now, 1983* From the lead-off single to Beauty Stab, album that effectively killed Sheffield neo-glamsters' career. Frontman Martin Fry later excused himself by claiming, 'The most memorable lyrics are often the stupidest.' NB: not that it's to do with rhyming, but to further prove point, Unzip from same LP features the line, 'She's vegetarian except when it comes to sex'.

**hall/'faster than a cannonball'** *Oasis, Champagne Supernova, 1995* Much-mocked rhyme from their biggest LP, though other candidates abound: if only for its blank awfulness, witness rhyme of 'liar' and 'sitting by the fire' in I Can See A Liar (2000), or same year's Little James, first of Liam's songs to go public, notable for coupling 'plasticine' and 'trampoline', and 'toys' and 'they make noise' – along with startling claim that titular character (his stepson, then seven) swims 'like a child'.

**'I know you well'/'I know your smell'** *James Blunt, Goodbye My Lover, 2004* No comment required, really.

**Jamaican rum/some/'spit out your gum'** *Bob Dylan, 4ᵗʰ Time Around, 1966* Given fact that song was a sarcastic reply to John Lennon's Dylan-influenced Norwegian Wood, meant to be funny, but still a clunker – not for nothing did Lennon allege that by now, BD was 'getting away with murder'.

**Japan/dishpan** *The Sex Pistols, EMI, 1977* Woeful comparison used in song taking aim at New York Dolls (NB: a 'dishpan' is what British people know as a washing-up bowl).

**jumpy/'you wanna pump me'** *Poison, Unskinny Bop, 1990* Opening rhyme in global 'hair metal' hit that amounted to strong argument for arrival of grunge. You don't expect Philip Larkin, but really.

**lairy/'I tell thee'** *Kaiser Chiefs, I Predict a Riot, 2004* Very bad attempt to decisively root images of closing-time violence in the band's native Yorkshire. Sung with vim by Ricky Wilson – but reet clunky, to adopt the requisite idiom.

**language/'Vegemite sandwich'** *Men At Work, Down Under, 1983* As occasionally happens with such howlers, sung – by lead singer Colin Hay – with same knowing quality that pervades matching of 'Brussels' and 'muscles'. Still crap, though.

**least/'infected yeast'** *Lou Reed, Last Great American Whale, 1989* In otherwise OK lyric with green overtones (from his morale-raising album New York), attempt at an analogy for how little the modern USA values human life. Lame, in a word.

**litres/'las senoritas'** *Sting, Love Is Stronger Than Justice (The Munificent Seven), 1993* Attempt at Mexican-flavoured knockabout from ex-Police man which is frankly too crap to succeed. Worse still, also rhymes 'burritos' with 'los banditos'.

**Monday/Sunday/'fun-day'/'run-day'** *The Bangles, Manic Monday, 1986* Authored by Prince, who recorded own version in 1984, before thinking better of it and donating it to guitar-driven Californian all-female quartet, who sent it to No 2 on both sides of the Atlantic. 'Fun-days' indeed.

**the moon/'a big balloon'** *Travis, Turn, 1999* In artistic terms, something of a war crime, indicative of fondness for homespun, greetings card-esque wisdom that occasionally suggested work of optimistic eight-year-olds.

**neck/'oh heck'** *Adam Ant, Desperate But Not Serious,1982* Second bit of very bad rhyme is muttered, as if to betray his shame. In fact, one of his better post-Ants tunes, though long forgotten by wider world.

**New York/'feel like a dork'** *Madonna, I Love New York, 2005* Manhattan-centric tommyrot that also finds Madge rhyming the 'off' in 'F off' with 'golf'. All apparently sung with a very straight face, too.

**Norman Mailer/'a new tailor'** *Lloyd Cole & The Commotions, Are You Ready To Be Heartbroken, 1984* Undergraduate-level one-upmanship, from transparently insecure native of Buxton, Derbyshire. Album from which it comes (Rattlesnakes) also contains references to Truman Capote, Joan Didion and Simone de Beauvoir. Zzzzz.

**Oven/'I need some lovin''** *Marvin Gaye, Sexual Healing, 1982* In otherwise classic tune, very easy to miss – though there again, the ultra-crap cooker/lust analogy is first thing Gaye sings. ☛

**Posse/'German Nazi'** *Vanilla Ice, Play That Funky Music, 1990* From the single whose B-side was Ice Ice Baby, before it was 'flipped' and white rapper born Robert Van Winkle was (briefly) sent skyward. Not even a half-rhyme, for what it's worth.

**Rolls Royce/'good for my voice'** *T.Rex, Children Of The Revolution, 1972* No poet, Marc Bolan – as evidenced by endless songs full of cheapest rhymes (e.g. Hot Love: 'gold'/'not very old'/'most'/'coast'). Such, in fairness, was his none-more-pop aesthetic.

**sadder/madder/ladder** *Emerson, Lake & Palmer, Still…You Turn Me On, 1973* Terrible guff from perplexing lyric that may or may not pay tribute to a woman, included on prog gods' LP Brain Salad Surgery. On this evidence, they perhaps should have got some of it (whatever it was, as usual).

**Sean Connery/the economy/sodomy** *Robbie Williams, Kids, 2000* Lowlight of spoken-word section from hit duet with Kylie Minogue, perfectly embodying gauche, egotistical and downright awful aspects of ex-Take Thatter's solo career. Take note: white people from Stoke-on-Trent should probably never attempt to rap, even in a Butlins Redcoat 'stylee'.

**shot/'in my opinion, there's a bigger plot'** *Stereophonics, Nice To Be Out, 2001* Rhyme from risible on-tour travelogue in which writer Kelly Jones visits site of JFK's shooting in Dallas, and makes claim relating to possible conspiracy. Never! Really? Wow! etc.

**'shuffles in'/'tonic and gin'** *Billy Joel, Piano Man, 1973* His breakthrough US hit, which managed to surmount crime of reversing name of iconic drink in first verse. In that sense, notice of the Joel howlers to come, especially 1989's We Didn't Start The Fire, protest on behalf of his generation about alleged responsibility for world going up in flames; they 'didn't light it', but rather 'tried to fight it'. That's right, Billy.

**Silly/'stepped in some Caerphilly'** *Rod Stewart, Italian Girls, 1972* Subsequently mis-transcribed by online Rod fans as 'stepped in soaking beer', but baffling Welsh cheese reference clear enough. Also rhymes 'tarty' and 'Maserati', and 'creep' and 'army surplus jeep'. Co-written by Ron Wood, which may tell you something.

**Soy latte/'double shottay'** *Madonna, American Life, 2003* From yet another 'rap' section (see R.Williams, above), full of several other sins: 'Mini Cooper' and 'super-duper', 'pilates' and 'hotties', and 'point of view' and 'I'm not a Jew'. Brilliant!

**stops/'some shops'** *The Human League, The Lebanon, 1984* Bamboozling nadir of song in which once-ace Sheffield pop group decided to go serious and address problems of Middle East (and, equally woefully, use guitars). In second verse, man leaves refugee camp and notes absence of 'some shops' – phrase surely more redolent of drizzly South Yorkshire than world-renowned trouble spot.

**'tension mounts'/'score an ounce'** *Wings, Rockshow, 1975* Highlight/lowpoint of Paul McCartney's evocation of a big gig – cleverly, also rhymes 'stacks' and 'glimpse an axe' (i.e. guitar) and 'rock show' and 'Concertgebouw' (it means 'concert building' in Dutch, and there's a famous one in Amsterdam).

**tonight/'overwhelmed with shite'** *Ride, I Don't Know Where It Comes From, 1994* Used in protest about music on the radio in song by future Oasis bassist Andy Bell. Oxford indie quartet weren't on airwaves much: this kind of thing was maybe why.

**toilet paper/ozone layer** *Neil Young, Rockin' In The Free World, 1989* May suggest blank verse, but no: in last verse of rabble-rousing piece from career-reviving Freedom LP, Young really does attempt rhyme, worsened by inclusion of bathetic phrase 'toilet paper' in words meant to bemoan consumerism and associated threat to environment. Mercifully, lines in question cut from song's acoustic version, which begins album.

**twenty-two/boo hoo** *The Stooges, 1969, 1969* Iggy Pop's attempt at nailing the misery of progressing through one's twenties. Surely implies silent third rhyming element: 'Will this do?'

**yacht/apricot/'watched yourself gavotte'** *Carly Simon, You're So Vain, 1972* Great song and everything, but this triple verbal car-crash is a crying shame. Oxford English Dictionary defines 'gavotte' as 'a medium paced dance popular in the 18th century'; given supposed identity of famous person who is song's subject, fellow party-goers implied in lyrics must have thought, 'Oh look, there's Warren Beatty – watching himself gavotte again.'

# Gimme some truth...

### Or, if you fancy, write a song with a howling factual error. Roll the corrections…

**The Divine Comedy, Sweden** *1998*
In the mid-to-late 1990s, Derry-born Neil Hannon – who effectively was/still is The Divine Comedy – was hailed as an indie-pop Noel Coward. Who else, after all, could manage a backhandedly witty tribute to the Northern European country where the people are icily good-looking and the welfare state will always sort you out? One problem: as well as such notable Swedes as the film director and dramatist Ingmar Bergman, the late 19th/early 20th century domestic designer Karin Larsson and The Cardigans' Nina Persson, it mentions the playwright Henrik Ibsen, who was Norwegian.

*Ibsen: Norwegian, actually*

**U2, Pride (In The Name Of Love)** *1984*
Why white rock musicians should approach the black liberation struggle with caution, Part 1: the Dubliners' impassioned tribute to the late Dr Martin Luther King Jr begins its last verse with the claim that he was murdered in the 'early morning' of 4 April 1968. If he'd employed a fact-checker, Paul 'Bono' Hewson would have discovered he was some way out: MLK was in fact gunned down at 6.01pm. At some subsequent live performances, he's dutifully changed the line to 'early evening'.

**Sade, Smooth Operator** *1984* A simple lesson in bad geography from the London-born queen of '80s pseudo-sophistication. Contains the regular refrain 'Coast to coast, LA to Chicago', which is so wrong it almost hurts. Chicago sits next to Lake Michigan, and the Chicago and Calumnet Rivers, but some 700 miles from a coast; needless to say, in the US, 'coast to coast' denotes any trip between the Eastern and Western seaboards. The next line in the song references Key Largo in Florida, so it presumably needed a rhyme, but that's surely no defence.

**Squeeze, Pulling Mussels (From The Shell)**
*1980* A brilliant portrait of the British holiday ritual from Squeeze's two-headed core, Glenn Tilbrook and Chris Difford. But! The narrator has a bit of the other behind a chalet, and feels like 'William Tell', with 'Maid Marion on her tiptoed feet'. Think about it.

**Busted, Year 3000** *2002* Back To The Future-esque fantasy from the now-defunct pop-rock trio, in which someone called Peter travels almost 1000 years into the future and reports back that 'your great, great, great granddaughter is pretty fine.' A spot of back-of-a-beermat maths blows the gaff: there are at least a couple of generations missing from this scenario; one online truth-fiend with far too much time on his hands calculated that human beings would have to live to be at least 166 for the lyric to make sense.

**Primal Scream, Star** *1997* Why white rock musicians should approach the black liberation struggle with caution, Part 2: on this single from the album Vanishing Point, Bobby Gillespie and his psychonauts pay tribute to some of the

*Parks: alive, at the time*

key African-American leaders and figureheads of past decades: Malcolm X, the aforementioned Dr King and 'Sister' Rosa Parks – who, in December 1955, refused to give up her bus seat to a white passenger and sparked a bus boycott in Montgomery, Alabama. 'Their bodies may be gone,' sings Gillespie, 'but their spirits still live on.' One snag: at the time the song was released, Parks was alive.

**Coldplay, Speed Of Sound** *2005* They had to be in here somewhere. Finds the often-confused Chris Martin looking at the night sky and observing 'planets moving at the speed of light'. At which point, we give up.

# OPEN TUNINGS
### The standard guitar is tuned E A D G B E. But never mind all that…

## Joni Mitchell

| | | | | | | |
|---|---|---|---|---|---|---|
| C | G | C | G | C | E | ............................................................ *Raised On Robbery* |
| C | G | D | F | B♭ | D | .............................. *Edith And The Kingpin* |
| D | A | D | G | B | D | ..............................................*Free Man In Paris* |
| C | G | B♭ | E♭ | F | B♭ | ..................................................... *Woodstock* |
| C | G | D | F | C | E | .......................................................... *Coyote* |
| D | A | D | F | A | D | ...............................*The Pirate Of Penance* |
| A♭ | A♭ | E♭ | A♭ | C | E♭ | ................................*This Flight Tonight* |
| F | F | C | G | A | C | ................*I Don't Know Where I Stand* |

## Nick Drake

| | | | | | | |
|---|---|---|---|---|---|---|
| C | G | C | F | C | E | ....................... *Which Will, Time Has Told Me* |
| D | A | D | G | D | G | .................................................*Northern Sky* |
| D | G | D | G | B | D | ........ *Black Eyed Dog, Rider On The Wheel* |
| C | G | C | F | C | F | ........................................ *From The Morning* |

## Jimmy Page (Led Zeppelin)

| | | | | | | |
|---|---|---|---|---|---|---|
| E | C | G | C | A | C | .......................................*Bron-Yr-Aur Stomp* |
| D | G | C | G | C | D | ...................................... *The Rain Song* |
| D | A | D | G | B | E | ....................... *Going To California* |
| D | A | D | G | A | D | .................*Kashmir, Black Mountain Side* |
| C | G | C | E | G | C | ...............................*Hats Off To (Roy) Harper* |
| E | A | C | F | A | C | ...................... *When The Levee Breaks* |
| E | A | E | A | C♯ | E | ...................................*In My Time Of Dying* |

## John Martyn

| | | | | | | |
|---|---|---|---|---|---|---|
| D | A | D | G | C | E | ..................................................... *Go Down Easy* |
| C | G | C | G | B♭ | D | ................................................ *Solid Air* |

## Keith Richards (The Rolling Stones)

| | | | | | | |
|---|---|---|---|---|---|---|
| D | A | D | F♯ | A | D | ......................... *Street Fighting Man, Jumpin' Jack Flash* |
| x | G | D | G | B | D | .....*Brown Sugar, Wild Horses, Happy, Start Me Up etc. etc.* |

## Some other notable examples

| | | | | | | |
|---|---|---|---|---|---|---|
| E | E | E | E | B | E | ...............Stephen Stills (CS&N): *Suite: Judy Blue Eyes* |
| E | B | D | G | A | D | ........................... David Crosby (CS&N): *Guinnevere* |
| F | A | D | D | G | D | ...............................The Edge: *The Unforgettable Fire* |
| D | A | D | G | B | D | ................................Neil Young: *Cinnamon Girl* |
| C | A | D | G | B | E | ....................Bob Dylan: *It's All Over Now, Baby Blue* |
| E♭ | A♭ | C♯ | F♯ | B♭ | E♭ | ..................................... Syd Barrett: *Octopus* |
| D | G | C | F | A | D | ...........................Paul McCartney: *Yesterday* |
| E | A | E | A | C♯ | E | ..... Jack White (The White Stripes): *Seven Nation Army* |
| C | G | D | G | B | E | .......Richard Thompson: *1952 Vincent Black Lightning* |
| E♭ | A♭ | A♭ | G♭ | B♭ | D | ..........Billy Corgan (Smashing Pumpkins): *Mayonaise* |
| C | G | C | G | G | E | .....................Kim Thayil (Soundgarden): *Pretty Noose* |
| D | G | D | G | B | D | ...........................................Jeff Buckley: *Last Goodbye* |
| E | B | E | G♯ | B | E | ....................................Bob Dylan: *Tangled Up In Blue* |
| D | A | D | F♯ | B | E | ..............Jose Gonzalez: *Crosses, Hints, Heartbeats* |

# GREAT SONG ARCHETYPES #3: HEY JUDE

In Ian MacDonald's peerless Beatles book Revolution In The Head, Hey Jude (1968) was described as 'the first of many such anthem-like singalongs to arise in response to rock's compulsive self-mythologisation'. Covered by such singers as **Wilson Pickett** and **Elvis** (who got the words very wrong indeed), its essential approach soon bled out into the Fabs' solo work – witness **George Harrison**'s borderline parodic Isn't It A Pity (1970); **John Lennon**'s Imagine (1971); and McCartney's own Maybe I'm Amazed (1970), and My Love (1973). Given their sizable debt to The Beatles, it was no surprise to find **ELO** dabbling in Hey Judery with 1977's Telephone Line – and while we're here, we'll also mention a long line of **Elton John** examples, from Don't Let The Sun Go Down On Me (1974) to I Want Love (2001). There's a strong case to be made for Hey Jude's role in the invention of the power ballad, as evidenced by **Guns N' Roses**' November Rain (1992), but it was the mid-1990s Britpop period that saw a decisive Hey Jude revival. **Oasis**'s Don't Look Back In Anger (1995) started the ball rolling – see also Stop Crying Your Heart Out (2002), Let There Be Love (2005) and I'm Outta Time (2008) – after which came such **Robbie Williams** hits as Angels (1997) and his cover of **World Party**'s She's The One (1999), along with lachrymose songs like Come Back To What You Know (1998) and Gravity (2004) by the West Yorkshire quartet **Embrace**. The latter song was written for them by **Chris Martin**, which brings us to **Coldplay**, and the likes of Fix You (2005), and the almost absurdly Imagine-esque 42 (2008). This one, it seems, is going to be with us for some time yet.

# GREAT SONG ARCHETYPES #4: THE MOTORIK BEAT

Drummer **Klaus Dinger** (1946-2008) was a member of a very early line-up of **Kraftwerk** before he and fellow Düsseldorfer **Michael Rother** formed **Neu!**, and made three of the most influential albums ever: Neu! (1972), Neu! 2 (1973), and Neu! 75 (1975), which spent much of the next three decades deleted and much-bootlegged before being belatedly reissued in 2001. To quote from Julian Cope's jaw-dropping German rock field-guide Krautrocksampler, 'the fall-out and repercussions from those three albums was (and is) immense', and much of that story is bound up with what Dinger did on the drums. As **Brian Eno** saw it, 'there were three great beats in the 1970s: Fela Kuti's Afrobeat, James Brown's funk and Klaus Dinger's Neu! beat.'

Most references to music being reminiscent of so-called Krautrock are implictly referring to the latter: Dinger called it the 'Apache' beat, but it's better known as the motorik (it translates as 'motor function') rhythm, an incessant 4/4 pulse – whose roots arguably lie with **The Velvet Underground**'s Mo Tucker – that you can also hear in the work of **Can** (e.g. 1973's Moonshake), the quick-paced middle section of Kraftwerk's Autobahn (1974), and stuff by Dinger's unhinged post-Neu! project **La Düsseldorf**. With Eno at his side, that great Germanophile **David Bowie** enthusiastically soaked up motorik's influence (witness, for example, Red Sails from 1979's Lodger), and it was later introduced to UK indiedom by **Stereolab** (e.g. 1991's Super Electric). For further enlightenment, have a listen to scores of other songs, such as **Primal Scream**'s Shoot Speed Kill Light (2000), **Sonic Youth**'s New Hampshire (2004), **Stereophonics**' deeply unlikely motorik hit Dakota (2005), the knowingly-titled Son Of Rother (2004) by dance experimentalists **Death In Vegas**, Monkey Bee, from **Damon Albarn**'s Monkey: Journey To The West (2008), and Bodysnatchers (2007), by enthusiastic Neu! fans **Radiohead**. 'Neu's music is like a brand-new motorway, and you are the first person to drive along it,' Thom Yorke once claimed, and though it sounded slightly odd, he wasn't far wrong.

# The Rock'n'Roll Radio Times

From rom-com to sci-fi: 32 story-songs , in a home-made CD/TV listings style

## CD 1

### 0.00 - 12.59

**Early learning**
**0.00** Norwegian Wood (This Bird Has Flown), The Beatles
*An inconclusive tryst in a London flat: does Lennon take revenge via arson?*
**2.05** You Know I'm No Good, Amy Winehouse
*Romantic intrigue, including giveaway carpet burns.*
**4.24** Smoke On The Water, Deep Purple
*Band travel to Switzerland, only for their intended recording location to burn down. Also stars Frank Zappa.*
**10.06** Streets Of Baltimore, Gram Parsons
*Marital drama: wife persuades husband to relocate to Maryland; disaster ensues.*

### 13.00
### Ode To Billie Joe
 *Bobbie Gentry, 1967*
American period drama and deserved No 1, featuring only voice, guitar and strings. In the Mississippi Delta, a poor farming family goes about its business, though a dark secret threatens to ruin their fragile stability. Billie Joe MacAllister has jumped off the nearby Tallahatchie Bridge, but the truth behind his suicide is going to be hard

to discover. Also stars Mama, Papa, Brother Taylor and Becky Thompson.
Writer BOBBY GENTRY

### 17.17
### The Saturday Boy
 *Billy Bragg, 1984*
The author looks back at his Essex schooldays, and an unrequited fixation with a classmate. They would 'sit together in double history twice a week' , but did they have any future? Well, what do you think? 'That's the great self-effacing song, isn't it?' says Bragg. 'Nothing comes to anything – he loses all the way through. But that's what touches people.'
Writer BILLY BRAGG

### 20.49
### The Night They Drove Old Dixie Down
 *The Band, 1969*
A personal account of the American Civil War: Southern Soldier Virgil Caine – played by drummer/singer and Arkansas native Levon Helm – served on the Danville Train, the main supply line into Richmond, Virginia, the Confederacy's capital. Among memories of the hungry winter of 1864-65, Caine pays tribute to his fallen brother, only 18. 'It took me about eight months in all to write that song,' said Robbie Robertson. You can tell.
Writer ROBBIE ROBERTSON

### 24.24
### Promised Land
 *Chuck Berry, 1964*
Narrator travels from Norfolk, Virginia to California, via North and South Carolina, Georgia, Alabama, Mississippi and New Orleans – before he arrives in Houston, Texas, and makes a flight to the Golden State. Later covered by Elvis Presley, Meat Loaf and – perhaps most memorably, Lousiana 'swamp pop' star Johnny Allan.
Writer CHUCK BERRY

### 26.49
### No Thugs In Our House
*XTC, 1983*
Police drama set in 1980s suburbia. Teenager Graham is wanted on suspicion of racist violence. The police pay his parents an early-morning visit, and are assured that their quarry is actually a 'good boy'. Says writer Andy Partridge: 'It's still the case now: kids are out there drinking Butane fuel and smoking crack and even though the parents can smell the crack and the butane on their breath, they say, "Oh, little Lenny hasn't been doing anything bad."'
Writer ANDY PARTRIDGE

### 32.00
### The Laughing Gnome
*David Bowie, 1967*
Period children's comedy, and by no means a

---

**KEY**  *Drama*  *Romance/Romantic comedy*  *History*  *Children's*

Bowie classic. In '67 it was his ninth consecutive flop single, though in 1973 it belatedly reached No 6. Warning to parents: the gnome smokes. Warning to everybody: contains such woeful puns as 'the Gnome Office' and 'Metrognome'.
Writer DAVID BOWIE

## 35.03
## W*O*L*D
*Harry Chapin, 1973*
Somewhat mawkish but affecting one-act piece based around a telephone conversation between a faded DJ – now employed on radio station W*O*L*D – and his estranged wife, full of pathos and regret. Cheerily, the themes addressed include alcoholism and arrested development: he feels 'all of 45 going on 15'. Story-song specialist Chapin managed four US singles hits (this one reached No 34) before dying in 1981, aged only 38; he suffered a heart attack and was killed in a car crash, though in what order they occurred remains a mystery.
Writer HARRY CHAPIN

## 40.16
## The Killing Of
## Georgie (Part I & II)
*Rod Stewart, 1976*
Rather Dylan-esque dramatic work that points up the author's long-lost talents as a storyteller. The hero – in real life, a close friend of Stewart and Faces keyboard player Ian 'Mac' McLagan – travels to New York and becomes 'accepted by New York's elite', only to meet his

end thanks to a bigoted New Jersey gang. Truly trailblazing stuff: 'I think it was a brave step, but it wasn't a risk,' said Stewart in 1995. 'It was a subject that no one had approached before. And I think it still stands up today.'
Writer ROD STEWART

## 46.35
## Athlete Cured
*The Fall, 1988*
Characteristically surreal piece from North-west dramatist Mark E Smith. A famous East German athlete is gripped by an ongoing illness; the narrator's observation of events close to his house reveals that his brother Gert is in the habit of parking his Volkswagen car close to the athlete's bedroom window and turning over the engine 'for up to an hour'. A new parking space is secured and the athlete is cured, only for the plot to take a very East German twist…
Writer MARK E SMITH

## 52.28
## The Gift
*The Velvet Underground, 1968*
Fantastical black comedy written by Lou Reed, narrated by John Cale. Student Waldo Jeffers is missing his college girlfriend Marsha Bronson: he is in Locust, Pennsylvania, while she has returned to her native Wisconsin. Tortured by imaginings of infidelity but unable to travel 'in the accepted fashion', he decides to put himself in the mail, in a cardboard box, with truly unforeseen consequences.

*NB: if your stereo has a balance control, flip it left to hear Cale alone.*
Writer LOU REED (song by LOU REED, JOHN CALE, STERLING MORRISON and MAUREEN TUCKER)

## 60.46
## Lola
*The Kinks, 1970*
Risqué romantic comedy set in 'Old Soho' – and, according to its author, based on the experience of Kinks manager Robert Wace, who drunkenly paired off with a stranger, only to discover something rather unexpected. A new-to-town nightclubber is seduced by Lola, who has a 'dark brown voice' and a strange habit of back-breaking embraces. What could be the explanation?
Writer RAY DAVIES

## 64.54
## Fish, Chips
## And Sweat
*Funkadelic, 1970*
Touring American funk maestro George Clinton is in Britain, and pairs off with a woman in the small hours who escorts him back to 'this place called home' via a fish and chip shop. Passions are soon aroused: as Clinton puts it, 'Sweat was pumpin' offa my face, fish and chips all over the place.' Adults only, obviously.
Writers GEORGE CLINTON, WILLIAM NELSON, EDWARD HAZEL

## 68.17 Closedown

---

 *Travel*    *Comedy*    *Science Fiction*    *Adults Only*

## CD 2

### 0.00 - 14.10

### Early learning
**0.00** Sloop John B, The Beach Boys
*Traditional Caribbean tale of seasick sailor: 'Let me go home!'*
**2.58** Fit But You Know It, The Streets
*Holiday romance. Who will get lucky: Mike, or 'that fucking white-shirted man'?*
**7.13** Clothes Line Saga, Bob Dylan & The Band
*American soap opera, written as a parody of Ode To Billie Joe (see above).*
**10.13** Dixie Chicken, Little Feat
*Romance, marriage and separation in the Deep South – with a twist in the tale…*

### 14.11
### Smithers Jones
*The Jam, 1979*
Office intrigue, set just as Britain tumbled into lean times, in a rare piece of convincing songwriting by The Jam's bassist Bruce Foxton. Commuter Smithers-Jones heads for work via Waterloo, and is summoned by the boss. 'I hope it's the promotion you've been looking for,' says a colleague. D'oh!
Writer BRUCE FOXTON

### 17.15
### Living For The City
*Stevie Wonder, 1973*
Social-realist drama, and what Rolling Stone magazine called 'a bleak seven-minute narrative about the broken

98

dreams of black America'. Begins with an incisive portrait of life in Mississipi before our doomed hero sets off for Manhattan. Innocently dragged into drug-running, he's swiftly sentenced to ten years in jail. Most of the plot centres on its spoken-word middle section, in which the part of the racist jailer was played by a studio janitor.
Writer STEVIE WONDER

### 24.40
### 2000 Light Years From Home
*The Rolling Stones, 1967*
Fictional glimpse of future space travel, authored when Keith Richards and Mick Jagger were in and out of jail (the latter wrote the lyrics in Brixton prison). The journey's apparent destination: Aldebaran, the brightest star in the constellation of Taurus, which is only 68 light years from earth, but we'll have to let that pass. Included on their misfiring go at psychedelia, Their Satanic Majesties Request. 'I liked a few songs, like 2000 Light Years,' said Keith Richards, 'but basically I thought that album was crap.'
Writers MICK JAGGER and KEITH RICHARDS

### 29.26
### Tracy Jacks
*Blur, 1994*
Quintessentially British comedy in the vein of The Fall And Rise Of Reginald Perrin (kind of). Jacks is a civil servant on the wrong side of 40, increasingly convinced that normality is 'overrated'. Without warning, he leaves his house at dawn and travels to Walton-on-the-Naze, Essex, where rum doings

transpire – though there is worse to come. 'They fascinate me, all those dead seaside towns on the Essex coast,' Damon Albarn later explained. 'They're half-places.'
Writer DAMON ALBARN (music also by GRAHAM COXON, ALEX JAMES and DAVE ROWNTREE)

### 33.48
### Back On My Feet Again
*Randy Newman, 1974*
Tale in a similar(ish) vein, this time set in the USA and authored by a truly peerless storyteller (and taken from Good Old Boys, an album focused on the Deep South). A man is held in an institution, where he pleads with a doctor to release him and tells the story of his siblings – most notably, a sister who ran away with 'a negro from the Eastern shore', who took her to Mobile, Alabama, and revealed himself to be a white millionaire. 'I'm very interested in how weird Back On My Feet Again is,' said Newman in 2002. 'You know, you see fake weird sometimes …[but] that is a genuinely strange song.'
Writer RANDY NEWMAN

### 37.13
### Stay Free
*The Clash, 1978*
Impressionistic look at education, crime, punishment and much more in the South London of the 1970s. Focused on the friendship between Mick Jones and the aptly-nicknamed Robin Banks (aka Crocker), a close friend of Mick Jones who in 1973 was involved in an armed robbery,

and sent via Wormwood Scrubs to a high-security prison on the Isle of Wight (though here, while on a nicking spree, he merely 'hit the wrong guy' and spent three years in the aforementioned Brixton prison). In 2002, Banks/ Crocker travelled to Iraq as part of an anti-war protest in which participants volunteered to be human shields. Jones paid for the trip; his friend made it back alive.
Writers JOE STRUMMER and MICK JONES

## 40.54
## After We Shot The Grizzly
*The Handsome Family, 2006*
Camped-up survival thriller in the vein of the American TV blockbuster Lost, written by Rennie Sparks, lyricist with husband-and-wife alt-country duo. Having survived an airship crash, a man floats precariously on a raft made of 'skin and bones' and reflects on a grim run of events: the radio failing, the shooting and eating of horses and 'a tiny antelope', the chance discovery of a human skull, and several deaths. Will he survive? No, frankly.
Writer RENNIE SPARKS (music by BRETT SPARKS)

## 44.29
## 1952 Vincent Black Lightning
*Richard Thompson, 1991*
Jaw-dropping romantic drama centred on James Adie and 'Red Molly', two lovers whose passionate bond is sparked by his British motorcycle, one of a super-fast line manufactured

between 1948 and 1952. He warns her that he's a 'dangerous man', and shocking news soon awaits her. Arguably its author's most fondly-loved song, thanks to both the perfectly-chosen machine at the centre of the tale, and the way the plot unfolds. 'I suppose I'd thought it was harder for people in the 20th century to sit down and listen to a story in a song,' he mused, 'but I was wrong.'
Writer RICHARD THOMPSON

## 49.14
## Razzle In My Pocket
*Ian Dury & The Blockheads, 1977*
A few miles from his home-turf of Upminster, a young Dury is prowling Romford, Essex. He steals a copy of low-end soft-porn title Razzle from a local shopping arcade and is tempted to get 'more of this stuff', whereupon his luck runs out. But will the shopkeeper involve the law? NB: among porn aficionados, the consensus is that Dury is referring to a period when Razzle was a pocket-format title, featuring nothing more risqué than topless photographs and 'cartoons'.
Writers IAN DURY and CHAS JANKEL

## 52.13
## ♥ Raspberry Beret
*Prince & The Revolution, 1985*
Rites-of-passage story starring the young Prince Rogers Nelson, who holds down a part-time job and spies a woman wearing the titular item – in warm

weather, of course, 'she wouldn't wear much more' – and is sufficiently impressed to take her to a nearby farm building where he loses his virginity. Said to be about one Susan Moonsie, a high-school girlfriend who was later a member of the Prince-created female duo Vanity 6.
Writer PRINCE

## 55.47
## The Old Main Drag
*The Pogues, 1985*
A Play For Today, as done by a songwriter hardly minded to spare us the gory details. The narrator arrives in London with 'a fiver in my pocket and my ole dancing bag', only to fall into male prostitution and barbiturate use, and then be savagely beaten up the police (who 'ruined my good looks'). Not quite the stuff of happy Irish reels, then.
Writer SHANE MACGOWAN

## 59.18
## The Jack (live version)
(18) *AC/DC, 1978*
Leery and singularly unpleasant tale of deceit, S&M and gonorrhoea, included in modified form on their in-concert album If You Want Blood, You've Got It. In the original, on the 1975 album TNT, singer Bon Scott half-veils its story under card-game metaphors; here, everything is baldly obvious. You may, in fact, want to switch off.
Writers ANGUS YOUNG, MALCOLM YOUNG and BON SCOTT

## 65.01 Closedown

# MUSSOLINI, NEIL KINNOCK, LENIN, SHAUN RYDER...

## The strange roll-call of people mentioned in songs by the Manic Street Preachers

John Lennon (1940-80)
*Musician, Beatle*
**Motown Junk (1991)**

*Neil Kinnock,*
*referenced thus: 'Were we the*
*Kinnock factor?'*

Madonna (b. 1958)
*Singer*
**Slash'N'Burn (1992)**

Benito Mussolini (1883-1945)
*Italian Fascist dictator*
Miklos Horthy (1868-1957)
*Regent of Hungary and Nazi*
*collaborator*
Adolph Hitler (1889-1945)
*Nazi leader of Germany*
**Of Walking Abortion (1994)**

Arthur Miller (1915-2005)
*American playwright*
Norman Mailer (1923-2007)
*American writer*
Sylvia Plath (1932-63)
*Poet and author*
Harold Pinter (1930-2009)
*Playwright*
**Faster (1994)**

Boris Yeltsin (1931-2007)
*Russian politician*
Jean-Marie Le Pen (b.1928)
100

*French politician*
Vladimir Zhirinovsky
(b.1946)
*Russian politician*
Myra Hindley (1942-2002)
*Moors murderer*
Ian Brady (b.1938)
*Moors murderer*
Peter Sutcliffe (b.1946)
*Serial killer, aka The Yorkshire*
*Ripper*
Beverley Allitt (b.1968)
*Nurse-turned-murderer, aka*
*'The Angel Of Death'*
Idi Amin (1923-2003)
*Ugandan dictator*
Jeffrey Dahmer (1960-94)
*Serial killer*
Dennis Nilsen (b.1945)
*Serial killer*
Colin Ireland (b.1954)
*Serial killer, aka 'The Gay*
*Slayer'*
Eugene Terre'Blanche
(b.1941)
*South African fascist*
Yoshinori Ueda (1955-2005)
*Japanese serial killer*
James Pickles (b.1925)
*English judge-turned-tabloid*
*columnist*
**Archives Of Pain (1994)**

Winston Churchill
(1874-1965)
*British Prime Minister*
**The Intense Humming Of**
**Evil (1994)**

Tipper Gore (b.1948)
*Wife of ex-US Vice President*
Abraham Zapruder (1905-70)
*US clothing manufacturer who*
*filmed Kennedy's assassination*
**Ifwhite America told the truth**
**forone dayits world would fall-**
**apart (1994)**

Lenin (1870-1924)
*Communist leader of the*
*Soviet Union*
Joseph Stalin (1878-1953)
*Communist leader of the*
*Soviet Union*
Mikhail Gorbachev (b.1931)
*Communist leader of the*
*Soviet Union*
Napoleon Bonaparte
(1769-1821)
*French military and political*
*leader*
Neville Chamberlain
(1869-1940)
*British Prime Minister*
Leon Trotsky (1879-1940)
*Russian Communist*
Ernesto 'Che' Guevera
(1928-67)
*Argentinian revolutionary*
Pol Pot (1925-98)
*Cambodian dictator*
Louis Farrakhan (b.1933)
*African-American, Supreme*
*Minister of the Nation of Islam*
**Revol (1994)**

*Vladimir Ilyich Ulyanov,*
*aka Lenin: 'Mr Lenin -*
*awaken the boy'*

Prince William of Wales
(b.1982)
Prince Henry (aka Harry)
of Wales (b.1984)
*Members of the British royal
family*
**Sculpture Of Man (1994)**

*Morrissey: 'Morrissey and
Marr gave me choice'*

Kevin Carter (1960-94)
*South African photojournalist*
**Kevin Carter (1996)**

Willem De Kooning (1904-97)
*Abstract painter*
**Interiors (Song For Willem
De Kooning) (1996)**

Matthew Maynard (b.1966)
*Cricketer*
**Mr Carbohydrate (1996)**

Phil Bennett (b.1948)
*Welsh Rugby international*
Neil Kinnock (b.1942)
*Ex-Leader of the Labour Party*
Steve Ovett (b.1955)
*Middle-distance athlete*
Shaun Ryder (b.1962)
*Singer, lyricist, co-founder of
Happy Mondays*
**Prologue To History (1998)**

Jimmy McGovern (b.1949)
*TV dramatist*
**S.Y.M.M. (1998)**

Francisco de Goya
(1746-1828)
*Painter*
Pablo Picasso (1881-1973)
*Painter*
Bonnie Parker (1910-34)
Clyde Barrow (1909-34)
*American criminals*
William Payne Stewart
(1957-99)
*American professional golfer*
Jack Kevorkian (b.1928)
*US pathologist and euthanasia
advocate*
Brian Warner (b.1969)
*Musician, aka Marilyn Manson*
Alberto Juantorena
(b.1950)
*Cuban track athlete*
Klaus Kinski (1926-91)
*German actor*
Haile Gebreselassie (b.1973)
*Ethiopian long-distance runner*
Dante Alighieri (1265-1321)
*Poet*
Werner Herzog (b.1942)
*German film director,
screenwriter and actor*
**The Convalescent (2001)**

Paul Robeson (1888-1976)
*American singer and activist*
**Let Robeson Sing (2001)**

Elian Gonzales (b.1993)
*Cuban abductee*
**Baby Elian (2001)**

John Stith Pemberton
(1831-88)
*Inventor of Coca-Cola*
The Dalai Lama (currently
Tenzin Gyatso, b.1935)
*Religious leader*
Richard Gere (b.1949)
*Actor*
**Freedom Of Speech Won't
Feed My Children (2001)**

Richard Nixon (1913-94)
*US President*
**The Love Of Richard
Nixon (2004)**

George Orwell (1903-50)
*Author and journalist*
Jayne Torvill (b.1957)
Christopher Dean
(b.1958)
*British ice dancers*
Friedrich Nietzche
(1844-1900)
*Philosopher*
Johnny Marr (b.1963)
*Former Smiths guitarist and
songwriter*
Morrissey (b.1959)
*Former Smiths singer and
songwriter*
**1985 (2004)**

Emmeline Pankhurst
(1858-1928)
*Campaigner for women's
suffrage*
**Emily (2004)**

Jack Lemmon (1925-2001)
*Actor*
**Rendition (2007)**

Lee Harvey Oswald
(1939-63)
*Alleged killer of President
John F. Kennedy*
**I'm Just A Patsy (2007)**

*Norman Mailer:
'I am stronger than Mensa,
Miller and Mailer'*

# Chapter 5

# THE LOOK

'Ridicule,' sang Adam Ant in 1981, 'is nothing to be scared of.' He was living proof. Having been launched at the public with a white stripe across his face and a dapper military jacket, he was now on to his next image: 'Prince Charming', clad in Regency finery and caked in make-up, with his supporting players not far behind. Remember them all? 'Marco, Merrick, Terry Lee, Gary Tibbs and yours tru-lee.' What times! What larks! What nonsense!

Now, for better or worse, rock music tends to be a rather more dowdy affair, and even those who want to somehow brighten the party often can't quite pull it off: witness Coldplay's recent attempt to evoke the French Revolution via a look that rather suggested the aforementioned Ants as re-imagined by Uniqlo. Still, one shouldn't be too dismissive of current developments, so let us instead salute at least a few people who still have roughly the right idea. Think, for example, of those 'nu-metal' survivors Slipknot, and in particular a fella called Craig Jones, who wears a head-covering thing that makes him look like an S&M pin cushion; or Karen 'Karen O' Orzalek of cult New Yorkers the Yeah Yeah Yeahs, who is given to dressing in the manner of someone at the rough end of a car boot sale trolley dash. These people know the basis of the true aesthetics of rock: that a life spent well away from the thin line that divides the divine from the ludicrous is no life at all.

Behind such latter-day flamboyance lies a long tradition of preparing for live performances, TV shows and photo sessions by ditching your at-home look and going barmy. At different ends of the rock-historical timeline, Elvis briefly favoured a gold lamé suit, and R.E.M.'s Michael Stipe has been known to face his public with a big blue stripe painted across his head. That great rock'n'roll pioneer Little Richard invented a gloriously absurd look quickly ripped off by Jimi Hendrix, and later dusted down and reused by Prince – central to which was the moustache, the acceptability of which underwent an unexpected revival among male musicians circa 2003.

On a rather different 'tip', back in the mid 1970s, Bob Dylan took to painting his face white and occasionally wearing a transparent plastic mask. By that time, however, the USA had delivered the sartorial and cosmetic coup-de-grace, in the form of four New Yorkers who trowelled on the make-up, tottered on to the stage in seven-inch high-heels, and reinvented themselves as 'The Demon', 'The Starchild', 'The Spaceman', and 'The Catman'. They were also known as Gene, Paul, Peter and Ace, and they were called Kiss; give or take a lot of cod-intellectual hoo-hah, Marilyn Manson specialises in the same essential idea.

Out in the real world, music's relationship with image has long created regular fashion-spasms that convulse the High Street. Just as even the dullest British town once had its obligatory hippy, so there have followed punks, mod revivalists, Goths, rockabillies, neo-Goths and nu-metallers. I recently spoke to a successful British musician who spent some of his childhood and teenage years as a punk, in an unremarkable North-western suburb called Handforth. Back then, he was the embodiment of how ideas can pass from cutting-edge bohemia to the local shopping precinct. 'My nana made my bondage trousers: proper tartan ones, and I used to put soap in my hair,' he said, matter-of-factly. If Britain has ever been great, it is this kind of thing that made it so.

Most of what's just been mentioned is in this chapter: bondage trousers, hair, make-up, footwear, sunglasses, moustaches, cross-dressing, smudged lipstick, you name it. A lot of this is delicate stuff to mess with: in most cases, it depends on the arrogance of youth, a particular set of historical circumstances, and a mystical process whereby what was out-of-the-question yesterday is exactly the right idea today, and vice versa.

Jimmy Page was right to wear trousers with dragons down the side in the mid 1970s, but it's a good job he didn't put them back on for Led Zeppelin's reformation in 2008. There are good reasons why you no longer see David Bowie with a zig-zag on his face, let alone an 'astral sphere' on his forehead. If you want quick proof of this truth, consider what happened when Kiss reconvened their classic line-up in 1996. Would you want to be knocking 50 while dressed up as a hard-rock kabuki monster, breathing fire and spewing up fake blood? I'm really not sure you would, though in an adulterated form, they're still at it.

Anyway, let us finish this bit by focusing on the rock look at its most glorious and remembering what the aforementioned Adam said. If you are young and daft enough, 'ridicule is nothing to be scared of' is surely a thought that should cross your mind most days. Now, the fun starts…

# THE LIPPY LIPPY SHAKE

### Six icons of the music/cosmetics interface, and what's in their make-up bags

## MICHAEL STIPE

### ...and his big blue stripe

You might like to think of it as the old-school British sit-com anti-hero Albert Steptoe pretending to be The Riddler from Batman – though when Michael Stipe took to wearing a big blue stripe across his face he preferred to call it his 'Blade Runner' look. Such was his chosen image when R.E.M. toured in 2004 and 2005 – preceded by equally eccentric make-up regimes whereby he favoured fistfuls of electric-blue eye shadow (c.1999, known by fans as his 'goblin' image) and streaked a big fluorescent orange line across his eyebrows (c.2003).

The explanation? The warpaint got him over 'basic insecurity', by allowing him 'to present something theatrical onstage'. Should anyone want to adopt the Blade Runner/Riddler look, the solution lies in a trip to New York, a Stipe-favoured shop called Make Up For Ever, at 409 West Broadway, and a 'dark blue body paint' called Color Cream, which sells for around $30. 'It's the normal make-up that I don't really do,' Stipe said in 2004, before explaining those all-important extra touches that too many musicians ignore. 'Stylists always want to bring down the colour in my ears, but I like it, so I pinch my ears and make them darker. They also want to powder my head, but I think it looks really good shiny.'

---

Now here lies a story. Like so many English box-bedroom androgyny merchants of a certain age, the singer-cum-boss of The Cure claims to have been partial to make-up since he was at school, on account of seeing David Bowie on an early '70s Top Of The Pops.

'I immediately borrowed someone's older sister's make-up and put it on,' he later recalled. 'I loved how odd it made me look, and the fact that it upset people.

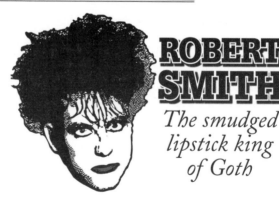

## ROBERT SMITH

### The smudged lipstick king of Goth

You put on eyeliner and people start screaming at you. How strange, and how marvellous.'

His big image breakthrough came some time prior to the release of Pornography in May 1982, seemingly thanks to time spent with Siouxsie And The Banshees (with whom he played in 1979, and between late 1982 and 1984). According to one important source, once he'd settled on his big and tousled hair, the other aspect of Smith's enduring and iconic image was chanced upon in a nightclub toilet – where, though he was already in the habit of wearing eyeliner and lipstick on- and offstage, he accidentally found his trademark.

'We added opium or LSD to our mix of drinks and, moments after, Robert borrowed Siouxsie's lipstick – then he stood up to go to the bathroom,' Banshees bassist Steven Severin later remembered. 'And when he came back he had that characteristic stain. And it was like that forever and ever'. Would-be Smith copiers take note: his lipstick of choice is made by the British Mac company, and the shade in question is called 'Ruby Woo'.

104

**ADAM ANT**

*...and his little white stripe*

The look that convinced millions of school-age Adam And The Ants fans to try putting Tipp-Ex on their faces was created in early 1980, when the aspiring icon born Stuart Goddard – back then, still managed by ex-Sex Pistols svengali Malcolm McLaren – came up with what he called an 'Apache/gypsy warrior look, with knee bells to make my moves percussive, kilt flying and a white stripe across my nose.' McLaren subsequently prised the first incarnation of the Ants away to form Bow Wow Wow – but Adam swiftly got himself a new band, and the white stripe remained.

By 1981 he was a star and about to do his first tour of the USA. There was one snag: some native Americans had taken exception to his appropriation of their culture, so Adam suggested a meeting with a group of community leaders led by one George Stonefish, a New Yorker whose mixed blood linked him to the Delaware and Chippewa tribes. In Adam's version of the story, he convinced them of his knowledge of their culture and history, and offered to remove the stripe for good and all if they objected to his act. 'Luckily,' he wrote in his autobiography, 'they loved our American debut performance in Boston, and I kept my stripe.' Phew!

By the end of the year, however, his most popular cosmetic trademark was gone, replaced by the look that accompanied the Prince Charming album, based on big boots, a double-breasted tailcoat, ludicrous painted-on eyebrows and two big red marks on the right side of his face. Needless to say, it was not in the same league.

---

Danny 'Dee' Snider was born in 1955 and raised in a very strict home in the Long Island suburbs, being forced at one point to have his long hair hacked off and undergo a crew cut. So, by the time he joined a local hard rock band called Twisted Sister in 1976, he wasn't going to hold back. 'I went for an outrageous form of expressing myself,' he later recalled. 'It seemed to be a way that I could show that I was somebody.'

'Our slogan was always "look like women, talk like men, and play like motherfuckers",' Snider later explained. 'And we were not your typical glam band – we were like football players and bikers wearing make-up.' In his case, this resulted in a look that suggested either a very eccentric transvestite, or someone auditioning for a British pantomime, though we shouldn't scoff: over two decades on, you can still buy an officially-licensed

**DEE SNIDER**

*Heavy Metal's Widow Twanky*

'Dee Snider make-up kit' (replete with sponge applicator), which retails in the US for $19.99.

The Sisters' sole big(ish) UK hit was I Am (I'm Me), which made it to No 18 in March 1983. Before that, however, on 24 July 1982, they famously played Wrexham football stadium in North Wales, on a bill topped by Motörhead. The band, in Snider's recollection, was 'shitting a brick', and fully expecting their trannie-biker schtick to be met with a hail of bottles. But the inestimable Lemmy introduced them and thereby gave them his blessing, and the crowd apparently lapped it up. 'I think it would have been a very different story if Lemmy hadn't introduced us,' said Snider. 'And the rest is history.' ☛

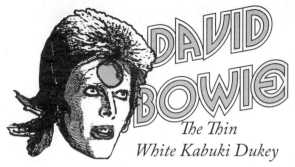

*The Thin*
*White Kabuki Dukey*

By the time of the release of The Rise And Fall Of Ziggy Stardust And The Spiders From Mars in June 1972, David Bowie's hair was cut into a style inspired by a model he'd seen in a show by the Japanese designer Kansai Yamamoto, and modelled on three different pictures from Vogue (a French issue inspired the front, and two different German copies were the source of the sides and back – it was essentially a turbocharged mullet). From then on, as he toured that album and Aladdin Sane, Bowie's level of barnet-centred ambition was matched by the intricacy of his stage make-up – and by the time he announced that a July 1973 show at Hammersmith Odeon was 'the last show that we'll ever do', it took him up to two hours to apply his slap.

As with the period's costumes – many of them designed by Yamamoto – his big inspiration was Japanese Kabuki theatre, which 1)was partly built on an androgyny that Bowie presumably found pretty appealing, and 2)may explain the line in Ziggy Stardust's de facto title track about Ziggy's charisma being up there with 'some cat from Japan'. Whatever, Bowie's white foundation, rouge and eyeliner were eventually joined by an 'astral sphere' suggested by a make-up artist named Pierre La Roche – who also applied the lightning-flash to Bowie's face for the cover of Aladdin Sane. For Bowie-philes, the effect was jaw-dropping: his whey-faced disciple Gary Numan later claimed that Bowie's look c.1972-73 was 'the greatest rock'n'roll image there has ever been'.

In a 1973 article in Mirabelle magazine, La Roche explained that Bowie bought most of his make-up 'from a little shop in Rome', but got his 'white rice powder' from 'Tokyo's Woolworth's equivalent' – and used a 'German gold base in cake form' for the sphere. Moreover, when the fancy took him, he would sometimes 'outline that gold circle in tiny gold rhinestones, stuck on with eyelash glue'. So now you know.

---

'It's not like I wear make-up to look like a mime, or a clown, or Gene Simmons – all of which are essentially the same to me,' said Marilyn Manson in 2007. 'I wear make-up like a girl wears make-up. I *always* wear make-up. I even have the no-make-up make-up look, which is a trick that college girls will use on you.'

Since his decisive breakthrough in 1996 as a vampire-esque neo-Goth, Manson has regularly changed the grim work of art that is his face with his use of zombie-esque contact lenses (used on one or both eyes) and white panstick as the main constants.

*The Antichrist*
*Superstar, aka*
*Brian Warner*

On-and-off innovations have included a big red triangle intruding on his forehead (c.1999), a Michael Stipe-type big blue stripe (c.2000), one eye covered in eyeliner and the other left untouched (c.2002), and red flame-type marks above each eye (c.2005). Plans in the mid-noughties to launch his own cosmetics brand came to nothing; for what it's worth, his favoured lines are the Japanese brand Shiseido, the Franco-American Nars, and Robert Smith's beloved Mac. Oh, and one other thing: he looks like that even when he's asleep. 'I don't take my make-up off to go to bed,' he once claimed. 'I have to shave, because I am a man, whatever you may think, but that's about the only thing I do that disturbs my make-up.'

# YOU ARE THE WALRUS!

## A razored-down history of the rock moustache

Thanks in part to post-war America's massed aversion to facial hair, the first dozen or so years of rock history saw precious few moustaches, apart from those belonging to two African-American pioneers: **Chuck Berry** and **Little Richard**, the second of whom minted a look (pencil-thin 'tache, garish attire, piled-up hair) that was partly lifted by **Jimi Hendrix** and then comprehensively nicked by **Prince**.

In the wake of the '50s, all was quiet on the moustache front until 1966, when the increasing fondness of hip London for all things Edwardian – witness the King's Road boutique I Was Lord Kitchener's Valet – prompted an upsurge of facial hair-growing in some of the capital's most high-end circles. By the end of that year, all four **Beatles** had 'taches of one kind or another (**Ringo Starr**'s, give or take his beard, remained in place for the next four decades, and is still here), as did The Rolling Stones' **Charlie Watts** and **Bill Wyman**, and, a little later, Pink Floyd's **Syd Barrett**. Across the Atlantic, the first stirrings of hippiedom were causing parallel moustache-growth: the best example was – and still is – **David Crosby**'s Walrus-esque trademark: like Ringo's, a four-decade stayer. 'Everybody had a moustache,' George Harrison later reflected. 'I think even **Engelbert Humperdinck** got one.'

From there, it was only a short hop to a phase of rock history in which the droopy Zapata moustache was king: witness the Allman Brothers Band's **Duane Allman** and **Berry Oakley**; Ian 'Lemmy' Kilmister (first of Hawkwind, then Motörhead); at least three members of the **Electric Light Orchestra**, and ELO co-founder **Roy Wood** (later of Wizzard). A little later, the proudly moustachioed **Steve 'Dobby' Dawson**, the bassist with British metallers Saxon, was the inspiration for Harry Shearer's portrayal of **Derek Smalls** in This Is Spinal Tap. On a different plane entirely, any discussion of rock moustachery should also include **Ron Mael** of the '70s art-rock duo Sparks, whose toothbrush 'tache made him look uncomfortably like a certain German dictator. Indeed, when John

*Ron Mael of Sparks and Nick Cave: 'toothbrush' and 'handlebar'*

Lennon first saw him on American TV, he is alleged to have exclaimed, 'Christ, they've got Hitler on the telly!'

In the meantime, punk rock had arrived, which seemed to throw rock moustaches on the same bonfire as flares and long hair, but had at least two 'taches hanging round its fringes: those worn by **Peter Hook** (a quick convert to a full-ish beard) and **Bernard Sumner** in the very early days of Joy Division. By the time of New Romanticism, **Midge Ure** was evoking Clark Gable with a pencil job that formed the basis of Ultravox's visuals in 1981, by which point a cultural sea-change was afoot: the appropriation of moustaches by the gay community, which was fixed in the public mind by **Freddie Mercury** and **Paul Rutherford**, and enough to make a lot of hung-up male musicians leave them well alone.

Not much happened to change any of that, though in 1995 **Paul Weller** briefly paid tribute to John Lennon circa 1967 with a short-lived moustache only glimpsed in one live photograph (according to apocryphal Weller legend, he swiftly shaved it off again after running into an incredulous Elvis Costello). And then, in 2004, something rather interesting happened: the opening of a half-decade in which splendid moustaches were worn by such musicians as **Frankie Poullain** of The Darkness, The Killers' **Brandon Flowers**, The White Stripes' **Jack White**, **Nick Cave**, and **Paul Thomson** of Franz Ferdinand. The moustache was back! For a bit, anyway.

107

# I WANT YOUR SPECS!
## Iconic rock 'bins', and the pioneers who wore them

## Elton John

Elton John's taste in eyewear reached its absurd peak in 1974 when he was fond of specs that were variously heart-shaped, spangle-encrusted, attached to huge metal rings or fashioned to spell the word 'Zoom'. The tropical-flavoured shades above were briefly the pair du jour, but soon, out-there spectacles were beginning to pall. 'When anyone does a send-up of me,' he said in 1976, 'it's still the monster boots, the orange hair and the huge glasses. I'm stuck with it.'

## John Lennon

In September 1966, John Lennon flew to Spain to film How I Won The War, a black comedy overseen by Beatles-movie director Richard Lester. He played Private Gripweed, a character whose portrayal required a pair of round-framed National Health glasses. From thereon in, a pair of the wire-rimmed variety remained in place, until around 1973. Thirty-six years on, with Yoko Ono's say-so, there's a glasses range called 'Lennon Lifestyle'. Make of that what you will.

## Roy Orbison

Early photos of Orbison attest to the fact that his trademark black shades – RayBan Wayfarers, in the main – arrived some way into his career, thanks to a famous mishap. According to his widow Barbara, it happened when he toured the UK with The Beatles in May 1963: 'He forgot his regular glasses, so he ended up having to wear sunglasses, [and] he turned them into his trademark.' Needless to say, the shades remained in place until his death in December 1988.

108

# Roger McGuinn

When their version of Dylan's Mr Tambourine Man made them stars in 1965, the effective leader of The Byrds wore so-called 'Ben Franklin' glasses, named after the square spectacles favoured by the US Founding Father and pioneer of electricity (and inventor of bifocals). The idea came from John Sebastian of the Lovin' Spoonful: 'I was walking down MacDougal Street in Greenwich Village one night,' McGuinn recalled, 'and Sebastian was walking towards me with these little shades. He said, "Try 'em on, man…they're groovy."' McGuinn soon moved on, but the same specs were adopted by such punk rockers as Johnny Rotten/Lydon and The Damned's Captain Sensible.

# Buddy Holly

Pre-fame, in his hometown of Lubbock, Texas, Holly had an abortive go at wearing contacts, and then looked for the most inconspicuous frames available. But his optician, Dr J. Davis Armistead, claims to have persuaded him to try something different – and found two pairs in heavy plastic on a trip to Mexico City. 'I showed them to Buddy,' he recalled. 'I put his prescription in them, and he picked the black pair. He said they were great.' Holly paid no more than $20; in 1998, a civic organisation in Lubbock had to find $80,000 for the pair he was wearing when he died in 1959.

# Bootsy Collins

When he played bass with James Brown, the virtuoso born William Collins was a very modest-looking figure – but after he fell in with George Clinton's Parliament-Funkadelic collective in 1972, in came costumes, a star-shaped 'Space bass', and Collins's trademark star glasses (the pair here date from 1978). 'If I didn't have the star glasses,' he once reflected, 'people said, "Where's those glasses, man?" So I had to make sure I got those thangs so I wouldn't disappoint nobody.'

# 'You write 'em – I'll sell 'em'

**Glam-rock godheads Slade, and their very sartorial sub-plot**

## Dave Hill

### 'It was all about major impact'

What grim old times the early-to-mid '70s were: strikes, power-cuts, oil price hikes, only three channels of TV, and a quite unnecessary amount of bad music (e.g. Yes). It was fortunate, then, that a slew of glam rock icons took it upon themselves to lighten up an otherwise tiresome era, not only with some thrilling records, but dizzyingly ludicrous clothes – and on both scores, no-one did it better than Wolverhampton gonzo-rock quartet Slade, the creators of a run of 12 Top 5 hits that stretched from 1971 to 1974.

On the costume front, their key weapon was lead guitarist Dave Hill, who pioneered one of the strangest haircuts in rock history (effectively two styles on one head – as he once put it, 'Shorter fringe, long sides – it allowed me to put a bit of glitter on my forehead'), and brought in two Midlands design students called Steve and Barbara Megson to work on some truly mind-boggling attire. 'It was all about major impact to me,' he later recalled. 'If I was on Top Of The Pops, I was going to be more noticed than anybody else. I knew what I was doing.'

'We didn't know what he was coming up with next, which was part of the fun of it,' says singer-guitarist Noddy (aka Neville) Holder. 'Usually, the unveiling wouldn't be at a gig. He'd have to test them on TV first, because they might be too cumbersome. Top Of The Pops was where it happened. He used to go to the toilet in the dressing room. He didn't want us to see it going on a bit at a time; we had to see it

as the audience would see it. So he'd go in the bog to change, and he'd be in there for hours at at a time. You could hear all the taps running, and all this scuffling about. But nobody was allowed in until he'd finished. And then things would quieten down, and we knew he was almost ready. We'd all shout, "Come on, H! Reveal all!" And he'd come out in whatever was the new thing.'

Among the outfits Hill premiered were costumes known by his colleagues as The Metal Nun ('a Cleopatra headpiece with a gown,' as Holder recalls), and Foghorn

*Dave Hill in full sci-fi bacofoil 'Super Yob' effect: 'ready for tomorrow', or what?*

Leghorn ('like a spacesuit with feathers coming out'). For one Japanese tour, the Megsons worked up a kind of sci-fi kimono – though Hill's archetypal get-up was probably the 'Super Yob' costume, replete with matching guitar. 'I was wearing futuristic, space-like clothes,' he explained. 'There were a lot of things going on in space, and we were just coming out of black and white telly. The Yob guitar was meant to look like a ray gun. You know: *spacey.*'

Three decades later, he reflected on his all-time favourite, worn to promote Merry Xmas Everybody, the single written to raise Britain's spirits in the winter of 1973. 'It was all white, with silvery bits, and I had boots with a big dollar signs on them. It looked like next year, rather than the tired year that had just finished. It looked like, "I'm ready for *tomorrow*".'

## Noddy Holder
### 'Like having a dozen torches on my head'

*Noddy Holder, Coachman's hat and glued-on mirrors: gasping crowd presumably out of shot*

When the hits began, Slade's singer and de facto boss had one key sartorial gimmick: tight-fitting tartan. But he soon wanted more. 'I saw Lulu on TV,' says Noddy Holder, 'and she was wearing a sparkly dress, and all these beams of light were flicking off it. And I thought, "Bloody hell – it would be great if we could do that onstage".'

The answer came on a visit to London's groovesome clothing emporium Kensington Market, where Holder found a second-hand Coachman's hat. Whereas a bog-standard top hat has curved edges, this one's sides were flat, so he could glue circular mirrors around it and create nothing short of 'a giant mirrorball'.

'It was fate,' he later recalled. 'It was bloody heavy, but it worked. We had this pin-point spotlight; at a given point in the show, we'd drop all the lights, and it would just go, Zap! A pin-point spot would hit the hat, and all these beams of light would go out. It was like having a dozen torches on my head. It was just mind-blowing. Onstage, you could hear the crowd gasp.'

## Jim Lea
### 'We can't do this – it's stupid'

One member of Slade, unfortunately, thought that sci-fi kimonos, feathered spacesuits and mirror hats were rather getting in the way. Drummer Don Powell – who was fond of garish cat-suits – just about got with the glam programme, but as Slade footage and photos reveal, bassist, violinist and co-songwriter Jim Lea, known by the band's road crew as 'the Midlands Misery', was having none of it.

'I always thought the wacky side would haunt us,' he says now. 'It made us look as if we weren't serious about what we were doing. And it got wackier and wackier. I walked out of photo sessions – it was, "Fuck that". So we'd end up with one shot with Dave in his chicken suit, and one without.'

'Jim's argument was: Well, Led Zeppelin and Pink Floyd don't do that,' says Noddy Holder. 'And I used to say to him, "But we're not Led Zeppelin or Pink Floyd. This is Slade!"' One apocryphal Slade story has Dave Hill turning up at Top Of The Pops in another insane creation, Lea expressing his disapproval, and Hill uttering the immortal words, 'You write 'em – I'll sell 'em.'

*Jim Lea: the none-too-chuffed 'Midlands Misery'*

# SOME UNHOLY WARDROBES

A six-decade, edited history of rock costume – from Bill Haley to the Yeah Yeah Yeahs

## 1950s

*December 1954* A cover of Big Joe Turner's Shake, Rattle And Roll becomes the first rock'n'roll hit in British music history. The man chiefly responsible: Bill Haley, a 29-year-old, Pennsylvania-raised musician whose look of choice is based on a kiss-curl and the red plaid jackets also worn by his band The Comets. Thus – possibly, anyway – is born a tartan-centric rock tradition stretching on to such names as The Bay City Rollers, Sex Pistols and 'celtic rock' specialists Big Country. And, if you think about it, the plaid-centric look favoured by devotees of grunge music.

*November 1956* Ohio-born Screamin' Jay Hawkins (b. Jalacy Hawkins, 1929-2000) releases I Put A Spell On You, a US Top 40 hit he apparently recorded while drunk. Cleveland DJ Alan Freed (the man who supposedly coined the term rock'n'roll) quickly suggests he reflect the 45's deranged spirit by starting his act emerging from a coffin. Thus, with the aid of leopard-print jackets, vampire-esque capes and a skull on a stick, Hawkins is reborn as a pioneer of rock's collision with a camp version of the occult (i.e. Goth, eventually).

*March 1957* Elvis Presley opens a US tour in Chicago, where he premieres a gold-leaf suit made for him by LA 'Rodeo Tailor' Nudie Cohn (see page 118). It enters history as the '$10,000 suit', though its actual cost is nearer $2500.

*Johnny Kidd & The Pirates: Yo ho ho!*

*The Spotnicks: Gagarin-esque*

*July 1959* Please Don't Touch is the first British hit for Johnny Kidd (b. Frederick Heath in 1935) And The Pirates, arguably the best pre-Beatles British rockers. Their onstage schtick involves the inevitable costumes and Kidd/Heath's eye patch, as well as one particular stunt. 'Johnny would take out a cutlass while I was doing a heavy blues solo,' guitarist Mick Green later recalls, 'and at the crescendo of the solo he would throw the cutlass at my feet and it would stick into the wooden stage.'

## 1960s

*October 1960* The Beatles make their first visit to Hamburg, where they will adopt their pre-suits look of black leather jackets and trousers, clothes favoured by the Hamburg art students who call themselves 'exis' (as in existentialists). Thanks to Brian Epstein, they will be abandoned within two years – partly because, as one writer later put it, 'Black leather, to most people in 1962, still signified Nazis.'

*June 1962* A single called Orange Blossom Special enters the British charts, and thereby announces the arrival of The Spotnicks – a Swedish, Shadows-esque quartet who dress in stylised versions of spacesuits, modelled on the get-up of Soviet cosmonaut Yuri Gagarin, who they meet on a visit to the USSR. Strangely, despite being the early '60s incarnate, they manage to stay together until 1970.

*October 1962* James Brown performs the show in Harlem recorded for the glorious album Live At The Apollo. Earlier that year, he had introduced his so-called 'cape routine' (whereby he was presented with a cape and escorted from the stage, only to insist on returning) in Baton Rouge, Louisiana. 'It really began with a Turkish towel,' his long-standing MC, Danny Ray, later recalled. 'He would drop to his knees, I would bring out the towel, he would rip it off and rush back to the microphone onstage. The crowd came to expect it, so we finally got a cape and decided to work it into the show.'

*Dr John:*
*Mardi bum*

*May 1965* The Who – more of whom later – play a concert at Dublin's National Stadium. At least one newspaper report claims that the IRA has given them word that if they appear wearing the union jack jackets already modelled by Pete Townshend and John Entwistle, they will be swiftly killed. Irish-themed green, white and gold replacements are quickly worked up at a Dublin tailor's.

*February 1967* The Jimi Hendrix Experience sit for a deservedly iconic session with the London-based photographer Gered Mankowitz. Hendrix is wearing a soon-to-be-famous braided military jacket bought from London outfitters I Was Lord Kitchener's Valet, pioneers of the Edwardiana boom also crystallised on the cover of The Beatles' Sgt Pepper.

*July 1968* New Orleans musician Malcolm 'Mac' Rebennack announces his reinvention as Dr John, The Night Tripper with the release of the album Gris-Gris. From hereon

in (and though he eventually tones things down) his onstage image is bound up with feathers, headdresses and out-there costumes, inspired by the African-American 'tribes' of 'Mardi Gras Indians' that took root in the Crescent City during the 19th century. The look is later nicked by Elton John – as evidenced by a performance of Crocodile Rock on a 1977 edition of The Muppet Show.

*July 1969* At The Rolling Stones' free concert in Hyde Park, Mick Jagger wears what one writer later calls 'a girl's party dress'. In fact, it's a men's outfit invented by Michael Fish (the designer, not the weatherman), originally made for aristocratic photographer Lord Lichfield, put off it by the warning 'you'll look like a big girl's blouse wearing that'. So Mick gets it instead.

# 1970s

*August 1970* The Who play the Isle of Wight Festival, with Pete Townshend in his then-regulation white boiler suit and Roger Daltrey giving it the rock-god fringed jacket look. But never mind them: John Entwistle is wearing his new skeleton jumpsuit. He later recalls: 'The shoulders to the crotch – I'd had it made so tight that I couldn't sit down in it.' In tribute, similar suits are later worn by such bassists as Red Hot Chili Peppers' Michael 'Flea' Balzary and The Flaming Lips' Michael Ivins.

*October 1972* Genesis release Foxtrot, and their live rendition of the hulking 23-minute suite Supper's Ready finds the dependably theatrical Peter Gabriel

*Gabriel: floral stimulation*

wearing costumes known as 'The Flower' and 'Magog'. The latter is based on a kind of geometrical helmet; the former, by Gabriel's own admission, is partly inspired by the old-school kids' TV programme Flower Pot Men (featuring, of course, Bill and Ben).

*December 1972* David Bowie achieves his 👉

*Labelle: pioneered the disco/space crossover*

biggest British hit yet with The Jean Genie. Much of his attire is designed by friend-cum-collaborator Freddie Buretti (aka Freddie Barrett, and also 'Rudy Valentino'). For a flavour of Bowie's look, there is no beating a salacious 1986 biography entitled Stardust, which describes 'Freddie's version of the designer pants of the moment', featuring 'a codpiece effect that makes the crotch bulge'. The text goes on: 'Ziggy Stardust may be an alien creature, but he is hung like an earth bull.'

*March 1973* Roxy Music put out For Your Pleasure. On the inside gatefold sleeve they are caught in full glam effect. Their synthesiser specialist Brian Eno is pictured in an outfit created by his then-girlfriend, a sculptor called Carole McNicol: vast black bell bottoms and a cropped jacket topped off with feathers on the shoulders. 'These were clothes that you could only wear onstage,' he explained. 'They were impossible to do anything normal in.'

*May 1973* Suzi Quatro (b. Susan Quattrochio) gets a British No 1 with the single Can The Can, and simultaneously excites millions of teenage males by wearing her signature leather jumpsuit, at the suggestion of producer/svengali Mickie Most. She says now: 'I wanted to wear a leather jacket like Elvis did. He *[Most]* said, "Oh Suzi, you can't. It's been done." I said, "Not

*Young: no sweat*

by a girl."So he suggested a leather jumpsuit and I thought, Yeah! That would be practical. Easy to get out of. I had no idea it would look sexy.' D'oh!

*November 1973* Brothers Angus and Malcolm Young form AC/DC in Sydney. At the suggestion of his elder sister Margaret, the former – a mere 5´2˝ – soon settles on his signature image, initially using the uniform of his alma mater, Ashfield Boys' High School. 'I was moaning to her, "How can you move onstage when your jeans are stuck? You know, you get all sweaty up there,"' he later recalled. 'So she suggested I wear my school uniform.'

*December 1974* The release of the single Lady Marmalade, by all-female trio Labelle. The costumes worn by Patti Labelle, Nona Hendryx and Sarah Dash combine elements of Spotnicks-ish sci-fi and glam rock with touches of the Mardi Gras stuff last seen on Dr John. The record isn't exactly disco, but blazes a trail in that direction, and thus forever joins that genre with futuristic get-up: witness a crop of space-themed disco hits c.1978-79, and the sight of disco siren Amii Stewart's Barbarella-esque, three-ring headdress in the video for her 1979 US No 1 version of the soul standard Knock On Wood.

*March 1975* Release of the film version of the 'rock opera'Tommy – the original work of The Who – directed by Ken Russell. Elton John plays the Pinball Wizard and 'wears fibre-glass replica Doctor Marten's, made by Northamptonshire chemical firm Scott Bader. They stand 4´6˝ tall; in 1988, they're bought by the R. Griggs firm, who make DMs.

*September 1976* While punk rock gathers momentum, on a trip to Paris The Sex Pistols' Johnny Rotten wears a new 'bondage suit' designed by Vivienne Westwood, replete with several zips and a 'towelling bum flap'. On 1 December, the Pistols appear on the ITV programme Today, and swear a lot – whereupon punk prompts a national panic, just in time for Westwood and Pistols manager Malcolm McLaren to re-open their infamous Sex boutique as a new outlet called Seditionaries.

*November 1976* Having moved through a Jackson Pollock phase in which their clothes were covered in paint splashes, The Clash adorn their get-up with stencilled slogans: 'HATE AND WAR' (accompanied by 'HEAVY MANNERS' and 'HEAVY DUTY DISCIPLINE', taken from reggae artist Prince Far-I), 'STEN GUNS IN KNIGHT'S BRIDGE *[sic]*' (a line from their own song 1977), and the inevitable 'WHITE RIOT'.

*November 1978* Judas Priest release the LP Killing Machine, featuring a song called Hell Bent For Leather, and decisively adopt a trailblazing S&M/leather-and-studs look, driven by singer Rob Halford. So it is that a look born in the more outré parts of gay culture soon threatens to define the visual aspects of Heavy Metal, though Halford doesn't come out until 1998.

# 1980s

*July 1980* Akron, Ohio's post-punk subversives Devo release their LP Freedom Of Choice. They've long been fond of uniforms, but this one heralds a masterstroke: the so-called Energy Dome, a precisely-contoured plastic hat. In 2008, stories circulate that the band

are suing McDonald's over a Happy Meal toy called 'New Wave Nigel' who wears the same headgear. These turn out to be misplaced; according to their lawyer, the issue has been 'amicably resolved on mutually agreeable terms'.

*November 1980* The success of To Cut A Long Story Short by North London's Spandau Ballet acquaints TV-watching Britons with New Romanticism, and a dress code pitched somewhere between Lawrence of Arabia and the Edinburgh Woollen Mill chain. When it comes to questions of image, guitarist-songwriter Gary Kemp later claims that they 'never intended to create an artificial front for the band'. Hmmm.

*March 1981* Louisiana-spawned, California-based avant-gardists The Residents release their album Mark Of The Mole, followed by a tour on which they continue their career-long insistence on anonymity and unveil the costume-cum-disguise that will forever define them: huge eyeballs that cover each of their heads.

*April 1984* Release of the Talking Heads concert film Stop Making Sense, in which singer David Byrne wears a vast grey suit. In an interview sequence, he explains: 'I like symmetry and geometric shapes. I wanted

*Devo and their 'Energy Domes': subsequent Happy Meal character not pictured* ☞

my head to appear smaller – and the easiest way to do that was to make my body bigger. Because music is very physical, and often the body understands it before the head.'

*November 1984* Julian Cope releases Fried, his second solo album, and announces a very reductive take on rock costume: on the cover, he is naked save for a huge turtle shell. In his autobiography Repossessed, he explains: 'It cost £30…back at the studio, I stripped off my clothes and crawled underneath it. Awlright! It was me!'

*August 1986* Cameo manage a British hit with Word Up, bringing singer Larry Blackmon's jaw-dropping red codpiece to millions of TV screens. It's the work of French fashion imp Jean-Paul Gaultier, more of whom later.

*January 1987* Public Enemy release the album Yo! Bum Rush The Show. Among their number is Flavor Flav (born William Drayton), whose signature look is based around a huge clock (often made by the bog-standard firm Westclox). He later explains it's there to embody 'how precious time is'. In June 1994, he turns up six days late for an NME interview, with the words, 'Sorry I'm late, G.' Mancunian photographer Kevin Cummins replies, 'Well, you're the cunt with the clock round his neck.' True!

*Flavor: 'Sorry I'm late, G'*

# 1990s & beyond

*April 1990* The start of Madonna's Blond Ambition tour, in support of her Like A Prayer album. The most slavered-over story surrounds her conical-breasted bustiers, designed by Jean-Paul Gaultier (and, he says, inspired by his grandma). In April 2001, one sells at auction for $21,150.

*June 1993* The Pet Shop Boys perform Can You Forgive Her? on Top Of The Pops, accompanied by silver-clad women holding cricket bats. Neil Tennant sits on a step

ladder; Chris Lowe moves around a huge blue egg. They are both wearing orange suits and huge stripey, pointed hats. 'It was inspired – the dunce's caps, anyway – by the references to school in Can You Forgive Her?,' explains Tennant. 'But, you know, we never really worry about what anything means.'

*September 1993* Kurt Cobain appears on the front of British style magazine The Face wearing one of his collection of dresses (and heavy eyeliner). In a previous interview, he has already explained: 'Wearing a dress shows I can be as feminine as I want. I'm a heterosexual…big deal. But if I was a homosexual, it wouldn't matter either.'

*June 1994* Manic Street Preachers trail their deeply confrontational album The Holy Bible with the single Faster, and perform the latter on Top Of The Pops, introduced by Vic Reeves and Bob Mortimer. The group are dressed in various versions of military apparel; singer James Dean Bradfield also wears an IRA-style black balaclava, on which he has scrawled his first name. Via either letter or telephone, the BBC receives over 25,000 complaints.

*June 1995* A study in Britpop-era contrasts: following the release of the To Bring You My Love album, PJ Harvey appears at Glastonbury, dressed in a shocking pink catsuit and black Wonderbra (as well as electric blue eye-shadow and red lipstick). Noel Gallagher, fresh from the photo-shoot for the Oasis's single Roll With It, performs in a duffel coat.

*Madonna: king cones*

*Three of Slipknot: (l-r) Fehn, Jordison, Jones*

*June 1999* The White Stripes put out their self-titled first album, whose sleeve features Jack and Meg White clad in their red, white and black colour scheme (actually, Meg wears only red and white, but let's not nitpick). According to Jack, the duo's dress code has its roots in the spiral-patterned, red and white American sweets known as Peppermint Candies (featured in the LP's cover art, and reflected in the trademark design on Meg White's bass drum), an occasion when he threw one in a fire and it oozed a black residue, and his belief in the beauty of the number three: 'After two, three means many, and that's it, you don't have to go any further than that.'

*January 2000* In the US, the self-titled first album by borderline unlistenable Iowa nu-metal band Slipknot is certified platinum, denoting a million sales. At least some of their success is down to the fact that all nine of them insist on wearing grotesque masks. The illustration above shows Chris Fehn (percussion), Joey Jordison (drums) and Craig Jones (samples), aka 'The Silent One'. In the account of one British journalist, the latter's headgear c.2002 'is a black helmet into which he has hammered nine-inch rusty nails. When he removes it, his shaven head is scarred with bright purple weals where the nails have penetrated his skin.' Lovely!

*October 2002* The release of Your New Favourite Band marks a watershed for The Hives, the garage-rock quintet from Fagersta, Sweden. To date, they have always insisted on wearing various modes of black-and-white dress – an idea rooted in a quest to distance themselves from their home country's somewhat generic punk milieu. According to guitarist Niklas Almqvist (aka Nicholaus Arson), 'it made us look way superior.'

*August 2006* New York trio the Yeah Yeah Yeahs appear at the Reading Festival. As usual, singer Karen Orzalek (aka Karen O) is wearing an admirably outlandish outfit invented by NY designer Christian Joy. This one is based around a metallic green, hot-panted main feature, magenta tights, and what appears to be a mask-type thing, possibly based on a leaded window. Says Orzalek of her work with the designer: 'We're in it with this attitude of search and destroy, and push everything to the limit and see how much we can get away with.' A lot, by the look of it.

*Karen O: possibly based on a leaded window*

117

# NUDIE CAN'T FAIL!
## The story of country and rock's most fabulous tailoring business

*Nudie Cohn: suits good enough to be buried in*

Nuta Kotlyarenko was born to a Jewish family in Kiev in 1902, and followed his eldest brother to the USA in 1913 – whereupon, true to the archetypal immigrant experience, his first name was misunderstood at New York's Ellis Island reception facility, joining up with his brother's shortening of their surname to make him 'Nudie Cohn'. As a small child, he'd been a tailor's apprentice and after three decades of up-and-down experience, in 1947 he and his wife Bobbie opened a soon-famous business in LA.

The speciality of Nudie's Rodeo Tailors was rhinestone-encrusted, gloriously gaudy costumery favoured by the likes of country musicians **Hank Williams**, **Lefty Frizzell**, **Webb Pierce** and Dolly Parton's mentor **Porter Wagoner**. By the late 1960s, it was also the chosen stagewear of **Gram Parsons** and the just-founded **Flying Burrito Brothers**, who pitched up at the Nudie store – by now at 5015 Lankershim Boulevard, North Hollywood – just after signing to A&M in 1969.

Their suits were made by a Cohn employee named Manuel Martinez. Guitarist-singer

*The Gram Parsons suit: note pills, leaves and women (and no pterodactyls)*

**Chris Hillman** ordered a blue suit featuring peacocks and a 'golden sunburst'; pedal steel player **'Sneaky' Pete Kleinow** got a black outfit featuring a pterodactyl (a favourite creature in his days as a cartoon animator); and bassist **Chris Ethridge** went for a white number with red and yellow roses. Parsons, meanwhile, excelled himself. His Nudie Suit was embroidered with stylised marijuana leaves, pills, poppies and tattoo-esque images of naked females, one on each lapel, as well as a big red cross on the back. The group wore their get-up on the cover of the wondrous LP The Gilded Palace Of Sin; Parsons' is now on display in the Country Music Hall Of Fame in Nashville.

Other Nudie customers and collectors included **Elton John**, **ZZ Top**, R.E.M.'s **Mike Mills** (who was first seen wearing a suit in the video for What's The Frequency, Kenneth? and is said to own ten), and **Elvis Presley**, for whom Cohn made the gold lamé suit most famously pictured on the cover of 1959 compilation 50,000,000 Elvis Fans Can't Be Wrong. Cohn died in 1984, though the business carried on trading until 1994. Oh, and one other thing: Hank Williams and **Buck Owens** – the Californian country star who had the first hit with Act Naturally, later covered by The Beatles – were both buried in their Nudie suits, which tells you something.

# THE KING'S NEW CLOTHES
## Elvis Presley and the 'Vegas Jumpsuit' (which nearly came with lasers)

It's a short quote, but it takes you straight to the glorious insanity of Elvis Presley's stage costumes between 1969 and 1977: 'I know he liked the dragon suit. I know he liked the peacock. He liked the leopard. And of course, I think that possibly his favourite was the Aloha Hawaii suit: the American eagle.'

So said Bill Belew (1931-2008), the Virginia-born, LA-based costume designer who worked with Elvis for the entirety of what we now know as the Vegas Years. Just before they started, it was Belew who had the inspired idea of dressing Elvis in the black leather get-up he wore during his self-titled 1968 US TV show (aka the '68 Comeback Special), replete with its high-raised collar. The King was around six feet tall, but this latter design feature was inspired by history's most famous short Frenchman: as Belew would fondly explain, it was intended as a 'Napoleonic' touch.

On 31 July 1969, Elvis played the first of his celebrated Las Vegas shows. While we're here, it's worth bearing in mind that his music at this point was immeasurably better than the more crass accounts of his story suggest (for proof, listen to 1969's From Elvis In Memphis LP), the Vegas band were evidently superb, and as the American vernacular would have it, his best Vegas shows simply cooked.

But anyway. For that run of concerts, Belew came up with two-piece suits featuring tunic-type tops and knotted belts. The following year, however, he created the first costumes that minted the essential Vegas look: one-piece jumpsuits with his favoured Napoleonic collars and flared legs, made from 'stretch gab' (i.e. gabardine), much beloved of ice skaters. From then on, The King apparently impounded most of the USA's annual rhinestone output, and wore ever more gaudy designs.

They included the 'Flame', 'Dragon' and 'Peacock' suits, as well as the 'Burning Love' suit, featured on the 1972 single of the same name (which, to quote from the Los Angeles Times, was 'red with several pinwheel designs'). The most celebrated, though, was the aforementioned 'Aloha (or American) Eagle' suit, created for Elvis's Aloha From Hawaii TV spectacular, broadcast globally in January 1973. This most patriotic of ideas, Belew later recalled, was Elvis's: 'He came up with the American Eagle. It was one of only three times that he ever made any requests. We made an American eagle belt for it... about three or four inches wide with four or five ovals with American eagles on them. And, of course, the cape.' Of course!

As it will pain anyone with a love of Elvis to reflect, as the '70s wore on and The King got bigger, the costumes – in particular the belts – got more unwieldy, and the abiding impression was of a man squeezed into things he shouldn't really have been wearing (though a suit split only once). Fate, however, spared us one unseen design. In 1977, Belew cleverly came up with a prototype 'Laser Suit', that would bounce back beams shone in its direction. The day of The King's death, he recalled in 2005, 'the electrician and I were going to test it'. But the world never got to see that one: not necessarily a bad thing, when you think about it.

*Elvis in a Belew design: thank God for 'stretch gab'*

# THE GREATEST ROCK'N'ROLL BRAND

Kiss: The Demon, The Catman, The Starchild and The Spaceman. Plus two others…

## PAUL STANLEY – The Starchild

*b. Stanley Eisen, 1952* Vocals/guitar

In 1993, with uncharacteristic self-deprecation, Paul Stanley looked back on Kiss's early make-up regime. 'At first, we tried using only white-face with heavy eye make-up. Ace *[Frehley]* tried the silver eye make-up without the white-face. I even tried painting my face all red – I looked like a long-haired tomato.'

Prior to forming Kiss, Stanley, bassist Gene Simmons and drummer Peter Criss had spent time in a New York group called Wicked Lester, before rehearsing as a trio in white face make-up. Then they recruited guitarist Frehley, and decisively got to work. 'Before I settled on the star *[on his right eye]*,' Stanley recalled, 'I'd just paint a black ring around my eye. But by the time we did our first gig *[on 30 January 1973, at a club in Queens, glamorously named Coventry]* the make-up was the way the public saw it for the next decade.'

Stanley was 'The Starchild', what Simmons later called 'an exaggeration of what he thought a rock star was'. His make-up changed only once: in 1974, when he drew a mask across both eyes, a look known as 'The Bandit'. That one, for some reason, was never seen again.

*Stanley: sent from Coventry*

## PETER CRISS – The Catman

*b. George Criscuola, 1945* Drums/vocals

'I was sitting at home,' Peter Criss recalled in 1997, 'and I was just sketching…I had this black tom cat, and I started adding his face structure to mine…I tried it at rehearsal one time and everybody was like, "Wow, that's great! That fits you."' On the cover of Kiss's self-titled first album, an outside make-up artist made things far too complicated, but Criss soon found what he was looking for: four drawn-on whiskers, a silver nose, a bit of green eye shadow and a red bottom lip.

Criss left Kiss in 1980. In 1996, after 12 years of 'unmasked' line-ups, the original quartet reformed, complete with make-up. Criss once again went on his way in 2001 and was replaced by former Kiss drummer Eric Singer, who

*Criss: owned a cat*

adopted the 'Catman' look. In 2002 Ace Frehley also left, leading to one Tommy Thayer being roped in and made-up à la his predecessor – before Criss rejoined, only to go for good in 2004, whereupon Singer returned and dutifully put on the slap. 'You can take the mask off the Lone Ranger and put it on someone else, but it ain't the Lone Ranger,' Criss said in 2008. How true.

## VINNIE VINCENT – The Egyptian Warrior

*b. Vincent Cusano, 1952* Lead Guitar

Vincent replaced Ace Frehley in 1982, changing his name thanks to Gene Simmons' insistence that everyone should have 'a nondescript name where you couldn't figure out their ethnicity or anything else about them'. Paul Stanley had the idea of painting his face with an Ankh cross, a symbol associated with Egyptian gods, though Vincent's precise persona wasn't too clear: as well as The Egyptian Warrior, he was also known as 'The Wiz'. Post-unmasking, he was kicked out of Kiss in 1984.

*Vincent: fired*

# GENE SIMMONS – The Demon

*b. Chaim Witz, 1949* Bass/vocals

Simmons's signature persona is undoubtedly Kiss's most recognisable image, helped on its way by a costume that began to reach a peak of lunacy between 1975 and 1976, when he started to wear the gargoyle-like footwear known as 'dragon boots'. In addition, he has long added two key aspects to the group's gigs: breathing fire, and spitting out/throwing up fake blood, a trick aided by his unusually long tongue (contrary to urban myth, a completely natural phenomenon).

His face art is a matter of two bat-like black shapes, a vampire-esque widow's peak, and the obligatory white base. 'My make-up came as a result of a lot of things,' Simmons said in 2005. 'All things Americana: Godzilla, horror movies, science fiction, and Black Bolt, which was a Marvel comic book.' Obviously, Godzilla was actually invented in Japan, but anyway: Simmons aimed at his own approximation of a variety of schlock pitched somewhere between superhero fantasy and old-school frighteners at the cinema. As he later put it, 'I was never interested in being a rock star: I wanted to be Boris Karloff.'

Not entirely surprisingly, when Paul Stanley suggested ditching the panstick in 1983, Simmons seems to have been the most rattled Kiss member. 'We did a photo session just to see what it would look like,' he wrote in his autobiography, Kiss And Make-up (cheers!). 'We looked straight into the camera lens. We were defiant. I made one small concession to the fans – I stuck out my tongue.'

*Simmons: liked 'dragon boots'*

# ACE FREHLEY – The Spaceman

*b. Paul Frehley, 1951* Lead guitar/vocals

As well as advising Paul Stanley to put a star over his right eye – and designing the Kiss logo – Ace Frehley came up with his own look via a process he has suggested was borderline supernatural.

'I was always fascinated with the science-fiction stuff – that whole scene – and I just started playing around with it,' he later remembered. 'It's bizarre. It just happened. When I write a song sometimes, it's like I'm not writing it. It's like somebody's beaming the information to my head: as fast I can write the lyrics, it's coming out of me…The make-up was kind of the same thing. It's almost like somebody up there sent it to me.'

*Frehley: liked a drink*

Since 2002, the 'Spaceman' look has been worn by Tommy Thayer, while Frehley has gone back to a solo career and, as Spinal Tap would have it, a more selective appeal. 'What Kiss is doing right now reminds me of like what some great fighters have done in the past when they come out of retirement, when they should have just rolled up the towel,' he said. 'That's the way it seems to me now. It's getting embarrassing.'

# ERIC CARR – The Fox

*b. Paul Caravello (1950-1991)* Drums/vocals

Carr replaced Peter Criss in 1980, wore make-up until Kiss's unmasking in 1983, and stayed in the group until 1991. At first, he tried a look called 'The Hawk', based around a yellow nose/beak, as well as a suit partly made of feathers. According to inside accounts, this was ditched partly thanks to his resemblance to Big Bird from Sesame Street, and he quickly came up with 'The Fox'. Tragically, having developed cancer of the heart, Carr died from resulting complications when he was only 41.

*Carr: foxy*

# THE NEEDLE AND THE DAMAGE DONE
## Case studies of the rock/tattoo crossover

In 1967, The Who released a song called Tattoo, the tale of two brothers who decide to go through a traditional rite of passage and get some permanent body art. Pete Townshend's feelings about the subject were betrayed by one line in particular: 'I expect I'll regret you, but the skin graft man won't get you.' In those days, after all, rock stars did not tend to get tattooed. These days, by contrast, ink-on-skin is a recognised signifier of the devil-may-care rock mindset – so hats off to a few pioneers: **Janis Joplin** (a 'Florentine bracelet' and small heart), AC/DC's late singer **Bon Scott** (among other things, a tiger and a parrot), and Fleetwood Mac's taciturn bassist **John McVie**, who built the penguin into his band's iconography by getting a tattoo of one (on his right forearm) in 1971. From there, the story moves on to such tattoo enthusiasts as The Clash's **Paul Simonon** (a New York taxi, and a none-too-subtle gun), after which the kind of punk rock that decisively took root in the early 1980s, along with LA-style heavy metal, joined rock and tattoos together forever. These, though, are some of our favourites…

## Henry Rollins

Over to the man born Henry Lawrence Garfield (1961), launched into the mass consciousness as the singer with hardcore punk pioneers Black Flag: 'I got started in '81, in those grimy places in Hollywood. Nowadays, you have to stand in line behind a model and a housewife, but not then…I wanted to be different. I wanted to customize the chassis.' His first tattoo was a Black Flag logo on his left arm, followed in turn by multiple additions, such as the logo of German avant-gardists Einstürzende Neubauten and, in tribute to the Stooges song of the same name, the legend 'Search & Destroy' (along with a huge sun-face) on his back. He's since stopped: 'I used to think that by decorating the exterior you change the interior. I don't get tattooed anymore, but I don't regret anything that's on me.'

## Liam Gallagher *Oasis*

In 1997, Liam Gallagher and Patsy Kensit had each other's first names tattooed on their arms, courtesy of a London tattoo artist named Lal Hardy. 'When he came in and asked to have Patsy's name etched on his arm, we tried to tell him he might want to change it but he wouldn't listen,' Hardy later recalled. 'When you're in love, you're in love.' They divorced in 2000, and in 2001 – supposedly at the behest of Liam's new squeeze, Nicole Appleton – the 'Patsy' tattoo was completely covered by an admirably big design, pinched from the 'Taking care of business' patch Elvis Presley co-designed with his Karate teacher. But note: Liam (sometimes nicknamed 'Elvis' by Noel) copied the words 'Faith' and 'Spirit' but not 'Discipline'. Kensit, meanwhile, went for the option of changing 'Liam' to 'Lennon', the name of their son.

## Travis Barker *Blink-182*

If you desperately want to be a musician, you could always get so many tattoos that regular work won't be an option, which is what the drummer with Californian punkoids Blink-182 did. 'I tattooed my whole body so I wouldn't have to be a perfect person in a perfect world, working in a perfect job,' he once reflected. 'I made it so I had to play music…I had no choice.' His extensive body markings include the pictured boom-box, such words as 'Lover' and 'Cadillac', and a pair of praying hands on his head. Nice.

## Tommy Lee *Mötley Crüe*

Among other tattoos, the drummer-cum-DJ and former Mr Pamela Anderson has a vast 'tribal design' on his back, and two 'dragon heads' on his chest. A 1996 court case involving his assault of a Jewish photographer saw a hoo-hah about an alleged swastika on one of his arms, since removed, and described by his lawyer as 'simply a stupid tattoo' (as opposed to writing 'Mayhem' on your stomach, which is obviously quite clever). Anyway, according to the Crüe's autobiography The Dirt, Lee agrees with a theory postulated by his analyst: 'He pointed out that a lot of the tattoos were symbols of things that I wanted in my life, like koi fish, which I got inked long before I ever had a koi pond in my house. I also have a leopard tattoo, and one of these days I'm going to have a fucking leopard. I want one on my couch just chilling when I get home from a tour.' That's right!

## Amy Winehouse

'I like looking at pretty pictures,' she said in 2007. 'I get bored looking in the mirror and seeing the same thing, so I just keep getting more and more.' Winehouse paid for her first tattoo aged 15 – a 'semi-permanent' image of Betty Boop – and then really got going. 'I got my eagle, and then my feather and my lightning on my arm…And then I got my horseshoe, and then I got the busty girls and my little love hearts…Then I got my tittie-girl, and then I got "Never clip my wings" [pictured].' Two other stories: when Winehouse performed at the 2008 Grammys, the 'tittie-girl' had an inked-on bikini; and in 2009, stories circulated that the tattooed tribute to her estranged husband Blake Fielder Civil (also pictured) was about to go. At the time of writing, its fate was unknown.

# BARBER-ISM BEGINS AT HOME
### Eight classic hairdos (or don'ts)

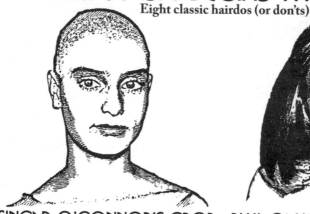

## SINEAD O'CONNOR'S CROP
### Nothing compares to it

'People always ask me if I shaved my head to look aggressive, but I shaved my head because I didn't want another boring hairdo. I did it because I'd done everything else that I could possibly do to my hair.'

So said Sinead O'Connor in 1990, when her version of Prince's Nothing Compares 2 U had rendered her and her somewhat minimalist haircut pretty much inescapable. Two years before, she had first appeared on Top Of The Pops, standing alone in a cloud of dry ice, miming to a single titled Mandinka. As was often the case when Britain's youth tuned in en masse on a Thursday night, part of the following day's national conversation duly concerned the singing woman with the shaved head – and very quickly, a set of clichés was born, most revolving around the idea that O'Connor had somehow managed to make a very close crop a byword for a new kind of feminine beauty.

'The way I looked didn't represent the kind of music I do,' she later claimed – though at the time of her greatest notoriety (the autumn of 1992 when, in protest against the Catholic Church's complicity in child abuse, she tore up a photograph of the Pope on the US TV institution Saturday Night Live), her haircut seemed to perfectly fit her persona, and so it has remained since. The crop has come and gone – it grew out, for example, in '94 and '97 – but in the public mind, Sinead is an elfin skinhead for keeps.

## PHIL OAKEY'S WONKY 'DO
### Who dares wins

Circa 1980, Phil Oakey was an aspirant pop star, working in his native Sheffield as a hospital porter and wondering how to get himself and the nascent Human League (then including Ian Craig Marsh and Martyn Ware, who would soon split and form Heaven 17) some attention. 'I really wanted to be noticed,' he explained in 2008. 'I was looking for something that no-one else had.'

The answer came thanks to South Yorkshire public transport. 'I stole the look off a girl who was a hair model in Sheffield,' he said. 'This beautiful girl got on a bus…and I went and half-chatted her up and she told me where she got it [her hair] cut and who did it. I never met her again, but I went to her hairdresser.'

Thus was born the short/long collision that slightly harked back to the 1940s Hollywood actress Veronica Lake (with the emphasis on 'slightly'), and ensured that when the League managed their first big hit, tongues would hyperactively wag. It came in May 1981 with the success of The Sound Of The Crowd, whereupon Phil's mind-boggling locks did most of the work, and they were off.

A more strait-laced version of the same basic idea was worn by Paul Weller in 1985, around the time of The Style Council album Our Favourite Shop; he later described it as 'sort of androgynous mod, and part casual'. For better or worse, it lasted mere months, and on the wonky barnet front, Phil deservedly remains king.

# MIKE SCORE'S SCI-FI THING
### 'It freaked everybody out'

A copper-bottomed classic. Liverpudlian quartet A Flock Of Seagulls crash-landed in the UK's consciousness in late 1982 when, after managing two minor hits with I Ran (a Top 10 sensation in America) and the cleverly-titled Space Age Love Song, they released a single called Wishing (If I Had A Photograph Of You). At that point Britain was decisively introduced to the bizarre barnet invented by keyboardist and singer Mike Score: two sculpted blonde horns balanced either side of a wedge-shaped clump of hair that covered his left eye. The single also perpetuated AFOS's success in the States, and worldwide iconic status was assured, kind of.

'It kind of happened by accident,' Score later recalled. 'I was a hairdresser. I used to have my hair in a Ziggy Stardust kind of thing. One day Frank *[Maudsley, bass player]* put his hand on my head and flattened it as we were about to go on stage. I liked the look of it and went for it. It freaked everybody out.'

It certainly did. He went on: 'It looked sci-fi, and we were into playing sci-fi sounding music. It was one of those things where everything came together.'

Note also the priceless moment in Quentin Tarantino's Pulp Fiction when, during the so-called 'Hamburgers' scene, Samuel L. Jackson menacingly turns to a character with slightly '80s-looking hair, and in tribute to the Score look, says: 'You – Flock Of Seagulls. You know what we're here for?'

# ERIC CLAPTON'S WHITEFRO
### Hail the 'obligatory Hendrix perm'

On The Wall, Pink Floyd's expansive concept album about the alienating effects of rock stardom, there lurks a song called Nobody Home, in which Roger Waters sings the line, 'I got the obligatory Hendrix perm' – a look back to Swinging London circa 1967 and the vogue among white rockers for adopting the same big-haired look as the freshly-arrived Jimi Hendrix (who had himself pilfered the look from Bob Dylan), usually via a perm. The Floyd's Syd Barrett was a prime example, as were the two English members of the Jimi Hendrix Experience – although history relates that bassist Noel Redding had an entirely natural 'do, and was already sporting it when he auditioned for the band.

Anyway, the modern world has come to know this style as a 'whitefro', and its most famous '60s exponent was Eric Clapton, who went for it on account of how much Hendrix impressed him. The latter famously sat in with the recently-formed Cream on 1 October 1966 and instantly turned an apparently terrified Clapton into a devout admirer. By the early summer of '67 the Hendrix-esque hair was present and correct.

According to Cream's bassist and singer Jack Bruce, the story behind Clapton's trip to the hairdressers was simple enough: 'When Jimi Hendrix came on the scene, Eric said, "One of us has to have a hairdo like that." I said, "OK, so long as it isn't me." So Eric went and got a perm.' ☞

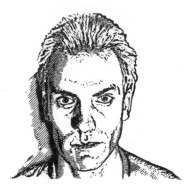

# THE PEROXIDED POLICE
## Blonde ambition, in a nutshell

In early 1978, The Police were starting to record their debut album Outlandos D'Amor at a less-than-glamorous studio in Leatherhead, and they were very strapped for cash. Sting *(pictured above)*, aka Gordon Sumner, was particularly feeling the pinch, and took roles in a handful of commercials. There was one for Brutus jeans, another for Triumph bras in which he 'had to grope Joanna Lumley's tits' – and, in the company of Stewart Copeland *(right)* and Andy Summers *(below)*, an ad for Wrigley's Spearmint chewing gum. As Copeland saw it, the plotline was simple enough: 'We're a pop group acting very obnoxiously pop-groupy and the day is saved by Wrigley's, or something.'

Sting had already dyed his hair blonde (for the full peroxide horror, have a look at his performance as 'Ace Face' in Quadrophenia), and suitably impressed, Copeland had followed suit. Now, Wrigley's insisted that to give the ad a zeitgeisty 'punk' look, Summers had to bow to the inevitable – and thus the punks who already saw the band as opportunistic interlopers had another stick with which to beat them. The ad was shot on 22 February 1978. Surprisingly, the band stuck with the blonde look for the duration of their career.

# KEITH FLINT'S MOHICANS
## Look at him! Two on one head!

Look back at early photographs of Essex-raised rave/techno/'electronica' titans The Prodigy, and what's particularly striking is the appearance of their chief shouter-cum-diabolic mascot Keith Flint: back then, a fresh-faced, smiling fella dressed in what might be called Rave Pyjamas, with soft and flowing locks. In the wake of 1994's much-praised album Music For The Jilted Generation, however, he began to affect a slightly more threatening look – first smearing on eyeliner and opting for some cumbersome piercings, and then, at 1995's Glastonbury, premiering a new hairdo: short, and dyed pink.

The main event arrived later that year, when the Prodge began playing a new, punk-esque song called Firestarter and Flint – giving it the old, 'I'm the firestarter/twisted firestarter' – unveiled what was soon known as a 'double Mohican': two coloured and teased-up clumps of hair, one on each side of his shaven head, which quickly rendered him 1)The Prodigy's instantly-recognisable public face, and 2)iconic. The explanation? 'It's about trying to get a "fuck the world, I'm not answerable to anyone" syndrome,' he level-headedly explained. 'You just do what you want, you just express yourself to the full. I am my own boss, it's just a natural process. Full on expressionism, you know what I mean?'

So now you know. Incidentally, for all Flint's devil-may-care affectations and air of nihilistic menace, his dad Clive once told a Daily Mail journalist this: 'If he saw a caterpillar in the road while he was doing 70mph in his sports car, he would stop and put it in the nearest bush.'

## LIMAHL'S REVERSE SKUNK
**Well, that's what we're calling it**

In early 1983, Kajagoogoo managed a big hit in both the US and UK with a song called Too Shy, co-produced by Duran Duran's Nick Rhodes and sung by one Limahl, known to his mum as Christopher Hamill (it was an anagram, see?). Unfortately, the fun didn't last: by that summer he had left, and though they tried to make a go of being a four-piece, the 'Googoo – as they were known – were soon on the slide.

Limahl, to be fair, managed to sustain his profile into the following year, a feat partly based on a quintessentially '80s hairstyle that somehow captured just about everything wrong with that decade and was copied by a certain kind of embarrassment-free suburban desperado. It had its roots, he later explained, in his early years as a jobbing actor: 'I was in a theatre show in Westcliff on Sea – it was called Godspell, and all the guys had mousy brown hair…so I went to the director and said, "Look, I've always fancied being blonde and it would look good in the show, is that OK?" He said, "Yeah, go for it", and that's really what started it off.' On a different occasion, he explained his hair's development thus: 'Originally, I had it done all white, then I put a black streak on one side, then later I added another bit on the other side, then a bit behind, and so on. It progressed, you could say.'

You certainly could. After 25 years apart, the original line-up of Kajagoogoo reconvened in 2008, and a thinned-out version of Limahl's 'do was present and correct, though he was now sounding slightly apologetic. 'I created a wave of dodgy hair,' he admitted. 'It's all my fault.'

## AMY WINEHOUSE'S BEEHIVE
**A towering triumph**

As proved by the video for Rehab, when the UK's most notorious soul-pop chanteuse released Back To Black in late 2006, her hair was pretty voluminous – but she had not yet adopted the feature that would lead to a key sign of her success: the fact that hairdressers all over the industrialised world soon knew exactly what 'an Amy Winehouse' was.

By early 2007, however, the Winehouse beehive had arrived. Was it, one interviewer asked, part of some carefully thought out attempt at an iconic look? 'Not consciously,' she said. 'But I know that over the last year my hair has got significantly bigger.' A few months later, she clarified the point as follows: 'I'm very insecure about the way I look. I mean, I'm a musician I'm not a model…The more insecure I feel, the bigger my hair has to be! I tell my hairdresser…make it bigger! Bigger! Bigger!'

Though Winehouse has occasionally claimed the beehive is all her own work, photographic evidence proves that it's actually a giant hairpiece – whose on-off status has prompted such affectionate headlines as 'Back to bald: emaciated Amy leaves the beehive behind to reveal her thinning locks' (cheers, the Daily Mail). By July 2008, when Winehouse was the most high-profile quarry of the tabloid press, it had reached its peak height: apparently a good two feet tall.

Anyway, one last Amy quote is worth repeating, given to an interviewer who wondered whether – perhaps with all that hard living – she had good hive days and bad hive days. 'Never,' she said. 'My hair is always on point, even if the rest of me is really naff.'

# Chapter 6

# THE BEATLES

The most influential, innovative, epochal rock group the human race has ever seen formally broke up in 1970, when Paul McCartney served formal notice of a split that had actually taken place, à la Bryan Adams, in the summer of '69. Back then, John Lennon was fond of a pretty dismissive approach to The Beatles' myth. 'People talk about it as if it was the end of the world,' he said. 'It's just a rock group that split up. It's nothing important.'

Relative to life, death and the universe, he was probably right. Nonetheless, there are millions of people for whom The Beatles are not just important, but bordering on the divine. From time to time they crowd into convention centres across the world to hear the memories of former Beatle girlfriends, ex-barmen from Hamburg and people who used to clean their cars. With very little persuasion, they will happily rhapsodise about the version of I Am The Walrus with no strings on, the endless hours of taped conversation from the Let It Be period, or how to find the site of the Southern English supermarket that John Lennon gave one of his closest friends as a present (it's on Hayling Island, in Hampshire – not hard to find if you ask a few locals). Contrary to what the latter Beatle said, it turned out that The Beatles failed to become bigger than Jesus – but there are times when the ongoing noise that surrounds them seems to denote a kind of secular religion.

Here's the thing, though. As ludicrous as it may look, all this shouldn't really be mocked, because if any of the thousands of musicians who have contributed to the 60-year progress of rock'n'roll music deserve that kind of adoration-bordering-on-faith, it is surely these four. You can argue about this or that album, or the meaning of the word 'genius', or the odd bad song – but presented with The Beatles' story, and the idea of four lives that apparently moved at 1000mph, and all that glorious music, how can your mind not boggle?

'From the Liverpool Docks to the Hollywood Bowl', as a song once put it – via London, New York, Manila, Tokyo – and, of course, India. A dozen albums that may have occasionally dipped, but contain not just scores of magical songs, but a story of almost supernatural artistic development, in double-quick time. In 1963, the world got Twist And Shout, Please Please Me, and She Loves You; by 1968, they were on to Happiness Is A Warm Gun, Revolution 9 and the seven glorious minutes of Hey Jude. That journey took five years, which kind of puts it all in perspective: comparisons are odious, of course, but can we realistically expect any similar growth-spurts from the musicians who are currently at the top of their particular tree? If so, they have until 2013, and they'd really better get going.

The following pages are a kind of crash-course in Beatledom. By way of a jump into the deep end, they begin with a guide to one of rock music's most incredible tangles of myth and nonsense: the theory, first propagated in 1969, that though Paul McCartney had been dead since 1966, John, George and Ringo had brought in a replacement, and then sent the world a series of clues about what they had done. After that, there's an A to Z of The Beatles' women, a walking tour of the dive-bars and flea-pits they frequented in Hamburg, a look at the insanity that took root at the offices of their Apple empire, stuff pertaining to the particular lives of each Beatle in turn – and, towards the end, an honest introduction to their wildly up-and-down solo careers. If you haven't yet heard a Wings album called Wild Life, don't worry about it; if you've yet to make the acquaintance of George Harrison's All Things Must Pass, you might want to give it a try.

Two solo Beatles, of course, are still with us. Ringo still occasionally tours and puts out well-intentioned, if unremarkable, albums, and was recently glimpsed on TV advertising a British insurance company. Paul, meanwhile, often seems to be omnipresent, playing scores of the old songs to delirious crowds and positioning himself as both the custodian of The Beatles' myth and, from time to time, yet another of those voices who'd have you believe that it was all a little more ordinary than most mortals would like to think; and from his perspective, theirs really was a fairly straightforward, workaday kind of story.

These days, he's often heard claiming that they were 'a good little band', which is just silly, though we should probably cut him some sympathetic slack. As the pages that follow suggest, they were most of the way to being superhuman – but maybe it's sometimes hard, looking in the bathroom mirror and seeing one of The Beatles.

# THE 'PAUL IS DEAD' MYSTERY

In October 1969 a Detroit-based DJ named Russ Gibbs made the first high-profile noise about rumours that Paul McCartney had died in a 1966 road accident, but The Beatles had 1)covered up his demise, and 2)attempted to alert more knowing members of their audience via a series of 'clues'. The 'Paul is Dead' stories quickly gave rise to something approaching a cult. The best of the alleged clues run as follows…

In the closing seconds of Strawberry Fields Forever, John Lennon is said to have uttered the incantation 'I buried Paul' (it happens at 3:57). Lennon and McCartney both subsequently insisted he actually said 'cranberry sauce'.

On the sleeve of Sgt Pepper's Lonely Hearts Club Band, there are a multitude of signs. On the front cover, a floral arrangement intended to represent a guitar is said to in fact read, 'Paul?', and a hand hovers over McCartney's head, as if he is being blessed before burial. Better still, if you bisect the 'Lonely Hearts Club' bass drum, it reveals the legend '1 ONE IX HE DIE'. This apparently gives away the date of Paul's passing: '1 ONE IX' = 11/9 = 9 November. An arrow before the word 'He' points up at Paul. Oh, and in the inner gatefold sleeve, Paul is also wearing a badge on his arm that reads 'O.P.D.', or 'Officially pronounced dead'. However, the man himself (if it was really him) was having none of it: 'I picked up the O.P.D. badge in Canada. It was a police badge. Perhaps it means Ontario Police Department or something.' It later turned out that the badge read O.P.P – it stands for Ontario Provincial Police.

On the back cover, Paul's back is turned, and next to him are the words 'WITHOUT YOU'.

*The giveaway 'I Was' sign*

In the booklet that accompanies the British Magical Mystery Tour EP, Paul is pictured sitting in front of a notice that reads 'I WAS'. In a still of the four Beatles from the film's closing sequence, John, Ringo and George are wearing red carnations, but Paul's is black (he later protested that 'I was wearing a black flower because they ran out of red ones').

130

In the centre spread of the Magical Mystery Tour EP and album, The Beatles are pictured miming to I Am The Walrus at West Malling Aerodrome in Kent. Ringo's bass drum is alleged to read, 'Love the 3 Beatles'. Think about it.

*Paul's Canadian police badge: 'O.P.P.' not 'O.P.D.'*

The lyrics to I Am The Walrus are supposedly smattered with clues. The refrain 'I'm crying' is said to be the sound of John expressing his grief over Paul's death. The references to 'pretty little policemen' and 'waiting for the van to come' allegedly refer to the police who were present after Paul's fatal accident. And the opening line of the song – 'I am he as you are he as you are me and we are all together' – is meant to suggest that the surviving Beatles were involved in the conspiracy to cover up Paul's demise.

On The Beatles, aka The White Album, I'm So Tired closes with some comical muttering from John Lennon (1:58–2:02). When played backwards, it sounds a bit like 'Paul is a dead man. Miss him, miss him, miss him.'

If you play it backwards, John (and Yoko's) White Album sound collage Revolution 9 allegedly throws forth – and we're quoting a 1969 issue of Life magazine here – 'the horrifying sounds of a traffic accident…a collision, crackling flames, a voice crying, "Get me out, get me out!"'

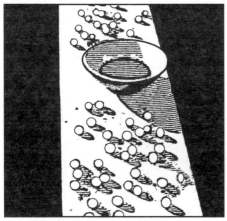

*The sleeve of 1970's 'McCartney' album*

The White Album came with two poster-sized collages of photos, including two creepy images of Paul. One pictures him in the bath, with his head surrounded by water, and is said to signify a 'decapitated corpse'. In another, Paul is seemingly being grabbed by a pair of 'ghostly skeletal hands'. Also, in one corner, there's a passport-type photo of what appears to be Paul in disguise – he's wearing glasses, and has a moustache – but may actually be one William Campbell, the musician secretly drafted in to replace him and persuaded to have plastic surgery so as to fool the world.

On the cover of Abbey Road, the picture of the four Beatles is said to represent a funeral procession. John, dressed all in white, is a clergyman. Ringo, in a black suit, is an undertaker. George, in denim 'work clothes', is playing the role of a gravedigger.

Paul, though left handed, is holding a cigarette in his right hand! And get this: his bare feet and closed eyes might represent a dead body.

In the background of the Abbey Road cover shot is a white VW Beetle, whose number plate ends with '28 IF' – or Paul's age IF he had lived. There is only one problem: when the picture was taken and the album released, Paul was only 27. By way of a last word, when McCartney released the album Paul Is Live in 1993 and parodied the Abbey Road image on its sleeve, a white VW's number plate read '51 IS'.

John's Abbey Road tune Come Together features the line 'One and one and one is three' – as in three surviving Beatles, rather than the full four. Also, on the back cover of Abbey Road, an arrangement of dots next to the titular street sign may suggest the number 3, the crack in the letter 'S' of 'Beatles' could denote a flaw in the band's myth, and a shadow close by might represent a skull. Or there again, perhaps not.

On the cover of the career-closing album Let It Be, John, George and Ringo are photographed in three-quarters view against white backgrounds, whereas Paul looks straight at the camera, against a backdrop that is coloured blood red.

On the front cover of Paul's first solo album, McCartney, is a bowl surrounded by red fruit, said to be cherries, though they look like more redcurrants. The bowl is empty, and if 'life is a bowl of cherries', this therefore signifies death. And that really is quite enough.

Mirror          Mirror

*The Sgt Pepper drum, with bisecting mirror trick*

# KNIGHTHOOD? SCHMIGHTHOOD!
## Overlooked facts about Richard Starkey (MBE)

**One of his favourite bands is alt-country duo The Handsome Family**
In 2003, he appeared on the NBC chat show presented by Carson Daly and raved about the New Mexico-based Brett and Rennie Sparks. His on-the-case host thought he meant the brotherly trio Hanson, which caused some confusion. But it's true: as Starr sees it, the Handsomes make 'gothic acid country pop – they're very good'.

**He doesn't want an airport named after him**
'I don't think John is getting anything he doesn't deserve. In Liverpool, Ringo Airport would have been more fun – but it's John Lennon Airport, and that's fine. I just want a conveyor belt: "The bags from Malaga are coming up on Conveyor Belt Ringo!"'

**He pretty much invented the drum riser, with good reason**
'The reason I had a drum riser, and also the smallest kit of drums, was I was going to make damn sure you could see me,' he said in 2001. 'Cos the drummer was always at the back, with cymbals hiding him. It wasn't going to happen to me. I just thought, Shit – I'm going to be out there too. So *[instead]*, it was John, Paul, George…AND RINGO!'

*Ringo: 'The Queen? Harumph!'*

**He's an anti-monarchist**
On his 2003 album Ringo Rama, there's a song called Elizabeth Reigns, which crisply advocates the British monarchy ending with the current Queen: 'God save the Queen, you know what I mean/We don't need a king.' He explained: 'I think it's time now. We've had enough of the Royal Family…I'm more opposed to it now than I used to be.' Neither was he too impressed by Paul McCartney's knighthood: 'I don't think me or George would have accepted it. Paul was getting it because he was a Beatle, really. That was how I felt about it: I thought, We all go, or none of us go. But we didn't and that's the end of it…I can't call him Sir. He wants it, he's got it. Let's hope he's happy.'

**He still meditates**
When The Beatles went to India to study Transcendental Meditation with the Maharishi, Ringo and wife Maureen left after a fortnight – which, he says, was always the plan. But he got his obligatory personal mantra, and now uses TM regularly: 'The benefits to me are quietening my mind and soul down. At the end of the day, I can end up totally wacky, because I've made mountains out of molehills. With meditation, I can keep them as molehills.' He didn't, however, do much TM when he was on the sauce: 'Drunks aren't big on meditation: *[Sarcastically]* "Give me another cognac – I've got to meditate".'

**He has two tattoos**
One was done in 1976, one in 1994. Of the latter, he says: 'I took my daughter *[Lee, born 1970]* to have her tattoo brightened up, and I thought, While I'm here, I'll have one too.' He refuses to explain what it means, but as he puts it, 'It looks like a bale of hay with a cross leaping out – it's supposed to be a volcano, with lotus flowers.' The earlier tattoo is of a shooting star going across the moon, a reference to his adopted surname. The variation in pain levels between the two was apparently down to alcohol, and the subsequent lack of it. 'In '76, there was no pain – in '94, lots of pain,' he says. 'Thank you, Martell.'

# BALLOONS, BUILDINGS, BUMS...

### John and Yoko's mind-boggling adventures in avant-garde movie-making

**Smile aka Film No.5** *1968*
Their celluloid debut: John, in the garden of his Surrey home, pulling faces, with the compelling twist that everything's so slowed down that very little of any consequence is spread over a whole 52 minutes (Yoko apparently fancied a four-hour version). Screened at the 1968 Chicago film festival; after 30 minutes only half the audience remained. To be honest, that was still pretty good going.

**Two Virgins** *1968*
More slo-mo tomfoolery, since glimpsed in Lennon documentaries. John and Yoko's faces blur together, and they also indulge in a bit of on-camera canoodling, while their borderline unlistenable debut collaborative album (the one with the nude cover) meanders on as intrusive incidental music. Not exactly Citizen Kane, really.

**Rape** *1969*
Probably their most ambitious and successful(ish) venture, though it was based on a somewhat cruel premise: as Yoko later put it, 'just following a girl, and keeping following her, and what would happen to somebody who's just totally exposed all the time, you know?' Inevitably, their chosen quarry – a 21-year-old Hungarian named Eva Majlata – 'freaked out'. Said John: 'We're showing how all of us are exposed and under pressure in our contemporary world. This isn't just about The Beatles. What is happening to this girl on the screen is happening in Biafra, Vietnam, everywhere.' Not exactly seen by millions, though for some reason shown on Austrian TV; an Evening Standard critic, meanwhile, reckoned it did 'for the age of television what Franz Kafka's The Trial did for the age of totalitarianism'. So, if you think about it, John and Yoko invented Big Brother. Almost.

**Self Portrait** *1969*
Oh, Mr Lennon! You spoil us! A 42-minute study of Beatle John's penis, sometimes in a state of partial arousal. 'The critics wouldn't touch it,' said Yoko. Arf!

**Apotheosis** *1970*
Filmed in late 1969. John and Yoko, dressed in monk-esque black hoods and capes, are driven to the Suffolk village of Lavenham, where they watch a hot air balloon take off and drift across the sky. From up above, we then get somewhat aimless views of the snow-caked English countryside, before the balloon enters the clouds and, for several minutes, there's nothing but a blank white screen. 'The onus is on the viewer to interpret,' reckoned one writer. It certainly is.

**Up Your Legs Forever** *1970*
Rather harks back to Yoko's infamous 1966 film Bottoms, for which 365 people were persuaded to remove their 'smalls' and have their buttocks filmed. Here, 300 pairs of legs are filmed, top to bottom – 'for peace', obviously – before the Lennons perform the finale by bringing up the rear and exposing their bums to public attention/ridicule.

**Freedom** *1970*
It lasts but one minute. Yoko tries to unclasp her bra, but the film – or, rather, 'film' – ends before she actually manages to do it. Spielberg-esque, obviously.

**Fly** *1970*
Over 19 thrilling minutes, a fly is filmed exploring a naked woman's body – only in reality, there were 200 of the little blighters. Put together in New York, during the same creative spurt as Up Your Legs Forever. 'The experience of making Fly was really hilarious, actually,' Yoko later recalled. 'The shooting was done in one night and was over by dawn... There was definitely a shortage of flies. One assistant finally got some in the subway and brought them back.' Incidentally, the solitary female star was called Virginia Lust.

**Erection** *1971*
Another penis movie? Thankfully not. It's a time-lapsed, 20-minute film of the building of the International Hotel on Cromwell Road, which is still there. It took nine months to film. Worth it? Well...

133

# DON'T FEAR THE REEPERBAHN
## A guide to The Beatles' Hamburg

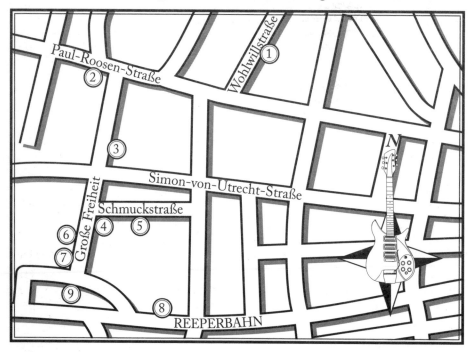

**1 Jägerpassage** *Wohlwillstraße 22*
During The Beatles' residency at the Top Ten club (see below), John Lennon posed here in a doorway for a photograph by Jürgen Vollmer, an associate of their close Hamburg friends who later cut John and Paul's hair in a proto-moptop style. The picture was used on John's 1975 covers album Rock'n'Roll.

**2 Bambi Kino** *Paul-Roosen-Straße 33*
Former cinema where the five freshly arrived Beatles – John, Paul, George, drummer Pete Best and bassist Stuart Sutcliffe – lodged on their first Hamburg trip in August 1960. According to one account, the facilities amounted to 'one filthy room and and two windowless cubbyholes, immediately behind the cinema screen.' Towards the end of The Beatles' first Hamburg visit (see below), Paul and Pete Best were arrested on suspicion of trying to burn the Bambi Kino down – as it turned out, they'd just set fire to a condom – and deported.

**3 Indra** *Große Freiheit 64*
Poky Hamburg club where they did their inaugural residency. After 48 nights, its owner Bruno Koschmider moved them down the street to the Kaiserkeller. 'The whole area was full of transvestites and prostitutes and gangsters,' George later recalled, 'but I couldn't say they were the audience. I don't recall there being many people at all at first.' Now a somewhat chi-chi bar and venue: at the time of writing, its forthcoming attractions included a 'poetry slam rumble'.

**4 Kaiserkeller** *Große Freiheit 36*
Spruced up and expanded, but still there. The second Hamburg club the Fabs played, where they ingested no end of beer and a refreshing German diet pill called Preludin, befriended Ringo Starr – then the drummer with Rory Storm And The Hurricanes – and first met Klaus Voormann and Astrid Kirchherr, the young German bohemians who would have a huge influence on them.

They would soon leave for the rival Top Ten (see below); according to most accounts, word of this led Bruno to tip off the police that George Harrison was under 18, leading to his deportation, and give or take a few George-less appearances at the Top Ten swiftly curtailed by Paul and Pete Best's deportation, the end of the Fabs' first Hamburg season.

**⑤ Chum Yuen Poon** *Schmuckstraße 9*
Former site of a Chinese restaurant. Said Paul: 'Its great attraction was pancakes – "Pfannkuchen mit Zitrone bitte, und Zucker"…It was the only place that sold them. Everywhere else was foreign food for us.'

*The Star Club, c.1962*

**⑥ Star Club** *Große Freiheit 39*
From 1969 onwards, a porno cinema, completely damaged by fire in 1983 and demolished in 1987. Their first gig here was in April 1962, soon after the death of Stuart Sutcliffe, who had by then left the band, remained in Hamburg with Astrid Kirchherr and enrolled at Hamburg's College of Art. There's a modest shrine-cum-gravestone commemorating the site of the only known recording of The Beatles in Hamburg, taped at their last Reeperbahn show, on New Year's Eve 1962 (having done three Star Club residencies, they played two last gigs in Hamburg, at the Ernst Merck Halle, on 26 June 1966). Now long deleted thanks to legal argy-bargy, you can still get second-hand copies of a double vinyl LP, brimming with such delights as John Lennon singing the chorus of an early soul song called (I Do The) Shimmy Shimmy as 'shitty shitty'.

**⑦ Gretel und Alfons** *Große Freiheit 29*
Bar-restaurant frequented by The Beatles and most other visiting British musicians. Still pretty much as it was: if you ask them nicely, they play Beatles records – and roughly the right ones, too (i.e. the Please Please Me LP and With The Beatles). When Paul came back here in 1989, he famously paid off all his old debts, with interest.

**⑧ Top Ten Club** *Reeperbahn 136*
Now a branch of Pizza Hut. The location of a club owned by one Peter Eckhorn, where The Beatles played (and slept) every night during their second

*Jägerpassage: doorway pose location*

Hamburg trip, beginning in April 1961. Their standard gigs lasted from 7pm to the early hours, and it was during this visit that they recorded a hyped-up version of the Scottish standard My Bonnie for German producer Bert Kaempfert, backing the London singer Tony Sheridan – though they also managed to record a John-sung treatment of Ain't She Sweet, and a Harrison-Lennon instrumental titled Cry For A Shadow.

**⑨ Beatles-Platz** *Junction of Reeperbahn and Große Freiheit*
Small plaza intended to look like a 12-inch record, dedicated to the Fabs and featuring five rather unconventional statues (which look like giant biscuit cutters) including a Pete Best-Ringo hybrid. The idea came from a Hamburg radio station; it was opened in September 2008, and estimated to have cost €500,000 (£450,000).

# WHEN I FIND MYSELF IN TIMES OF TROUBLE...

### Edited highlights of the bad-vibes Let It Be tapes, also starring Peter Sellers...

*On 2 January 1969, The Beatles started work on the film and album that would be called Let It Be, at Twickenham Film Studios. The rough plan was to work up new songs and then perform them at an unspecified, movie-ending spectacular live show (proposed locations included an ocean liner and a Roman amphitheatre in Tunisia). It didn't quite work out like that, and the much-bootlegged tapes endlessly recorded four men – and Yoko Ono – in the throes of a grim divorce...*

## Paul v George
### 6 January

*Mid-way through working on Two Of Us, then titled On Our Way Home, George and Paul reflect on their progress...*

**Paul:** We've just gone round, like, for an hour, with nothing in our heads.
**George:** There's no riffs.
**PM:** You and I... it's not together, so that it's not sounding together...
**GH:** So we can only play it until we...
**PM:** Or we can stop and say, 'It's not together.'
**GH:** If we had a tape recorder now, and put the tape on playback, we'd throw that *[the arrangement]* out straight away.
**PM:** It's complicated now. So if we can get it simpler, and then complicate it where it needs complications...
**GH:** *[Sharply]* It's not complicated.
**PM:** You always get annoyed...I'm trying to help, you know. But I always hear myself annoying you.
**GH:** You're not annoying me. You don't annoy me anymore.

136

**PM:** I'm not trying to get you. I really am trying to say, 'Look lads – *the band*. Shall we try it like this, you know?' With this one, it's like, 'Shall we play guitar all through Hey Jude?', *[a reference to George's rejected suggestions]* 'Well, I don't think we should.'
**GH:** OK. Well, I don't mind. I'll play, you know, whatever you want me to play, or I won't play at all if you don't want me to play. Whatever it is that'll please you, I'll do it.

## Paul v The Other Three
### 7 January

**PM:** We've been very negative since Mr Epstein *[Brian, Beatles manager]* passed away. We haven't been positive. That's why all of us in turn have been sick of the group...There's nothing positive in it. It's a bit of a drag. The only way for it not to be a bit of a drag is for the four of us to think, should we make it positive or should we forget it?...It's discipline we need. It's like everything you do, you always need discipline.

*Some time passes...*

**Michael Lindsay-Hogg (Director of Let It Be):** Do you want to perform to an audience, or do you just see yourselves as a recording group?
**PM:** I think there's something in the performing thing.
**GH:** I don't want to do any of my songs on the show, because they'll turn out shitty. They'll come out like a compromise.
**PM:** Look, last year, you were telling me, 'You can do anything you want'...I think we're very good. We can get it together, if we think we want to do these songs great. *[To John]* What do you think?
**John:** *[Distractedly]* About what?
**GH:** *[Pointing at Paul, John and Ringo]* Hear no evil, speak no evil, see no evil.
**Ringo:** I'm not interested.
**PM:** I don't see why any of you, if you're not interested, get yourselves into this. What's it

for? It can't be for the money. Why are you here? I'm here because I want to do a show, but I don't feel an awful lot of support.

*A few minutes later…*

**PM:** There's only two choices: we're going to do it *[the show]* or we're not going to do it. And I want a decision – because I'm not interested in spending my fucking days farting around here, while everyone makes up their mind whether they want to do it or not. If everyone else wants to do it, great. But I don't have to be here.

## Paul v John
### 8 January

**PM:** Haven't you written anything?
**JL:** No.
**PM:** We're going to be faced with a crisis, you know.
**JL:** When I'm up against the wall, Paul, you'll find me at my best.
**PM:** Yeah, I know – but I just wish you'd come up with the goods.
**JL:** Look, I think I've got Sunday off.
**PM:** Yeah, well I hope you can deliver.
**JL:** I'm hoping for a little rock'n'roller… Sammy With His Mammy.

## The Peter Sellers visit
### 14 January

*George temporarily bailed out of the sessions on 10 January, and returned on the condition that they dropped plans for a big live performance, whereupon filming and recording moved to the basement of the group's Apple offices (see page 144). In the interim, the three remaining Beatles carried on working at Twickenham Film Studios, where they were joined by Peter Sellers – soon to work with Ringo on the movie The Magic Christian. What follows is a kind of on-the-spot comic improvisation…*

**JL:** Remember when I gave you that grass in Piccadilly?
**PS:** I do – and man, it really stoned me out of my mind. Acapulco gold, wasn't it? It was really fantastic. I'm not holding any right now, I'm sorry.
**JL:** We've now given up, as stated by Hunter Danier in The Beatles' Actual Life Story *[a reference to the 1968 authorised biography by Hunter Davies].*
**PS:** I'm sorry about that, fellas. If I'd known I was going to see you, I'd have had some on me, cos I know how you love it.
**PM:** Gotcha, Pete. Can you dig it?
**PS:** Oh yes. I can dig it.
**PM:** You wanna make the scene for the Gents' lavatory?
**PS:** That's a groove, guys. *[Preparing to leave]* Well guys, see you.
**JL:** Bye bye.
**PM:** Too much, Pete.
**RS:** Way out.
**JL:** Just don't leave the needles lying around. We've got a bad reputation now, with John getting busted. I know what it's like for showbiz people: they're under a great strain, and they need a little relaxation…If it's a choice between that and exercise, drugs win hands down…
**Yoko Ono:** Shooting *[up]* is exercise.
**JL:** Shooting is exercise, oh yeah.

*Peter Sellers (left) and Ringo: 'You wanna make the scene for the Gents' lavatory?'*

137

# WITH A LITTLE HELP FROM MY GIRLFRIENDS

### An A-Z of notable Beatles women

**Nancy Lee Andrews**
American model turned photographer
(b.1947) who assumed role of Ringo's other
half between 1974 and 1980. They met in the
midst of the tomfoolery surrounding John
Lennon's supposed 'lost weekend' in LA. A
memory of their early courtship: 'Ringo turned
more melancholy as we approached two in
the morning, holding my hand, touching
my face, and looking at me with those big
blue watery eyes. He weaved his way to the
jukebox and punched in Charlie Rich's The
Most Beautiful Girl In The World, over and
over again.' Sounds lovely, but it wasn't to
be: she says they decided to marry, but then
Ringo met Barbara Bach (see below). Andrews
whacked him with a $5 million lawsuit – for
'palimony', as lawyers say in California – but
was unsuccessful.

*Paul and Jane: brimful of Asher*

**Jane Asher**
Actress and cake expert (b.1946) who partly
defined Paul's public profile between 1963 and
1968. Soon after the Fabs' first success, Paul
moved into her family's central London house
(at 57 Wimpole Street, W1), before the couple
made a home at Paul's new pad in St John's
Wood. Songs written for/about her include
And I Love Her, Here, There And Everywhere,
You Won't See Me and I'm Looking Through
You; the latter two point up tensions traceable
to her successful dramatic career and Paul's
interest in a traditional, career-lite notion of
housewifery. Having got engaged to Paul on
New Year's Day 1968, she travelled with the
Fabs to India, but by July had announced it
was all off. The public, Paul later reflected,
'didn't like me giving up Jane Asher. They
didn't like that at all.' She married barbed
cartoonist Gerald Scarfe in 1981, ten years
after they first met.

**Barbara Bach**
Model-turned-actress (b. Barbara Goldbach,
1947) who, having starred in 1977's Bond film
The Spy Who Loved Me, met Ringo on the
set of the execrable movie Caveman. They got
married in April 1981, with Paul and George
in attendance. She shared Ringo's booze/tax
exile lifestyle – 'We didn't have a lot of energy
and we didn't do much,' he later reflected –
until they both did rehab in Arizona in 1988.
They're still together, which is nice.

**Iris Caldwell**
Liverpool native born in 1945, and a very
early girlfriend of George – she was, he said,
'really nice and had cotton wool in her bra.'
Her brother was Alan Caldwell, aka Rory
Storm, who led Scouse band The Hurricanes,
also featuring Ringo Starr. She dated Paul
McCartney c.1962 (Fabs lore associates her
with Love Me Do and I Saw Her Standing
There), before marrying one Shane Fenton in
1964. He subsequently became Alvin Stardust,
and they got divorced.

**Alma Cogan**
Pre-rock British singing
celeb (b. Alma Cohen,
1932) who, despite his
usual sexual preference, was
courted by Brian Epstein.
She also had an
affair with John
Lennon circa
1964, sparked
at one of the
all-night parties
she threw in the London home shared with her
mother on Kensington High Street. Two years
later, she died of cancer.

## Shelley Duvall

Star of The Shining and Popeye (b.1949), and one of a handful of notables associated with Ringo in the early-to-mid 1970s, before his divorce (see Maureen Starkey, below), along with British singer and Eurovision entrant Lyndsey De Paul and a British TV actress called Vivienne Ventura.

## Julie Felix

Californian folk(ish) singer (b.1938) who was the resident musical turn on BBC1's The Frost Report, as well as hosting her own BBC shows, and eventually managed two Top 40 UK hits in 1970. She briefly dated Paul McCartney c.1967 – unbeknown to Jane Asher, obviously.

## Sonny Freeman

Berlin-born model who married Robert Freeman, the photographer responsible for the sleeve-shots of With The Beatles, Beatles For Sale, Help! and Rubber Soul. Between November '63 and July '64, the couple lived in the same house as John and Cynthia Lennon: 13 Emperor's Gate, SW7, near Gloucester Road tube – where the Lennons hid from overheated fans as the 'Hadley' family, and John would sneak downstairs for secret assignations with Sonny. In 2008, Philip Norman's Lennon biography claimed she was the woman at the centre of Norwegian Wood (This Bird Has Flown), a contention that chimed with her '60s habit of telling people she was from Norway rather than Germany, so as to avoid standard post-war British prejudice. As to one of the song's most memorable lines, whether John ever slept in her bath is unclear.

## Olivia Harrison

Mexican-born, LA-raised woman (b. Olivia Arias, 1948) who met George in 1974 while working as a secretary at his label Dark Horse. Once his divorce from Pattie Harrison (see below) was finalised in 1977, they married the following year, and their son Dhani was born soon after. A sample remembrance of her late husband: 'He was so generous and open, so much more patient with people than me. He took everybody along with him, like a driftnet fisherman. If we were going on holiday, everybody would come. If we were having dinner, everybody was welcome. He was Pisces, so he swam in a school.'

*George and Pattie: put-upon spouse*

## Pattie Harrison

Byword for rock wifery (b. Pattie Boyd, 1944) who met George on the set of A Hard Day's Night (she's in it, as a schoolgirl) and married him in 1966, drastically cutting down her work as a model and becoming a dutiful and apparently put-upon spouse – not least thanks to GH's affairs, up-and-down temperament and apparently all-consuming fondness for disappearing to meditate. By '69, things were not good; according to her autobiography, suicide sprang to mind, and 'I got as far as working out how I would do it: put on a diaphanous Ossie Clark dress and throw myself off Beachy Head.' The rest is now a rock cliché: having been endlessly pestered by a besotted Eric Clapton, she left GH and took up with EC ('I'd rather she was with him than some dope,' said George), though they broke up in 1986 (she also had a brief thing with Faces/Stones guitarist Ron Wood). While we're here, the obligatory mention of three famous Pattie-centric songs: Something, Layla and Wonderful Tonight. Oh, and her sister Jenny married Fleetwood Mac's Mick Fleetwood, as well as inspiring Donovan to write Jennifer Juniper.

## Astrid Kirchherr

Key player in the Fabs' Hamburg period whose influence on them was huge. Born in 1938, she befriended them on their first visit to the city in August 1960, and took up with bassist/artist Stu Sutcliffe. She called time on his quiff and cut his hair into the combed-forward 'pilzen kopf' (mushroom head) shape favoured by cutting-edge German youth, encouraged him to wear black leather, and also had the prescience to make him a Pierre Cardin-inspired collarless corduroy jacket – as well as endlessly photographing the group, occasionally in the half-shadow style later rendered iconic by 1963's With The Beatles. Sutcliffe died of a brain haemorrhage in April 1962. After 40 often troubled years, Kirchherr now co-runs a Beatles-centred photography and memorabilia business in Hamburg (www.center-of-beat.com).

## Cynthia Lennon

Arguably the most tragic ex-Beatle wife (b. Cynthia Powell, 1939), whose story – since told in two self-written books – amounts to a cautionary tale about unplanned pregnancy, and expecting stability, happiness etc. from self-centred and dysfunctional generational icons. 'When John discovered drugs I lost him,' she later reflected. 'He had decided his path in life and there was nothing I could do about it.' In May 1968, she famously returned from a holiday in Greece (with, among others, Jenny Boyd and Donovan) to find John breakfasting with Yoko Ono, and that was pretty much that; come the divorce, she settled for a mere £100,000. She claims to have been unimpressed by the sentiments captured in Imagine: 'always believe you practise what you preach, that's my philosophy in life and in my eyes John wasn't doing that.' For some reason, in 1995 she recorded a version of the 1968 Mary Hopkin hit Those Were The Days and put it out as a single. This is, obviously, best forgotten about.

## Linda McCartney

Born Linda Eastman in 1941, became a New York-based photographer, and first met Paul in 1967, doing her thing at the press launch for Sgt Pepper. And fair play to her and her husband: few rock marriages last nearly 30 years, survive under a barrage of rudeness and public antipathy (e.g. 'She was hairier than he was,' according to one of the fans who would stand sentry outside Paul's London home), or give rise to a enduring line of vegetarian convenience food, which will surely forever form one of the staples of the British student diet. Liked what some people call 'draw' as much as her husband, for what that's worth.

140

## Heather Mills

Oh lord. 'Model'-cum-campaigner-cum-celebrity (b.1968) with incredibly eventful life-story who married Paul in 2002, before the relationship headed for one of the most rancorous break-ups in living memory, and she was awarded £24.3 million in a divorce settlement, after being rebranded 'Lady Mucca'. For details of all that, go straight to the red-top archive; here, we'll somewhat arbitrarily recall Paul – while the marriage was still on – phoning a couple of tabloid journalists to somehow set them right on some of the relationship's details. 'It was a couple of lady columnists – I'd rather not give them the fame,' he said in 2005. 'One thing was *[the allegation that]* Heather's too old to wear above-the-knee boots. I said, "Do you actually know why that is? She's an amputee, love."'

*John and Yoko: copped off in '68*

## Yoko Ono

Where to start? Avant-garde artist born in Tokyo in 1933. First met John in 1966, decisively copped off with him in '68, married him in '69, spent two weeks in bed 'for peace' etc. etc. Here, though, are a few things you don't hear/read too often. The odd bit of her music is much better than the more malign accounts suggest (e.g. 1981's disco-rock classic Walking On Thin Ice, 1973's Move On Fast). Unless you're mad and/or extremely curious, there's no point going near the three avant-garde albums she quickly made with John in 1968 and 1969 (Two Virgins, Life With The Lions and The Wedding Album). And a quick word about her infamous 1966 film Bottoms, aka No. 4: to quote one archivist, 'the camera is very close to the skin with the buttocks actually filling the screen. The crack between the cheeks and the crease between the buttock and the leg divide the screen into four almost equal sections.'

**May Pang**

A memory from late 1973, when Pang (b.1950) was working as John and Yoko's secretary: 'Yoko walked in. She said, "I have to talk to you." I pulled out my pen and pad and she said, "Well, you know John and I aren't getting along?" And then, all of a sudden, she said, "You know, he's going to start seeing other people; he may even start dating…" And then she said, "You know, *you* don't have a boyfriend." I said, "Excuse me?" And that's how it started. She said, "I know that John likes you." And I said, "But I don't want your *husband*." But it seemed like she wasn't going to take no for an answer.' Ergo an 18-month(ish) relationship, largely played out in LA, before John got back with Yoko in 1975. Pang has always feistily disputed the 'lost weekend' thesis, pointing to the music made around that time (the Lennon song Sweet Bird Of Paradox was written about her), and claiming that a Lennon-McCartney songwriting reunion was back on circa January 1975, but it came to grief when JL moved back in with Yoko.

**Dorothy Rhone**

Girlfriend of Paul McCartney between 1959 and 1962, known as 'Dot', and – as with Cynthia Powell/Lennon – encouraged by her Beatle boyfriend to rock the Brigitte Bardot look. In his authorised biography Many Years From Now, PM recalls Dot and Cynthia Powell visiting him and John Lennon in Hamburg: 'I remember buying her a leather skirt and encouraging her to grow her hair long so she'd look like Brigitte…I remember [John] and I talking and saying, "Yeah, well, the more they look like Brigitte, the better we are, mate."'

**Francie Schwartz**

Aspiring American scriptwriter (b.1944), who came to London in the summer of '68, looking for financial help from the freshly-formed Apple organisation, whereupon she began a brief thing with Paul, which fed into his split with Jane Asher. Her slim kiss-and-tell book Body Count – published in 1972, and long out of print – is

a right old scream. Three illustrative quotes: 'With five cats, the sheepdog and Eddie *[a puppy]*, I was constantly cleaning up shit, and shit looks like shit, even on an oriental rug'; 'He never bitched when I went down on him at 90 miles an hour on the road'; 'I didn't hear from him for eight days. This time he showed up at five o'clock in the morning. He ran me up the stairs…half-singing, "It's F-day, it's F-day."' Oh, and one other thing: at 27, she looked very like Keeley Hawes from BBC1's Ashes To Ashes.

**Nancy Shevell**

At the time of writing, Paul McCartney's 49-year-old post-Heather Mills girlfriend-cum-partner. She's the New York-dwelling heiress to a vast family fortune made from road haulage, and the recipient of something called the Fred Hurley Memorial Scholarship for Excellence in Transportation. Which must have impressed him.

**Maureen Starkey/Starr**

*Ringo and Maureen, pre-'incest' interlude*

Born Mary Cox in 1946, married to Ringo between 1965 and 1975, and the mother of his three children (including sometime Oasis and Who drummer Zak Starkey). Later married the founder of the Hard Rock Cafe empire, and died of complications arising from leukaemia in 1994, aged 47. According to several accounts, in the early 1970s, the Starrs were visited at their home by George and Pattie Harrison. Somewhat unexpectedly, over dinner, George announced that he was in love with Maureen. Not long after, Pattie found the pair *in flagrante delicto*. George's alleged explanation? 'Incest.' A rum old do, it has to be said.

# HE CAN WORK IT OUT

'Vocals and bass', go the credits. But the omni-talented Paul did more than that...

*Paul: drums, lead guitar... recorder?!*

*NB: Beatles songs abound with Paul on piano and acoustic guitar, and they're not here. Neither are possible contributions that are a matter of speculation. Also, his guitar-playing is so omnipresent on 1969's Abbey Road that only the stand-out non-bass contribution is mentioned.*

**Ticket To Ride** (1965)
Paul on lead guitar: bluesy interjections, and some pretty cool improv in the fade-out. Nice.

**Another Girl** (1965)
Supposed confession of trysts beyond the knowledge of his then-girlfriend Jane Asher, peppered with guitar honks à la Ticket To Ride.

**Drive My Car** (1965)
Paul adds both the opening lead guitar passage and a cool solo, subtly laying the ground for what came next...

**Taxman** (1966)
A proper stinger: a repeated 13 seconds of squawking lead that fiercely underline George's dismay at having to hand over most of his earnings to pay for schools, hospitals, roads etc.

**Sgt Pepper's Lonely Hearts Club Band** (1967)
Among other things, three stabs of lead guitar before his first vocal line. Note: on the 'Reprise' version of this song, George is back.

142

**Good Morning, Good Morning** (1967)
Brilliant lead guitar that peaks at 1:46: 'Now you're in gear,' sings John, and Paul definitely is.

**The Fool On The Hill** (1967)
Paul does the recorder solo, a trick repeated after the mention of this song on John's 1968 piece Glass Onion. Clever fella.

**Back In The USSR** (1968)
On Thursday 22 August 1968, Ringo temporarily quit the band, leaving Paul to play the basic drum part on The White Album's dizzying overture. He also plays lead guitar, though not at the same time.

**Dear Prudence** (1968)
Still no Ringo, so Paul once again on drums.

**Helter Skelter** (1968)
By now, Ringo was back, powering the song later misinterpreted by Beatles fan and complete psycho Charles Manson. Paul plays lead guitar.

**Martha My Dear** (1968)
In all likelihood, McCartney on piano, bass, guitar, drums and handclaps. Much the same applies to the inconsequential White Album doodle Wild Honey Pie.

**Why Don't We Do It In The Road?** (1968)
Paul on everything apart from the drums. 'I was always hurt when Paul would knock something off without involving us,' John later moaned.

**The Ballad Of John And Yoko** (1969)
With Ringo and George unavailable, John recorded his diary of recent months with Paul on bass, piano, and drums.

**The End** (1969)
Effectively The Beatles' farewell to civilisation, with lead breaks taken in turn by George, Paul and John (in that order). Lennon gets the last one, whereupon it's Paul and piano, and the sound of the Fabs waving goodbye – although ten seconds later the McCartney throwaway Her Majesty barges in. But we'll ignore that.

# ONE WAY TICKET, YEAH?
## The three solo sojourns that changed Beatle George's life forever

### ① India, 14 September-22 October 1966
*The Great Eastern trip*

A fortnight after The Beatles' final paying show in San Francisco, George and his wife Pattie began five weeks in their newly-beloved India – where he took sitar lessons from Ravi Shankar, the pair of them learned yoga, and they ended up staying on a houseboat moored in the Himalayas. For the next year, he was barely interested in the guitar, and his flaming passion for India would lead The Beatles to Maharishi Mahesh Yogi, and from there to India in early 1968. Oh, and by way of a disguise, it was now that he started to grow his Sgt Pepper moustache.

### ② California, 1-9 August 1967
*The trip that ended the trips*

One week in which George – along with Pattie, road manager-cum-aide Mal Evans and infamous Greek Fabs hanger-on 'Magic' Alex Mardas – visited Ravi Shankar

*George: holiday tripper*

in LA, where George wrote the dirge-like Magical Mystery Tour tune Blue Jay Way. They then journeyed to San Francisco's Haight-Ashbury neighbourhood to experience the supposed nerve-centre of Hippiedom. 'It was full of spotty drop-out kids on drugs, and it turned me right off the whole scene,' he later recalled (he had already been 'spiked' by a local DJ, which didn't seem to have helped). Handed an acoustic guitar, George managed a few choruses from the recently-released Beatles tune Baby You're A Rich Man, but his mood was bleak indeed. 'I could only describe it as being like *[infamous New York version of Skid Row]* The Bowery: a lot of bums and drop-outs,' he reflected, claiming that any idea of the acid-and-weed culture representing 'spiritual awakenings and being artistic' now fell out his mind. His conclusion: 'That was the turning-point for me – that's when I went right off the whole drug cult and stopped taking the dreaded lysergic.'

### ③ LA and New York, 16 October-3 December 1968
*The trip that ended The Beatles (kind of)*

With The White Album pretty much done, George took his singing Liverpudlian protégé Jackie Lomax – an Apple Records artist, obviously – to LA, where the two of them worked with high-end session talent drawn from the city's so-called Wrecking Crew – like Hal Blaine, the drummer who played on such hits as The Byrds' Mr Tambourine Man and The Beach Boys' Good Vibrations. Having also been introduced to the newly-invented Moog synthesiser (which would be played on Abbey Road), George then spent Thanksgiving in Woodstock, where he shared the company of Bob Dylan and The Band. He told Ringo Starr The Band were simply 'too much – they're just *living*, and they happen to be in a band as well.' Then came the badly-vibed sessions for Let It Be, during which Paul McCartney's attitude to the man he posthumously called his 'little brother' rankled as never before – as proved by the infamous section of the film (see page 136) in which George informs Paul that, 'I'll play whatever you want me to play, or I won't play at all…whatever it is that'll please you, I'll do it.' Subsequent accounts have suggested George wasn't getting on with John either, though in his submission to the court case that dissolved The Beatles' partnership two years later, George said: 'In 1968, I went to the United States and had a very easy co-operation with many leading musicians. This contrasted with the superior attitude which for years Paul had shown to me.' Whatever, on 10 January 1969, he temporarily quit The Beatles, whose break-up – what with John also wanting out, and Yoko not exactly discouraging him – became even more inevitable.

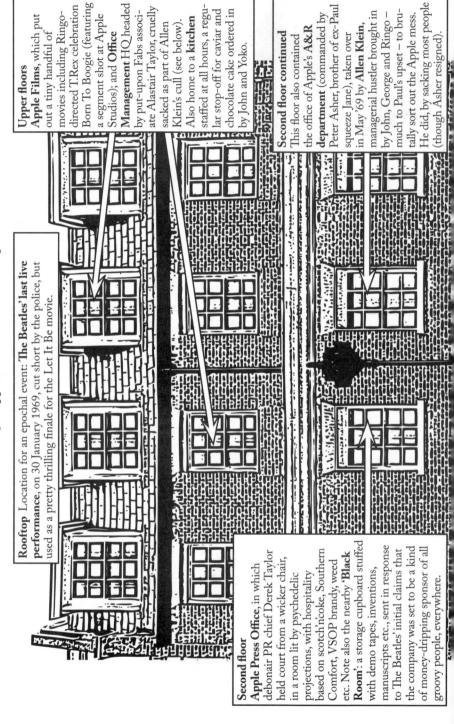

# THE HOUSE THE FABS BUILT

3 Savile Row, W1: the HQ of Apple, where the Beatles' empire crumbled into dust

**Upper floors**
**Apple Films,** which put out a tiny handful of movies including Ringo-directed T.Rex celebration Born To Boogie (featuring a segment shot at Apple Studios); and **Office Management** HQ headed by put-upon Fabs associate Alastair Taylor, cruelly sacked as part of Allen Klein's cull (see below). Also home to a **kitchen** staffed at all hours, a regular stop-off for caviar and chocolate cake ordered in by John and Yoko.

**Rooftop** Location for an epochal event: **The Beatles' last live performance,** on 30 January 1969, cut short by the police, but used as a pretty thrilling finale for the Let It Be movie.

**Second floor continued**
This floor also contained the office of Apple's **A&R department** (commanded by Peter Asher, brother of ex-Paul squeeze Jane), taken over in May '69 by **Allen Klein,** managerial hustler brought in by John, George and Ringo – much to Paul's upset – to brutally sort out the Apple mess. He did, by sacking most people (though Asher resigned).

**Second floor**
**Apple Press Office,** in which debonair PR chief Derek Taylor held court from a wicker chair, in a room lit by psychedelic projections, with hospitality based on scotch'n'coke, Southern Comfort, VSOP brandy, weed etc. Note also the nearby '**Black Room**': a storage cupboard stuffed with demo tapes, inventions, manuscripts etc., sent in response to The Beatles' initial claims that the company was set to be a kind of money-dripping sponsor of all groovy people, everywhere.

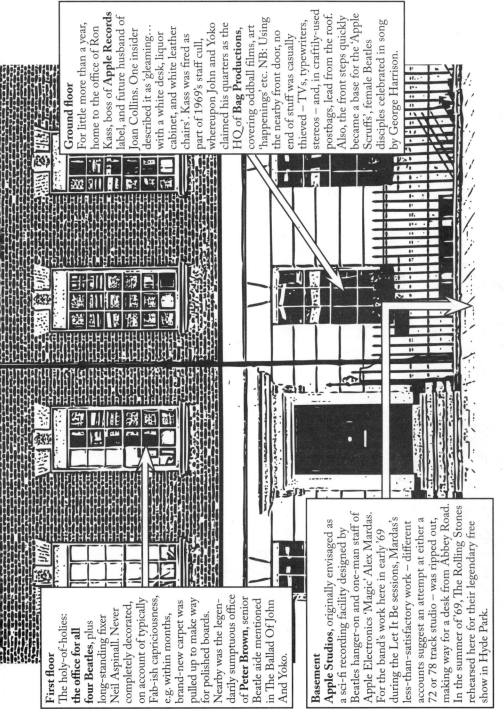

## First floor

The holy-of-holies: **the office for all four Beatles**, plus long-standing fixer Neil Aspinall. Never completely decorated, on account of typically Fab-ish capriciousness, e.g. within months, brand-new carpet was pulled up to make way for polished boards. Nearby was the legendarily sumptuous office of **Peter Brown**, senior Beatle aide mentioned in The Ballad Of John And Yoko.

## Ground floor

For little more than a year, home to the office of Ron Kass, boss of **Apple Records** label, and future husband of Joan Collins. One insider described it as 'gleaming… with a white desk, liquor cabinet, and white leather chairs'. Kass was fired as part of 1969's staff cull, whereupon John and Yoko claimed his quarters as the HQ of **Bag Productions**, covering oddball films, art 'happenings' etc. NB: Using the nearby front door, no end of stuff was casually thieved – TVs, typewriters, stereos – and, in craftily-used postbags, lead from the roof. Also, the front steps quickly became a base for the 'Apple Scruffs', female Beatles disciples celebrated in song by George Harrison.

## Basement

**Apple Studios**, originally envisaged as a sci-fi recording facility designed by Beatles hanger-on and one-man staff of Apple Electronics 'Magic' Alex Mardas. For the band's work here in early '69 during the Let It Be sessions, Mardas's less-than-satisfactory work – different accounts suggest an attempt at either a 72 or 78 track studio – was ripped out, making way for a desk from Abbey Road. In the summer of '69, The Rolling Stones rehearsed here for their legendary free show in Hyde Park.

# THE RISE AND FALL OF CAPITOL-ISM
## The extremely weird way America heard The Beatles

Most people who are partial to The Beatles have at least a rough idea of how their albums proceeded. Please Please Me, then With The Beatles, A Hard Day's Night, Beatles For Sale, and Help!, on through Rubber Soul and Revolver…and all the way through to Let It Be: simple, really.

In the States, things were very different, thanks to the Capitol label and one Dave Dexter Jr, the A&R man who gleefully messed about with the LPs he was sent from the UK, adding plenty of reverb and repackaging them according to an apparent handful of unbreakable rules. They went something like this: 1)every last drop had to be wrung from the Fabs' catalogue; 2)their reluctance to include hit singles on their LPs was so much English nonsense; and 3)royalty payments could be kept down by strictly limiting albums to 12 songs.

In 1964 alone, Capitol put out five Beatles albums. The run began with **Meet The Beatles**: essentially With The Beatles stripped of most of its cover versions and fattened up with I Want To Hold Your Hand, This Boy and I Saw Her Standing There. Three months later came **The Beatles' Second Album**: Dexter's With The Beatles off-cuts, plus two songs from the British Long Tall Sally EP and You Can't Do That. **Something New** glued the remaining Long Tall Sally songs to most of A Hard Day's Night, and – oh, go on then – the German-language version of I Want To Hold Your Hand. Then **Beatles '65** sent out a seasonal message of goodwill to American fans by taking Beatles For Sale, cutting out five of its tracks, and adding I Feel Fine, She's A Woman and I'll Be Back. On top of all that, there was a monstrous creation called **The Beatles' Story**:

146

bits and bobs of music, and a voiceover that gave an absurdly camped-up account of their rise to glory ('Liverpool, a poor but proud British seaport, has lifted her head…there's now a sound of hope').

And so the madness continued. In 1965, Capitol put out a cut-down version of the Please Please Me album called **The Early Beatles**, a very strange LP called **Beatles VI** (pictured – on the cover, the Fabs appear to be ceremonially cutting a big cake), a chopped-up version of **Help!**, and a completely baffling version of **Rubber Soul**, which cleverly missed out four songs, including Nowhere Man and Drive My Car.

In 1966, they duly appeared on **Yesterday… And Today**, the album that initially featured the infamous 'Butcher sleeve': a picture of the Fabs amidst decapitated dolls and pieces of meat, interpreted as a protest against Vietnam. Then came **Revolver**, deprived of all but two of John Lennon's songs. As one US fan later moaned: 'That was really, really odd. There were only two Lennon tracks on it: Tomorrow Never Knows and She Said She Said. I remember buying it and thinking, Where was he this month? Was he ill? Come on John! You've just got these two songs about dying and stuff. Paul's doing way better.'

While we're here, it's worth also bearing in mind the chilling sins committed by the Vee Jay label, who briefly had the rights to a handful of early Fabs music (**The Beatles vs The Four Seasons**, anyone?). Anyway, normal service belatedly arrived with Sgt Pepper – though if you want to hear The Beatles' music as a whole generation of Americans did, Capitol brought out two box-sets of their US albums, in 2004 and 2006 – though Yesterday…And Today and the American Revolver have yet to appear. Funny, that.

# THE BEATLES 1970-80
## A user's guide

In December 1970, Paul McCartney started High Court proceedings to dissolve The Beatles' legal partnership, and endured something of a dark night of the soul. The Beatles had effectively called it a day in the autumn of 1969, but this development brought the uglier side of their split into sharp focus. 'The fact that I had to sue the Beatles was something that was very, very difficult,' he later reflected, 'cos I could see what that would do in terms of perception of me. People could quite easily say, "You know what? I'd never do that, no matter if it meant losing everything. He's a hard-hearted bastard. And a mean bastard. And a money-grabbing bastard."'

The public didn't seem to think he was any kind of bastard, though John Lennon was soon in the midst of some searing Macca-hatred. Nine months later, in response to supposed pops at him and Yoko Ono on Paul and Linda's 1971 LP Ram, he released the album Imagine, featuring a lovely little piece entitled How Do You Sleep?, an attempted demolition of his one-time partner ('Those freaks was right when they said you was dead'), on which, just to hammer the point home, George Harrison played lead guitar.

In turn, just before the year's end, Paul's new vehicle Wings put out the decidedly shabby Wild Life, which nonetheless contained a fascinating musical olive-branch called Dear Friend. By this point, unfortunately, John had moved to the US and apparently had his mind on other things: hanging around with what remained of the '60s counterculture, and singing about such subjects as feminism, the state of American prisons, and the British presence in Ireland, all of which were pretty crassly dealt with on his career-nadir Some Time In New York City, one of the few solo Beatles albums that succeeds in being downright embarrassing.

Such, anyway, is the fun to be had listening to the Beatles' early solo records: spotting the veiled and not-so-veiled references to each other, and keeping pace with their feelings about Fabdom. John's inaugural solo album contained God, in which he baldly served notice that he was no longer the Walrus, and didn't believe in Beatles. On George's 1971 tour de force All Things Must Pass – and title-wise, think about it – Wah Wah was about an occasion when Paul gave him a headache, and Isn't It A Pity contained a backhanded quotation of the 'na-na-na' bit from Hey Jude. By way of more intrigue, there was Wings' 1973 album Band On The Run, and Let Me Roll It – which referenced John's Cold Turkey, and extended yet another hand of friendship (or there again, it might just be about smoking weed).

---

One thing is certain: like most half-decent rock groups, The Beatles' four-way bond gave rise to a unique magic, and their solo stuff tended to get nowhere near it. There are flashes of genius, for sure, but by around 1974, all of them had rather surrendered to the essential spirit of the pre-punk '70s, and were indulging in soft-rock bland-out and worse (poor old Ringo's progress through the latter half of that decade is, it has to be said, woeful).

Contrary to his posthumous deification, this applied just as much to John as to the other three, and characterised even his and Yoko Ono's 1980 comeback album Double Fantasy, a portrait of contentment made in collaboration with highly-paid sessioneers: his half was alright, but really no masterpiece. Indeed, by this point there was a strong argument for Paul being the most creatively interesting Beatle, as proved by his second Paul-only album McCartney II – which, as with bits of 1970's McCartney, sounds a little like an early try-out for the home-baked aesthetic later picked up on by the likes of Beck and The Beta Band (no, really).

If you're new to the solo Fabs, you may want to tread carefully. By way of remaining on the safe side, there is a strong argument for going no further than the handful of compilation albums that anthologise the ex-Beatles' solo stuff, and throw forth the odd revelation – like the fact that, for a short period, Ringo was actually a tidy singles artist. But for the brave or curious student of post-Beatles history, the first ten years of the story goes something like this...

**Great**

**Pretty Good**

**Average**

**Not Good**

**Awful**

After a run of top-hole solo singles, his post-Fabs progress decisively began with the Phil Spector-produced **John Lennon/ Plastic Ono Band** (1970), the album that invented angst-rock, and remains essential.

## John

**Imagine** (1971) was another dose of the same soul-baring medicine, sugared by a bit more of Spector's magic. Thus, Jealous Guy, Crippled Inside and Oh Yoko! sound almost MOR by comparison, though the latter remains a real diamond. Note also the ace Gimme Some Truth and How Do You Sleep?, a borderline nauseating dig at Paul (with a mocking George guitar solo) that's grimly compelling.

Oh lord. John and Yoko moved to Manhattan, befriended counter-culture politicos, and made **Some Time In New York City** (1972), a lamentable rent-a-cause album. Feminism, Irish Republicanism and Black Power abound – though the best track is the live Frank Zappa collaboration Well (Baby Please Don't Go), originally done by doo-wop troupe The Olympics in 1958.

**Great**

**Pretty Good**

## Ringo

**Average**

**Not Good**

**Awful**

To begin: **Sentimental Journey** (1970), a pretty pointless set of covers of pre-rock 'standards'. By way of predicting the travails to come, the cover features Ringo emerging from a huge pub.

Such Fabs tracks as Act Naturally, What Goes On and Ringo's own Don't Pass Me By had marked him down as the Country Beatle. Ergo **Beaucoups Of Blues** (1970), made in double-quick time with high-end Nashville sessioneers whose CVs included stuff by Elvis and Dylan. It works pretty well, though the public were somewhat bamboozled: in the US, it got no higher than No 65.

Reunion alert! On the career-high that was **Ringo** (1973), John and George backed him on the Lennon-written I'm The Greatest, Paul helped out on his own Six O'Clock, and there was also the pretty glorious Harrison co-write Photograph. Further musical heavy-lifting was delivered by four-fifths of The Band, Motown's Martha Reeves and Marc Bolan. All told, not quite great art, but more than OK.

And so to **Mind Games** (1973). Such songs as Bring On The Lucie (Freeda People) and One Day (At A Time) are OK – though the bland-out that would soon grip all the ex-Fabs is present and correct. That said, the title track is rather fine – as John later explained, 'the middle eight is reggae. Trying to explain what reggae was to American musicians in 1973 was pretty hard.'

John and Yoko now temporarily split up, and he hit the sauce. His then-squeeze May Pang argues that the 'lost weekend' was more creatively fertile than the brandy/insanity myth suggests, and she may be right: **Walls And Bridges** (1974) – featuring the hit Elton John collaboration Whatever Gets You Thru The Night – is a tad more interesting than Mind Games, but maybe only just.

Five years of retreat now beckoned, but not before **Rock'n' Roll** (1975), an album of classic covers begun with Phil Spector before no end of craziness put it on hold. It has its moments: Stand By Me is great, and the closing cover of Lloyd 'Lawdy Miss Clawdy' Price's Just Because sounds movingly valedictory. That said, the phrase 'Cavern Club cabaret' often springs to mind.

The return: **Double Fantasy** (1980) was split between John and Yoko songs and hyped as a portrait of domestic bliss. 'I wish that Lennon had kept his happy trap shut until he has something to say that was even vaguely relevant to those of us not married to Yoko Ono,' said the man from the NME. He had a point, but then fate tragically intervened and made this Lennon's last word.

Harrison and McCartney were absent, but the title track of **Goodnight Vienna** (1974) was provided by Lennon, and there were also turns from two other esteemed Johns: New Orleans titan Dr John, and Elton. More slapdash than its predecessor, though the drugs/booze ode No No Song is something of a laugh, and the 1992 CD reissue also features the top 1972 single Back Off Boogaloo.

Then came the anthology **Blast From Your Past** (1975), packaging up his best solo stuff so well as to make buying Ringo albums proper the preserve of the hard-bitten or crazy. To prove it, then came **Ringo's Rotogravure** (1976 – the title refers to an arcane US name for a Sunday supplement), featuring contributions from John and Paul and a song by George, but no real magic.

Yowsa! Thanks to Bee Gees producer Arif Mardin, **Ringo The 4th** (1977) was Starr's disco album, giving off the whiff of expensive cocktails and artistic irrelevance. In the USA, it reached No 162; back home, Polydor Records followed it with the kids' album **Scouse The Mouse** (1977), on which Ringo voiced the titular role of a Liverpudlian rodent. Which was nice.

Did the world need a Ringo cover of the Supremes' Where Did Our Love Go? Was there really much mileage in a version of Gallagher and Lyle's soft-rock classic Heart On My Sleeve? Wasn't it shameless to take a track from Scouse The Mouse called A Mouse Like Me and retitle it A Man Like Me? All questions prompted by the woeful **Bad Boy** (1978) – after this, it was essentially all over.

Great

Pretty Good

Average

Not Good

Awful

His first solo stabs were occasionally ditzy, but fair play: **McCartney** (1970) has real charm, and **Ram** (1971) is peppered with such treats as the US No 1 single Uncle Albert/ Admiral Halsey.

After that, things took a rum turn. **Wildlife** (1971) was the first Wings' album, put to tape in little more than a week, and as half-cocked as that sounds – though Dear Friend, his reply to John's anti-Paul tirades, is a jaw-dropper. **Red Rose Speedway** (1973) was way more polished, but not much of an improvement – aside from My Love, a titanic weepie about Linda (obviously).

Whereupon he got it back, and how. **Band On The Run** (1973) was recorded in Lagos, Nigeria, after two of Wings quit. Gleefully, Paul played the drums, and just about everything turned out right: witness the three-part title track, Jet, Bluebird, and another Lennon-reply, Let Me Roll It. Note also the celeb-strewn sleeve, starring – among others – Michael Parkinson and Clement Freud.

**Paul**

Great

Pretty Good

Average

Not Good

Awful

**All Things Must Pass** (1970) briefly made The Quiet One the world's favourite ex-Beatle. A frazzled Phil Spector – who, said George, would down '18 cherry brandies' before work – produced, and minted a rock version of the Wall Of Sound, with the assistance of musicians including Eric Clapton. An accredited classic, and arguably the best solo Fabs album.

A big delay, and then an unfortunate slip. Oozing a slightly pompous dissatisfaction with the human race – which would define more and more of GH's lyrics – **Living In The Material World** (1973) reached No 1 in the US, toppling Wings' Red Rose Speedway. In comparison to ATMP, however, it sounds muted and underwhelming – though worse, unfortunately, was to come…

**George**

By now, Wings were mulleted international arena-gods, but standards quickly slipped. **Venus & Mars** (1975) has its moments, but is too bland (it closes, for some reason, with a rock version of the theme from TV soap Crossroads), and **Wings At The Speed Of Sound** (1976) was rather let down by the weird idea of letting everyone else sing a song – even Joe English, the new drummer. No!

Back to a three-piece for the period that also threw forth the huge-selling Mull Of Kintyre. The long-forgotten **London Town** (1978) was based on the kind of inoffensive, grown-up pop that defined so much of the 1970s, but the love-soaked and weirdly guitar-free With A Little Luck is still irresistible. One other thing: whose idea was Morse Moose And The Grey Goose?

**Back To The Egg** (1979) did precious little business at the time, but is worth re-visiting. Ignore Spin It On's attempt to ally Wings with punk rock, and instead go straight to cod-soul tune Arrow Through Me, the Macca-does-metal Old Siam Sir, and the gloriously stupid Rockestra Theme, recorded with John Bonham, Dave Gilmour, John Bonham, Hank Marvin, Pete Townshend et al.

**McCartney II** (1980) was a belated companion piece to his first solo album, and similarly variable-though-impressive. John Lennon rated Coming Up ('a good piece of work', he reckoned), Waterfalls is a borderline classic, and the electro-ish Temporary Secretary was revived by achingly hip London clubbers circa 2004. But be warned: avoid Bogey Music as you would gout.

And then things went really wrong. **Dark Horse** (1974) soundtracked a broken-up personal life, and the vocals often sound like the work of someone gargling with broken glass. One or two songs are OK, but the yuletidey Ding Dong Ding Dong says it all. 'George Harrison belongs in a daycare centre for counterculture casualties,' said rock writer Lester Bangs. On this evidence, he was on to something.

**Extra Texture (Read All About It)** (1975) was his last solo album for EMI, and thus widely viewed as a matter of contractual obligation. In that context, it was predictably not much cop, though You – an off-cut from 1971 – harked back to the All Things Must Pass aesthetic with reasonable success. Still, perhaps ignoring Dark Horse, George maligned this as his worst solo album.

**Thirty Three and & 1/3** (1976) didn't really improve matters. As with its two predecessors, the overwhelming air is of high-paid sessioneers, wicker chairs and expensive loon pants, and the trademark George slide guitar sound rather gets on one's wick. All that said, there are a few points of historical interest – like See Yourself, started in 1967 as a song about Paul's admission that he'd taken LSD.

For some reason, he now had a perm. **George Harrison** (1979) is the sound of George lapsing happily into de facto retirement: breezily lightweight, though not unpleasant. Fabs enthusiasts should sample Not Guilty, finally released 11 years after being cut from The White Album. It also includes the clunky single Faster, a somewhat Jeremy Clarkson-esque tribute to GH's beloved motor racing.

# NOT A SECOND TIME!*

Some of the best – and worst – Fabs cover versions, starring Liza Minelli, Stevie Wonder, Mae West and Bono (a lot)

## A Hard Day's Night

Ignore **Billy Joel**'s *dummkopf* musical photocopy (1997), have a quick giggle at **Peter Sellers**' famous Shakespearian spoof (1965), and go to a handful of covers by female icons that turn it into a vampish hymn to getting it on even when you're knackered. **Ella Fitzgerald**'s live version (1965 – done in Hamburg, fittingly) is ace, as are the slinky rendition by **Peggy Lee** (1965), and **Dionne Warwick**'s treatment from her southern soul album Soulful (1969 – the interpretations of Hey Jude and We Can Work It Out aren't bad either).

## We Can Work It Out

**Stevie Wonder** managed one of the greatest Fabs covers ever (1970) with this, not least because he grafted on his own brilliant riff. **Deep Purple**, by contrast, glued it to a classical-meets-rock thing called Exposition (1968) on their second LP – the song itself briefly threatens to be built on an endearing proto-baggy shuffle, before pomposity once again kicks in. There again, the fact the album was called The Book Of Taliesyn probably served as some kind of warning.

## Day Tripper

Plenty here, though you may want – arf, arf – to take the easy way out. **Jimi Hendrix**'s ragged BBC version (1967) has long been rumoured to feature John Lennon on backing vocals, but the consensus is that this is a lie. Compared to, say, his top-hole go at the Stones' Satisfaction, **Otis Redding**'s reading (1966) is a scrappy travesty, **Nancy Sinatra**'s effort (1966) sounds Austin Powers-esque, and **Mae West**'s go (1967) is entertainingly barmy, though it's a matter of laughing at rather than with (also, points off for faffing about with personal pronouns – 'I'm a day tripper' indeed). The wooden spoon, however, should be used to beat David Coverdale's **Whitesnake**, whose half speed cock-rock version (1978) should be handed to the International Criminal Court.

*Emmylou Harris*

## For No One

Easily done in a Cabaret style, as proved by **Liza Minelli** (1968), who also commits personal pronoun crimes over and above standard-issue gender alteration. But hats off to country siren **Emmylou Harris** (1975), who stretches Paul McCartney's original into something schmaltzy, but in a very good way. Her take on Here, There And Everywhere (1976) is also worth attention.

## With A Little Help From My Friends

There can be only one: **Joe Cocker**'s version (1968), which decisively turned this into a hymn to countercultural solidarity, even if his onstage loon-dancing in the Woodstock movie was bit much (his version of She Came In Through The Bathroom is pretty great, too). Nineteen years later came a charity-aiding treatment by Glaswegian laughing boys **Wet Wet Wet** (1988), which was No 1, with a much better double A-side featuring **Billy Bragg** doing She's Leaving Home. Good cause and everything, but with this song, you're best off sticking with Joe C.

## Lucy In The Sky With Diamonds

**Elton John** managed a hit re-tread (1974) that was pleasant but pretty pointless. Ditto the reliably shameless **Bono**, who turned in a version (2007) for the OST of a very forgettable musical called Across The Universe, in which characters called Jude, Lucy, Sadie, Jojo, Prudence etc. (think about it) tumble through the 1960s. His try amounts to expensive-studio karaoke, whereas Star Trek actor **William Shatner**'s barmy spoken-word version (1968) is deservedly legendary.

*1963 Lennon/McCartney song covered by Robert Palmer (1980) and The Pretenders (1990)*

## Hey Jude

A heap of stuff here, but let's zero in on three of the greats. Good on him and everything, but **Bing Crosby**'s stab (1968, from the brilliantly-titled LP Hey Jude/Hey Bing!) is kind of ugly, not least when the 'Da-da-da' bit begins with him singing 'Pommm-pom-pom-pom-pom-pom-pom'. **Elvis**'s version (1972), on the out-takes rag-bag Elvis Now would be OK if he tried a bit harder to get the words right. By contrast, you can only salute **Wilson Pickett**, whose understatedly groovy take (1969) is a real treat.

## Helter Skelter

Thanks to its associations with US serial killer Charles Manson, an obvious one for rock'n'rollers keen to flag up their dark side, which may partly explain the witless version (1983) by hair-metal viscounts **Mötley Crüe**. **U2** had a live crack (1988) on Rattle And Hum ('This is the song Charles Manson stole from The Beatles – we're stealing it back'), which is way too precious, but perhaps that bit better than readings by **Oasis** (2000), **Pat Benatar** (1981) and **Stereophonics** (2007) – though for its snotty audacity, the prize has to go to **Siouxie And The Banshees**, for a caterwauling version (1978) with music that has delightfully little to do with what's on The White Album.

## Happiness Is A Warm Gun

Most people would probably leave this one well alone, but **U2** – and do you see a pattern emerging here? – did it as a B-side (1997) during the disco-dad phase crystallised by the Pop album, which chops up the words to a trip-hop beat and is not pretty. The treatment by sometime Guns N' Roses guitarist **Gilby Clarke** (1997) may actually be worse, which is going it. But! The version by sometime Pixie Kim Deal's vehicle **The Breeders** (1990) is way better, benefiting from being re-interpreted by women (all the 'mother superior' stuff is done very well indeed).

## The Ballad Of John And Yoko

Nothing much doing here, aside from the inevitable karaoke and pan-pipes versions. But respect to top Scots indie-rock funsters **Teenage Fanclub**, whose rendition (1990) suggests a load of Beatles fans drunkenly proving that they know all the words, as well as who Peter Brown was, why the titular couple were eating chocolate cake in a bag etc.

## Here Comes The Sun

On her album of the same name (1971) **Nina Simone** gets the words a bit wrong, but George's tribute to solar inspiration suits her voice just fine, and all is warmth and good vibes. **Steve Harley And Cockney Rebel** took their effort (1976) to No 10 in the British singles charts, but it's really just a feeble re-tread with horrid prog-rock keyboards. By contrast, the treatment by acoustic king **Richie Havens** (1971) is simplicity itself, and therefore a thousand times better.

*Nina Simone*

# SPECIAL PRIZES

Not many people have thought to have a go at whole(ish) Beatles albums, so let's briefly pay tribute to some who did. **George Benson**'s half-instrumental, jazzed-up The Other Side Of Abbey Road (1969) mixes up the track listing and misses out a few songs, but it's mostly good, in a subtly strange way. The idea was obviously catchy: **Booker T And The MGs**' McLemore Avenue (1970) rolls through the same album – *sans* Maxwell's Silver Hammer, Oh! Darling and Her Majesty – in their trademark groovesome fashion, though it's kind of uneventful. For a true mind-boggler, go straight to Let It Be by the infamous Slovenian faux-totalitarians **Laibach** (1988), which puts the songs in a nightmarish new Teutonic context. NB: there's no title track, and Maggie Mae is replaced by a traditional German toe-tapper called Auf der Lüneburger Heide ('On The Lüneburg Moor' – it's in Lower Saxony). 'The Beatles record stands as a cheapskate epitaph, a cardboard tombstone,' they explained. 'What we are doing is rewriting history, which every now and then has to be corrected and reinterpreted to be useful for the future.'

# Chapter 7

# THE ALBUMS
# (AND SINGLES)

What a pleasure it is to be a consumer of rock music in the early 21st century: devices the size of a packet of ten fags that can carry an entire record collection, obscure videos of your heroes and heroines on tap – and at least one computer-based application-cum-entertainment service (Spotify, to name names) that's essentially a pub jukebox crossed with the Tardis, holding out the promise of almost infinite musical choice, and for free.

Imagine trying to explain such magic to someone stranded in a record shop in, say, the late 1970s, made miserable by the fact that the latest by their favourites wasn't in stock, and knowing that taping it off the radio just didn't cut it, what with Radio 1's own 'Hairy Cornflake' talking over the intro and everything. Those were perhaps not the days of wonder that some people claim: indeed, even if you got the record you were after, you could easily end up taking it to a teenage party, and having it soaked in cider, stamped on, and rendered unplayable. From that perspective, the MP3 age offers the world nothing but bliss and convenience.

Strange, then, that so many of us cling stubbornly to the black plastic coins that still seem to embody no end of magic. Vinyl records refuse to die, and not just because of the loyalty of people of a certain age. The 33rpm LP is still with us, now held to be an item aimed at the higher end of the market, and predicted to outlast the compact disc. In January 2009, the BBC marked the 60th anniversary of the 7-inch single with reports of increased sales, and enthusiastic quotes from the chirpy indie-rock singer Jack Peñate. 'What I love about 7-inch singles is the sound quality and the warmth,' he said, 'and also that they're physical, and I'll keep them forever and I cherish them. They're not throwaway.' When he said that, he was not yet 25.

For as long as records are still here, and the CD has a few years left, and iTunes still obediently bundles up music in album-sized packages, the two terms at the head of this chapter will still have some meaning. Which is, of course, a good thing, particularly when it comes to the one beginning with 'A'. How do you know if a group is any good or not? By whether they can find it within themselves to create at least 40 minutes or so of reasonably consistent art. What is more magical than the fizz of anticipation on a Monday morning, knowing that so-and-so's latest LP is about to be released? A few things actually, but you take the point. More conclusively, if you're going to map out rock'n'roll's progress – and, come to think of it, a certain kind of post-war history – doesn't a long line of LPs do the job almost perfectly?

Some of that information starts on page 156, where the roll-call includes Elvis's self-titled first album, James Brown's Live At The Apollo, Sgt Pepper's Lonely Hearts Club Band, Patti Smith's Horses, The Human League's Dare, Run DMC's Raising Hell, and Arcade Fire's Funeral (and, for reasons that will become clear, Ten Good Reasons by Jason Donovan). In among all that, there are mentions of such era-defining singles as Bob Dylan's Like A Rolling Stone, Aretha Franklin's Respect, Joy Division's Transmission, Kate Bush's Hounds Of Love and – but of course – (You Gotta) Fight For Your Right (To Party) by The Beastie Boys. By way of a contrasting selection of stinkers, there is a backhanded celebration of so-called Rock Follies, including misfiring records by a Duran Duran splinter group, Keith Moon, Billy Idol, Bob Geldof and good old Rick Wakeman.

There is, of course, much more than that: stuff about Bob Dylan, and Pink Floyd, and The Smiths' fondness for etching cryptic messages next to their records' labels, and plenty more besides. All of it is intended to evoke no end of things – among them, what happens when groups flee to the English countryside to make their masterpiece, the weird music that comes from once-great artists completely losing their bearings, the expectant thrill of unwrapping a new CD, and the smell of fresh vinyl in the morning.

A thought, to finish. In 1984, the gonzo hard-rock monarchs Van Halen released a thrillingly ludicrous single called Jump, whose passage into its chorus was marked by David Lee Roth pleading with some unnamed lover: 'Can't you see me standing here?/I got my back against the record machine.' If you doubt any of what you've just read, you should perhaps think about those last two words, and reflect on whether even the most poetic reference to portable music devices, streaming services and the like could get anywhere near it. At the risk of sounding hopelessly luddite, we thus rest our case.

# FROM SHELLAC TO iPOD

Humanity's journey to the download age – via records, 'MiniDiscs' and Dire Straits

*78rpm record c.1894*      *33 ⅓ rpm record c.1948*      *45rpm record c.1949*      *Cassette c.1963*

## Early records

**Launched** 1894, by the US-based Berliner Gramophone company.

**In brief** After Thomas Edison's invention of the phonographic cylinder, the race was on to produce a more manageable 'flat' record, with Germans and Americans fighting for pole position. A key breakthrough came around 1907 with double-sided records; in 1909, the first multi-disc 'album' appeared.

**In favour** Easier to use and store than the phonographic cylinders that preceded them, and better-sounding (just about).

**Against** 'Frying bacon' sound, the fact that it wasn't until 1925 that speeds from 60 to 120rpm were standardised at 78rpm, a limit of around three minutes per side, brittleness of Shellac material.

**Archetypal artists** Enrico Caruso, The Carter Family, Marie Lloyd

## LPs

**Launched** 1948, by Columbia Records.

**In brief** As in most things, war accelerated the progress of the record. Sending Shellac 78s to soldiers abroad resulted in breakage, prompting a rush to vinyl, accompanied by research into 'microgroove' long-players. And fair play: this format still lives, so posthumous hats off to such unsung American engineers as Peter Carl Goldmark and Jim Hunter.

**In favour** At an initial 17 minutes a side, less need to keep running back to the gramophone to put another one on; end of 'frying bacon' problem.

**Against** Pops and clicks, static and warping.

**Archetypal artists** Frank Sinatra, The Beatles, Pink Floyd

## 45s

**Launched** 1949, by RCA-Victor

**In brief** Essentially a replacement for the 78, and aimed at the single-song market. Prompted a 'battle of the speeds' only resolved by the quick invention of multi-speed record players.

**In favour** Cool size, and embodiment of the basic aesthetic of pop, thanks also to surprisingly impressive B-sides (e.g. The Beatles' I Am The Walrus, The Rolling Stones' Play With Fire, The Smiths' Is It Really So Strange?). Note also: with the introduction of 12-inch singles in 1975, the way was paved for the DJ creativity pioneered in hip hop.

**Against** Lo-fi sound, but let's leave that to the squares, yeah?

**Archetypal artists** Elvis Presley, The Dave Clark Five, Mel & Kim

## Cassettes

**Launched** 1963, by Philips

**In brief** Initially introduced for home recording, but the music industry launched pre-recorded cassettes in 1965.

**In favour**: Pocket-sized, and so perfect for home-made compilations that at least three generations used them as both romantic pulling-aids and classroom status symbols. Acme of aceness was surely marked by the launch of the Walkman in 1979, whereupon they became a byword for the '80s: their peak year was '86.

**Against**: Muddy sound, spaghetti-tape/'Dad, it's broken'-type disasters, concertina inserts folded into 88 layers.

**Archetypal artists** Duran Duran, Wham!, Bow Wow Wow (creators of 1980 single C30, C60, C90, Go! and 1980 album Your Cassette Pet)

156

   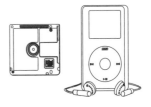

*8-track cartridge c.1965     CD c.1982     DCC c.1992     MiniDisc c.1992     iPod c.2001*

## 8-track cartridges
**Launched** 1965, by the Ford Motor Company, with help from RCA-Victor
**In brief** Weird innovation which went down well in the USA as an early roll-out for in-car entertainment. Began to dwindle c.1974.
**In favour** Essence of idea was tape-looping, meaning albums could be played forever.
**Against** Prone to extreme and unpleasant spaghetti-tape issues.
**Archetypal artists** The Eagles, Kiss, Chicago

## CDs
**Launched** 1982, by Sony and Philips
**In brief** In 1977, big audio firms got together with a view to introducing digital sound to the ordinary Joe. After a false-start based on LP-sized digital discs, the breakthrough came in 1980, when the two companies above settled on Philips' idea of the CD.
**In favour** Seemingly perfect sound quality.
**Against** Vinyl still sounds warmer; industry claims that you could eat your breakfast off one and still play it were bollocks; 78-minute running time led to albums that were too long.
**Archetypal artists** Dire Straits (Brothers In Arms was the first CD million-seller), David Bowie (first artist to put his old stuff on CD)

## Digital Compact Cassette
**Launched** 1992, by Phillips and Matsushita
**In brief** aka DCC. For much of the '80s, the music industry was fond of storing music on digital audio tapes (or DATs); the idea here was to somehow remodel the same idea for the High Street. It didn't work. At all.
**In favour** More portable than CDs; good for home recording.

**Against** Clunky, to be polite: though you could skip between tracks, you still had to wait for the tape to wind through.
**Archetypal artists** Dire Straits: their 1992 On Every Street was sponsored by Phillips as way of pushing DCC. It didn't work. At all.

## MiniDiscs
**Launched** 1992, by Sony
**In brief** Challenger – as if it needed one – to DCC that had more in common with a computer 'floppy'. Link to Sony supposedly guaranteed its success, ho ho (though, in fairness, they're still around).
**In favour** Small and recordable. But only once.
**Against** They felt cheap and nasty.
**Archetypal artists** Bruce Springsteen: Q Magazine gave away a free copy of his Human Touch album on MiniDisc in 1992. Inevitably, no one knew what to do with it.

## MP3
**Launched** First mass-production player came in 1998, from SaeHan Information Systems. The iPod was introduced by Apple in 2001.
**In brief** The nemesis of the music biz: downloadable music and true portability. Initially, the industry stuck its head in the sand; thus, even now, 95 per cent of music downloads are illegal.
**In favour** [Assumes voice of aged wonderment] 20,000 songs in one little box? Are you sure?
**Against**: Drawbacks in audio quality due to shortcomings bound up with 'bit rate'. Thanks to such online innovations as Spotify, even this technology may soon be obsolete.
**Archetypal artists** iPod commercial stars include U2, Bob Dylan and Paul McCartney

# IT'S A MIGHTY LONG WAY DOWN ROCK'N'ROLL, PART 1

### A history of albums, singles and the world in general, 1956-1982

*Author's note: each entry begins with that year's biggest selling single and album in the UK, and closes with alternative options. We describe these as 'groovy' – which, back when life was a bit simpler, was the chosen term. If you don't like it, you may prefer to think of them as 'cool', 'interesting' etc.*

## 1956

**Biggest selling single**: I'll Be Home **Pat Boone**
**Biggest selling album**: Carousel **Original Soundtrack**
*Soviet troops invade Hungary, the Suez crisis erupts, and Rock'n'Roll decisively arrives, as proved by the thrillsome movie The Girl Can't Help It.*
**Groovy single**: Roll Over Beethoven **Chuck Berry** *(pictured)*
**Groovy album**: Elvis Presley **Elvis Presley**

## 1957

**BSS**: Diana **Paul Anka**
**BSA**: The King And I **Original Soundtrack**
*The Soviets launch Sputnik, Patrick Moore presents the first edition of The Sky At Night, and John Lennon meets Paul McCartney.*
**GS**: Not Fade Away **Buddy Holly & The Crickets**
**GA**: Ray Charles **Ray Charles**

## 1958

**BSS**: Jailhouse Rock **Elvis Presley**
**BSA**: My Fair Lady **Broadway Cast Recording**
*Brazil win the World Cup, hosted in Sweden. Race riots convulse Notting Hill, and the UK opens its first stretch of motorway, near Preston.*

158

*Crazy times – though many Britons still gather round the gramophone to listen to musicals.*
**GS**: Good Golly, Miss Molly **Little Richard**
**GA**: The Everly Brothers **The Everly Brothers**

## 1959

**BSS**: Living Doll **Cliff Richard**
**BSA**: South Pacific **Original Soundtrack**
*Fidel Castro takes power in Cuba, Cyprus becomes independent, and Miles Davis puts out the earth-shaking Kind Of Blue. But who cares about that? 'Another musical, please,' say Mr and Mrs Average.*
**GS**: Bad Boy **Larry Williams**
**GA**: Go Bo Diddley **Bo Diddley**

## 1960

**BSS**: It's Now Or Never **Elvis Presley**
**BSA**: South Pacific **Original Soundtrack**
*Oh, no! South Pacific again! But never mind: Elvis leaves the army, the oral contraceptive pill is approved in the US and TV arrives in New Zealand, so who's complaining? There again, rock goes rather quiet.*
**GS**: Shakin' All Over **Johnny Kidd & The Pirates**
**GA**: Rockin' At The Hops **Chuck Berry**

## 1961

**BSS**: Are You Lonesome Tonight **Elvis Presley**
**BSA**: GI Blues **Elvis Presley**
*A clean sweep for the King, who's really not at his rockingest. The US puts a chimp called Ham in space; the USSR pings Yuri Gagarin up there. President Kennedy makes his first State of the Union address.*
**GS**: Ya Ya **Lee Dorsey**
**GA**: Lonely And Blue **Roy Orbison**

## 1962

**BSS**: I Remember You **Frank Ifield**
**BSA**: West Side Story **Original Soundtrack**
*Thanks to the Cuban missile crisis, the world nearly meets its end, so maybe listening to an Australian-English yodeller and yet another*

musical (one of the better ones, it has to be said) is understandable. Anyway, The Beatles and Bob Dylan release their first records, so all is well. Chile hosts the World Cup; Brazil win it again.
**GS**: Soldier Of Love **Arthur Alexander**
**GA**: Twist And Shout **The Isley Brothers**

# 1963
**BSS**: She Loves You **The Beatles**
**BSA**: With The Beatles **The Beatles**
Beatlemania arrives, after a particularly grim UK winter. JFK is assassinated. The Catholic Church accepts cremation, Martin Luther King makes his 'I have a dream' speech, and Britain marvels/recoils at the Great Train Robbery.
**GS**: Harlem Shuffle **Bob & Earl**
**GA**: Live At The Apollo **James Brown**

# 1964
**BSS**: Can't Buy Me Love **The Beatles**
**BSA**: Beatles For Sale **The Beatles**
The Fabs break America, and Harold Wilson ends 13 years of Conservative rule. Cassius Clay (who soon becomes Muhammad Ali) becomes Heavyweight Champion of the World, and London really begins to swing. Allegedly.
**GS**: You Really Got Me **The Kinks**
**GA**: A Girl Called Dusty **Dusty Springfield**

# 1965
**BSS**: Tears **Ken Dodd**
**BSA**: The Sound Of Music **Original Soundtrack**
What a rum do. Music is aflame: Dylan releases Bringing It All Back Home and Highway 61 Revisited, The Byrds do Mr Tambourine Man, The Who put out My Generation and The Beatles and Stones are on fire. Ken Dodd? Julie Andrews?! Other news just in: the first US troops see action in Vietnam.
**GS**: Like A Rolling Stone **Bob Dylan**
**GA**: Animal Tracks **The Animals**

# 1966
**BSS**: Green Green Grass Of Home **Tom Jones**
**BSA**: The Sound Of Music **Original Soundtrack**
Again, something of a baffler: this is the year of Revolver, the Stones' Aftermath, Dylan's Blonde

On Blonde, etc. etc. Ming The Merciless lookalike Anton Lavey founds the Church Of Satan in California and, less creepily, host nation England win the World Cup.
**GS**: Good Vibrations **The Beach Boys**
**GA**: Fifth Dimension **The Byrds**

Aretha: respect!

# 1967
**BSS**: Release Me **Engelbert Humperdinck**
**BSA**: Sgt Pepper's Lonely Hearts Club Band **The Beatles**
The crooner born Arnold George Dorsey not only sells most singles, but keeps The Beatles' Penny Lane/Strawberry Fields Forever off No 1 position. Israel wins the Six-Day War, Elvis gets married, and Che Guevara is executed.
**GS**: Respect **Aretha Franklin**
**GA**: The Velvet Underground & Nico **The Velvet Underground**

# 1968
**BSS**: Hey Jude **The Beatles**
**BSA**: The Sound Of Music **Original Soundtrack**
The post-war world's watershed year: Soviet tanks in Prague, strike and riots in France, the assassinations of Bobby Kennedy and Martin Luther King, and 3785 things besides.
**GS**: Jumpin' Jack Flash **The Rolling Stones**
**GA**: Electric Ladyland **The Jimi Hendrix Experience**

# 1969
**BSS**: Sugar, Sugar **The Archies**
**BSA**: Abbey Road **The Beatles**
Human beings set foot on the Moon and a cartoon achieves the year's biggest-selling 45. Richard Nixon takes over the US Presidency. Woodstock ☞

*gives the '60s a big old climax; the Stones' farrago at Altamont begins the comedown. For a moment, millions of people think Paul McCartney is dead.*
**GS**: I Want You Back **The Jackson 5**
**GA**: The Band **The Band**

# 1970

**BSS**: The Wonder Of You **Elvis Presley**
**BSA**: Bridge Over Troubled Water **Simon & Garfunkel**
*England crash out of the World Cup (in Mexico) after a rematch with West Germany; Brazil win the tournament. Edward Heath becomes British Prime Minister. The Beatles officially break up, and Jimi Hendrix dies.*
**GS**: All Right Now **Free**
**GA**: No Dice **Badfinger**

# 1971

**BSS**: My Sweet Lord **George Harrison**
**BSA**: Bridge Over Troubled Water **Simon & Garfunkel**
*The UK's currency goes decimal. Intel unveils the world's first microprocessor. Jim Morrison dies. So does Louis Armstrong.*
**GS**: Double Barrel **Dave & Ansell Collins**
**GA**: Untitled (aka Led Zeppelin IV) **Led Zeppelin**

# 1972

**BSS**: Amazing Grace **The Royal Scots Dragoon Guards Band**
**BSA**: 20 Dynamic Hits **Various Artists**
*Another weird year for record sales, split between a marching band going spiritual and a Now That's What I Call Music-esque compilation on the K-Tel label. Meanwhile, Nixon is re-elected as US President, though the odorous events that will lead to Watergate are underway.*
**GS**: Metal Guru **T.Rex** *(Marc Bolan, pictured)*
**GA**: Clear Spot **Captain Beefheart & The Magic Band**

160

# 1973

**BSS**: Tie A Yellow Ribbon Round The Old Oak Tree **Tony Orlando & Dawn**
**BSA**: Don't Shoot Me I'm Only The Piano Player **Elton John**
*In the year of the final American pull-out from 'Nam, pole singles position goes to an Easy Listening 45 honouring a custom to mark absent loved ones doing military service abroad. As of 1 January, Britain is in the EEC (the proto-EU). Pink Floyd release The Dark Side Of The Moon, and Paul McCartney's Wings manage a career peak with Band On The Run.*
**GS**: All The Way From Memphis **Mott The Hoople**
**GA**: Innervisions **Stevie Wonder**

# 1974

**BSS**: Tiger Feet **Mud**
**BSA**: The Singles 1969-73 **The Carpenters**
*Nixon resigns after a TV address to the USA, and is replaced by Gerald Ford (husband of rehab queen Betty). Harold Wilson re-enters Downing Street. West Germany hosts the World Cup (and wins it). The BBC starts its Ceefax teletext service (like the internet on a tight budget).*
**GS**: Rebel Rebel **David Bowie**
**GA**: Down By The Jetty **Dr Feelgood**

# 1975

**BSS**: Bohemian Rhapsody **Queen**
**BSA**: The Best Of The Stylistics **The Stylistics**
*Note a surprising feat pulled off by the Philadelphian soulers. Spanish dictator General Franco kicks el bucket, Margaret Thatcher becomes Tory leader, and Bill Gates starts Microsoft. In a referendum, the UK votes to remain inside what's then called the Common Market (now, naturellement, the European Union).*
**GS**: Autobahn **Kraftwerk**
**GA**: Horses **Patti Smith**

# 1976

**BSS**: Save Your Kisses For Me **Brotherhood Of Man**
**BSA**: Greatest Hits **Abba**
*A long hot summer in the UK, and the decisive arrival of British punk, capped by the Sex Pistols swearing on TV – though a silly old Eurovision*

winner is the top 45. Montreal hosts the Olympics; the Viking 2 probe takes the first decent pictures of Mars.

**GS**: Anarchy In The UK **Sex Pistols**
**GA**: Ramones **Ramones**

# 1977

**BSS**: Mull Of Kintyre/Girls School **Wings**
**BSA**: Arrival **Abba**
*Queen Elizabeth II celebrates her Silver Jubilee; the Sex Pistols – who this year put out not only God Save The Queen, but their only album – don't. Elvis Presley dies.*
**GS**: Egyptian Reggae **Jonathan Richman & The Modern Lovers**
**GA**: Exodus **Bob Marley & The Wailers**

# 1978

**BSS**: Rivers Of Babylon/Brown Girl In The Ring **Boney M**
**BSA**: Saturday Night Fever **Original Soundtrack**
*Argentina hosts the World Cup, and wins it; Scotland flounder, but manage to beat eventual finalists Holland 3-2. Come the cold season, the UK sees the start of the legendary Winter of Discontent.*
**GS**: Le Freak **Chic**
**GA**: All Mod Cons **The Jam**

*Debbie Harry: preferable to Art Garfunkel*

# 1979

**BSS**: Bright Eyes **Art Garfunkel**
**BSA**: Parallel Lines **Blondie**
*Islamic revolution hits Iran; in the UK, Margaret Thatcher becomes Prime Minister. At the year's*

end, the Soviet Union invades Afghanistan. Perhaps in retreat from a cruel world, Britain swoons to the keynote song of a film about rabbits (younger readers: ask your dad).

**GS**: Transmission **Joy Division**
**GA**: London Calling **The Clash**

# 1980

**BSS**: Don't Stand So Close To Me **The Police**
**BSA**: Super Trouper **Abba**
*Bad rhymes and pervsome lyrics serve Sting's chaps surprisingly well. Ronald Reagan beats Jimmy Carter and is elected President of the USA; Moscow hosts the Olympics, and for Afghanistan-related reasons America – busy backing those lovely Mujahadeen fellas – keeps its athletes at home. John Lennon is murdered in New York.*
**GS**: Ashes To Ashes **David Bowie**
**GA**: Back In Black **AC/DC**

# 1981

**BSS**: Don't You Want Me **The Human League**
**BSA**: Kings Of The Wild Frontier **Adam & The Ants**
*Arguably the record-buying public's finest hour: the Ants, Sheffield's greatest pop conceptualists, and not a musical in sight (apart from, erm, Cats). The Social Democratic Party is launched after a split in the UK Labour Party. In the midst of recession, the Conservatives unveil a controversial deflationary budget. IRA hunger striker Bobby Sands dies in Prison. 7500 people take part in the first London marathon.*
**GS**: Pull Up To The Bumper **Grace Jones**
**GA**: Dare **The Human League**

# 1982

**BSS**: Come On Eileen **Dexys Midnight Runners**
**BSA**: Love Songs **Barbra Streisand**
*UK unemployment reaches a post-war high of over 3 million. Britain and Argentina fight over the Falkland Islands. Welsh language TV station S4C is launched (but only in Wales). Spain hosts the World Cup, and Italy are victorious; more importantly, Hungary puts on the first world Rubik's Cube Championship.*
**GS**: The Message **Grandmaster Flash & The Furious Five**
**GA**: Pornography **The Cure**

# PINK FLOYD: FRIENDS OF DOROTHY?
## A guide to the great Dark Side Of The Moon/Wizard Of Oz synchronicity mystery

'Dark Side Of The Moon was meant to be simple and direct,' said Pink Floyd's David Gilmour, some 30 years after the release of the band's most revered album. 'Then letters started pouring in saying, This means this, and this means that…and then you get The Wizard Of Oz coming along to stun you. Someone once showed me how that worked, or didn't work. How did I feel? Weary.'

As with so many of the grim aspects of modern living, blame the internet. Though the origins of the idea are lost to history, in 1994 subscribers to the Pink Floyd newsgroup alt.music.pink-floyd began discussing the supposed synchronicity between Dark Side and The Wizard Of Oz. Not entirely surprisingly, the so-called Dark Side Of The Rainbow 'theory' rapidly gripped the imaginations of box-bedroom conspiracy theorists (and weed casualties) all over the world, and despite countless denials from the band, it refused to die. So, here it is: start up the DVD, let loose the album on the third roar of the MGM lion, and you'll be transported to the intersection between the Moon and Oz. Or there again, maybe you won't…

The intrigue begins in the first verse of Breathe. 'Look around,' go the lyrics, at the exact(ish) point that – and get this! – Judy Garland looks around. Creepy, or what?

Breathe's penultimate line is 'Balanced on the biggest wave', and it synchronises with Judy/Dorothy balancing on a fence – which is not anything like a wave. But bear with us…

Nothing doing as far as the next track (On The Run) is concerned, but the chimes that precede Time go off just as Mrs Gulch appears on her bike, and stop when she gets off!

Time briefly reprises the verse melody from Breathe, and includes the line 'Home, home again'. At this point, Professor Marvel tells Dorothy she should go home.

162

But enough scepticism. This is our favourite bit of 'sync': the fact that The Great Gig In The Sky is exactly – yes, *exactly* – the same duration as the storm that blows Dorothy to Oz.

Just when Dorothy opens a door and the film switches from black and white to colour, the ringing of tills begins Money. Which makes no narrative sense, but whatever…

Just after the Munchkins have danced in time(ish) to Money, the black-attired Wicked Witch appears, just as the lyrics to Us And Them mention the word 'black'. Woooo!

Dorothy leaves Munchkin-land as Money segues into the instrumental Any Colour You Like, which may not look like much on paper, but just you wait.

Brain Damage: Roger Waters sings 'the lunatic is on the grass' as the Scarecrow starts dancing – but on the road, not the grass (though note a later reference to 'the path').

Dorothy tries to find the Tin Man's heart, as Dark Side ends with a heartbeat. Aside from even more wacko theories about letting the film run on and resetting the CD, that's that.

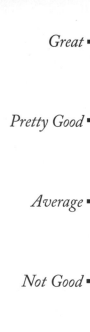

## Neil Young's weird period

Is this rock's most disastrous 'Lost it' episode?

You join us in the early '80s. **Hawks & Doves** (1980) and **Re-ac-tor** (1981, made with long-time Young aides Crazy Horse) were very patchy. Then, freshly in love with synths, he created **Trans** (1982), a futurist farrago full of vocals done with a vocoder (e.g. the inexplicable reworking of his old classic Mr Soul – no fun at all). Live, it caused booing – 'but they never made me run.' Bravo!

Next: how about a country record? NY had an abortive crack at a Nashville-oriented project called Old Ways, before his new overlords at Geffen records had a fright and asked for 'more rock'n'roll'. Ergo **Everybody's Rockin'** (1983), a lame faux-'50s creation that rather suggested the same aesthetic as Grease (the musical, that is). It was his lowest-charting US LP since his 1968 solo debut.

*Axis labels (top chart): Great, Pretty Good, Average, Not Good, Awful*

## The Rolling Stones in the 1980s

Knee pads! S&M! Crap 'raps'! Oh *lord*.

1978's Some Girls halted a spell of obvious creative decline. Then came the long-forgotten **Emotional Rescue** (1980), peppered with creative crimes: Where The Boys Go finds Mick Jagger delivering a cockernee-accented 'punk' impression, and on Send It To Me, he cleverly rhymes 'Australian', 'Ukrainian' and 'Alien'. The Keith track All About You isn't bad, though.

To tie in with 1981's world tour, the world was given **Tattoo You** (1981), largely a mish-mash of out-takes put together by Jagger and producer Chris Kimsey ('The rest of the band were hardly involved,' he said). As proved by Start Me Up and the appealing 1972 reject Waiting On A Friend, it was a bit better than that sounded – but up there with Let It Bleed, Sticky Fingers et al? Well, no. Of course not.

*Axis labels (bottom chart): Great, Pretty Good, Average, Not Good, Awful*

And then it got really odd. Geffen accused NY of making 'uncharacteristic' music and sued for damages. The result: he promised them that he'd soon make a proper Neil Young record – after he'd gone country again and finished off **Old Ways** (1985). Bits (e.g. Misfits) weren't bad, but it was no Harvest. Oh, and he was also loudly backing Ronald Reagan, which wasn't very clever.

It was now time for the 'characteristic' stuff, but only sort of: for **Landing On Water** (1986) he employed co-producer Danny Kortchmar, whose CV included Don Henley's '80s smash The Boys Of Summer. Naturally, the production was *disgusting*, and the songs weren't good either: as proved by Bad News Beat and Pressure, imagine Young being reluctantly pushed on to the set of Top Gun. Yeeeuch.

Then a partial recovery (with the emphasis on 'partial'). A la 1979's Rust Never Sleeps, **Life** (1987) was based on live stuff done with Crazy Horse – there were still too many '80s noises, but the old grit and mystery were in there. Next: the inevitable divorce from Geffen and **This Note's For You** (1988), partly a horn-laden R&B-ish effort which was OK, but still a tad 'uncharacteristic'.

A good year. The Berlin Wall fell, Bob Dylan got good again, and so did NY. The evidence: **Freedom** (1989), split between splenetic rock, a bit of horn-assisted business, and some of his trademark acoustic stuff. And let's face it: Rockin' In The Free World – in both electric and acoustic versions – simply *kills*. 'I just wanted this one to be a Neil Young album,' he said. Good attitude!

A souvenir of the tour that found Jagger 'rocking' the yellow jodphurs and knee-pads look, while Keith and Ronnie descended into self-parody, **Still Life** (1982) marked the birth of the stadium-based, oldies-cranking Stones we now love/hate (e.g. on this album, Under My Thumb is butchered). Note also the typically bizarre Jagger phonetics on the between-song announcements.

**Undercover** (1983) featured the fired-up de facto title track but not much else. Tie You Up (The Pain Of Love) was a crapola S&M tribute, the pub-rocking Pretty Beat Up took its lead from a Ron Wood demo tellingly called Dog Shit, and Too Much Blood was a lame go at Thriller-esque '80s pop featuring a grim Jagger 'rap': 'You ever seen the Texas Chainsaw Massacre – 'orrible, wasn't it?'

By the time **Dirty Work** (1986) was started, things were grim and getting grimmer: a grumpy Keith begrudged Mick his solo career, and Charlie Watts was so desperate that he briefly got a heroin habit. DW was effectively Keith's album, which meant no Thriller-esque '80s pop and the odd flash of the old sorcery (e.g. their version of Harlem Shuffle), but no fireworks, to put it mildly.

**Steel Wheels** (1989) was hailed – as with every Stones album since – as 'their best since Some Girls', which may have been true, though that wasn't saying much. Still, Mixed Emotions was pantomimically infectious and Rock And Hard Place stands as their last (half) great rocker. Voodoo Lounge (1995) and Bridges To Babylon (1997) were next, which partly explains why this graph has to end here.

# How to get into Captain Beefheart
### It's easy(ish)! And note: compilations are for cheats

① The supposed masterpiece of Captain Beefheart and The Magic Band – Don Van Vliet (b.1941) and a shifting cast of players – is the chaotic **Trout Mask Replica** (1969). To quote Andy Partridge of XTC, it can sound 'like a ball of rusty barbed wire' – so if you're new to Beefheart, go straight to **Clear Spot** (1972), a jaw-dropping album that's the ideal starter. **Song to start with**: Big Eyed Beans From Venus

② The blues-rocking **Safe As Milk** (1967) features the esteemed guitarist Ry Cooder, and was much liked by John Lennon. By way of a detour into a purple patch that arrived in the 1980s, there's nothing better than **Doc At The Radar Station** (1980), founded on musical fragments left behind by Beefheart earlier in his career, though you'd never know: it's a top-hole work that was a big influence on Franz Ferdinand circa 2005's You Could Have It So Much Better. **Songs to start with**: Electricity, Hothead

④ **The Spotlight Kid** (1972) preceded Clear Spot, and is way less consistent, though it's worth sticking with. It's also audibly downcast and self-doubting ('It was a horrible time for the band,' said guitarist Bill Harkleroad, aka Zoot Horn Rollo). So, after that, go to the more upbeat **Strictly Personal** (1968): an album partly disowned by Beefheart thanks to disagreements with its producer, but which sounds compellingly like the original spirit of the Delta Blues being bent completely out of shape. **Songs to start with**: Blabber 'N Smoke, Trust Us

*The Trout Mask*

③ And so to **Shiny Beast (Bat Chain Puller)** (1978), which followed the disappointing Unconditionally Guaranteed (1974) and Blue Jeans And Moonbeams (1974). This has some of TMR's growling scariness, but is also suffused with Clear Spot's swampy cool, and a surprisingly melodic aspect. Interesting fact: it was recorded at the San Francisco studio where Joe Strummer and Mick Jones were working on The Clash's second album. **Song to start with:** Tropical Hot Dog Night

⑤ **Ice Cream For Crow** (1982), Beefheart's last album to date, was partly a deliberate attempt to reawaken the spirit of Trout Mask, though it has its (relatively) approachable moments. Ditto **Lick My Decals Off, Baby** (1970), a close relation of TMR but a fraction less out-there. According to those who know him, Van Vliet thinks this is his best album. **Songs to start with**: Ice Cream For Crow, Woe-Is-Uh-Me-Bop

⑥ Now comes the big stuff: **Trout Mask Replica**. If you have soaked yourself in the aforementioned music, you will now be ready – as you'll ever be, anyway – for its endlessly disconcerting, unquestionably fascinating 79 minutes. By way of warning, back to XTC's Andy Partridge, and some more gloriously mixed metaphors. 'It sounds like a piece of the Somme, lifted up and put in an art gallery…You're running around stairs and gangways and gantries – it's like being trapped in a mad, giant watch. Do you know what I mean?' You will now. **Songs to start with**: Dachau Blues, Ella Guru

# HOW TO GET INTO P-FUNK

## A six-stage journey, commanded by President Clinton (George, that is)

*George Clinton: his mind was free, his ass followed*

(1) You may as well jump in at the deep end. Hairdresser turned musical adventurer George Clinton founded Funkadelic in 1968 (the name alone is surely one of rock's great mission statements). The wildly diverse **Maggot Brain** (1971) is their masterpiece, with an opening title track that's a cosmic/mournful 10-minute monster built around a guitar solo from Eddie Hazel, told by GC to play 'like your mother just died'. That it's followed by a beautifully approachable gospel-ish thing called Can You Get To That is Clinton's genius all over. **Song to start with**: Maggot Brain

(3) Funkadelic's very accessible **One Nation Under A Groove** (1978) is GC's most accomplished take on the disco period P-Funk helped create, with a renowned title track that – entirely deservedly – reached No 1 on the American R&B charts, and was their only UK hit. It also features the way cool Can A Funk Band Play Rock? **Song to start with**: One Nation Under A Groove

(2) To come back to earth, try **Osmium** (1971), the first album by Parliament – confusingly, Funkadelic in all but name, originally designed to be a bit more strait-laced and soul-ish, and the 'P' in the catch-all trademark-cum-genre P-Funk. It's not perfect, but at least half of it is pretty great, and on the 2001 CD reissue bonus tracks include Come In Out Of The Rain, a 100 per cent brilliant 1971 single. **Song to start with**: Little Ole Country Boy

(5) At this advanced stage, take your pick from the Funkadelic albums **Cosmic Slop** (1973) or **Standing On The Verge Of Getting It On** (1974). Despite its title, the former is largely built from shorter tracks than usual; the latter is much more jam-heavy, though the odd special cigarette might help. **Songs to start with**: Cosmic Slop, I'll Stay

(4) From there, pause to listen to Funkadelic's **self-titled first album** (1970), but leave space in your diary for their second LP, **Free Your Mind… And Your Ass Will Follow** (1970). According to GC, it was recorded in a single day. On acid. Of course. **Song to start with**: Friday Night, August 14th

(6) After four years during which the Parliament name was unused, GC relaunched it with the S&M-themed **Up For The Down Stroke** (1974). But you're best off with the politicised **Chocolate City** (1975), **Mothership Connection** (1976) – co-written by P-Funk star and bassist Bootsy Collins – or better still, the endlessly-sampled Parliament's **Funkentelechy Vs The Placebo Syndrome** (1977). If you're still with us, you are now 1)probably feeling confused, but 2)officially a P-Funk brother/sister, so all is well. **Song to start with (from Funkentelechy)**: Bop Gun

# DO YOU WANT TO SEE MY ETCHINGS?

## The story of the enigmatic run-out groove message

In the late 1960s, rock music began to pull away from the more staid aspects of the record industry, as managers flexed their muscles and new labels sprang into life. One aspect of this change has always been rather overlooked: the appearance of messages in the run-out grooves of singles and LPs. For the first stage of vinyl history, they tended to feature only nondescript matrix numbers; now, they began to embody some nicely subtle mischief.

As with so many things, **The Beatles** have a hand in the story – but first, here comes the science. To transfer sound from old-fashioned tape on to vinyl records required the cutting of the 'masters' used by pressing plants. During mastering treble, bass and the general sound could be tweaked via a technique eventually known as 'parametric equalisation'.

At the Fabs' Apple label, the in-house cutter was one George 'Porky' Peckham, an ex-member of the Merseybeat band The Fourmost, who got his nickname 'cos of all the ale I put away.'

At first, Peckham – who's now retired from cutting – made a habit of scratching 'PORKY' into his run-out grooves, a trademark quickly superseded by the legend 'A PORKY PRIME CUT'. Musicians eventually began to encourage him to scratch on more enigmatic stuff. Thus, Side 1 of 1971's **Led Zeppelin IV** (aka Untitled) featured the words 'PECKO DUCK', 'AUNTY B' was etched on to the B-side of **T.Rex**'s 1972 single Metal Guru, and on side 2 of **George Harrison**'s Extra Texture (1975) lurked the message 'OOH GEORGE, YOU'RE SUCH A DARK HORSE, LUV GEORGE'.

Towards the end of that decade, it was the arrival of dozens of independent labels – many of which used Peckham's services – that made the run-out message almost obligatory. Via etchings on records by the likes of **Ian Dury And The Blockheads** and **The Damned**, the Stiff label blazed the trail that led to what was written on the 1978 **Elvis Costello And The Attractions** album

This Year's Model, thanks to his manager and Stiff co-founder Jake Riviera. By then, Costello was signed to the major label WEA, which only made run-out groove tomfoolery all the more tempting. According to Peckham, Riviera told him to write, 'SPECIAL PRESSING NUMBER 003. RING MOIRA ON 434 3232 FOR YOUR SPECIAL PRIZE' on Side 1. 'That was WEA's number, and Moira was Costello's press agent,' he later recalled. 'WEA's phone lines were jammed. I was told by WEA that I'd never cut another record for them again.'

Come the great indie label explosion of early 1980s and beyond, the run-out etching idea went berserk, as illustrated by a few random examples.

Thanks to Peckham, the A and B-sides of **Joy Division**'s Love Will Tear Us Apart (1980) read 'DON'T DISILLUSION ME' and 'I'VE ONLY GOT RECORD SHOPS LEFT'. In 1988, Sub Pop released **Nirvana**'s first single Love Buzz, the A-side of which read 'WHY DON'T YOU TRADE THOSE GUITARS FOR SHOVELS', a quotation from bassist Krist Novoselic's dad.

And, just to prove you could be on a major label and get away with it, the respective sides of **Radiohead**'s The Bends (1995) read 'SHE'S OUT WITH HER ANSWERPHONE' and '(NICE DREAM)' – both references to the track of the same name (Side 1, track 6).

The true kings of the run-out groove, however, were George Peckham clients **The Smiths**, as proved on the facing page…

*The Smiths' Ask etching: Note the Mozzer's bad spelling*

168

# The run of cryptic epigraphs featured on The Smiths' LPs and 45s

**Hand In Glove** *May 1983*
7˝: KISS MY SHADES / KISS MY SHADES TOO
**This Charming Man** *November 1983*
7˝: blank on 'A' side / SLAP ME ON THE PATIO
12˝: WILL NATURE MAKE A MAN OF ME YET / blank on 'B' side
**Heaven Knows I'm Miserable Now** *May 1984*
7˝: SMITHS INDEED / ILL FOREVER
12˝: SMITHS PRESUMABLY / FOREVER ILL
**William, It Was Really Nothing** *August 1984*
7˝ & 12˝ with green cover: THE IMPOTENCE OF ERNEST/ ROMANTIC AND SQUARE IS HIP AND AWARE
7˝ with lilac cover: THE IMPOTENCE OF ERNEST / WE HATES BAD GRAMMER
12˝ with lilac cover: THE IMPOTENCE OF ERNEST / ROMANTIC AND [ ] IS HIP N' AWARE
**Hatful Of Hollow** LP *November 1984*
THE IMPOTENCE OF ERNEST / blank
**How Soon Is Now?** *January 1985*
7˝ & 12˝: THE TATTY TRUTH / blank
**Barbarism Begins At Home** limited edition 12˝, promotion-only *January 1985*
THESE ARE THE GOOD TIMES / blank
**Meat Is Murder** LP *February 1985*
ILLNESS AS ART / DOING THE WYTHENSHAWE WALTZ
**Shakespeare's Sister** *March 1985*
HOME IS WHERE THE ART IS / blank
**That Joke Isn't Funny Anymore** *July 1985*
7˝: OUR SOULS, OUR SOULS, OUR SOULS / OUR SOULS, OUR SOULS, OUR SOULS
12˝: OUR SOULS, OUR SOULS, OUR SOULS / blank
**The Boy With The Thorn In His Side** *September 1985*
7˝ & 12˝: ARTY BLOODY FARTY / 'IS THAT CLEVER'…JM

**Bigmouth Strikes Again** *May 1986*
7˝: blank, disappointingly
12˝: BEWARE THE WRATH TO COME / TALENT BORROWS, GENIUS STEALS
**The Queen Is Dead** LP *July 1986*
FEAR OF MANCHESTER / THEM WAS ROTTEN DAYS
**Panic** *July 1986*
7˝ & 12˝: I DREAMT ABOUT STEW LAST NIGHT / blank
**Ask** *October 1986*
7˝ & 12˝: ARE YOU LOATHESOME TONIGHT? / TOMB IT MAY CONCERN
**Shoplifters Of The World Unite** *February 1987*
7˝ & 12˝: ALF RAMSEY'S REVENGE / blank
**Sheila Take A Bow** *April 1987*
7˝ & 12˝: COOK BERNARD MATTHEWS / blank
**Girlfriend In A Coma** *August 1987*
7˝: AND NEVER MORE SHALL BE SO / SO FAR, SO BAD
12˝: EVERYBODY IS A FLASHER AT HEART / AND NEVER MORE SHALL BE SO
**Strangeways Here We Come** LP *September 1987*
GUY FAWKES WAS A GENIUS / blank
**I Started Something I Couldn't Finish** *November 1987*
7˝ & 12˝: 'MURDER AT THE WOOL HALL' (X) STARRING SHERIDAN WHITESIDE* / YOU ARE BELIEVING, YOU DO NOT WANT TO SLEEP
**Last Night I Dreamt That Somebody Loved Me** *December 1987*
7˝ & 12˝: 'THE RETURN OF THE SUBMISSIVE SOCIETY' (X) STARRING SHERIDAN WHITESIDE / 'THE BIZARRE ORIENTAL VIBRATING PALM DEATH' (X) STARRING SHERIDAN WHITESIDE
**Rank** LP *August 1988*
PEEPHOLISM / blank
*The Wool Hall (near Bath) was the studio where The Smiths recorded their final album; 'Sheridan Whiteside' was a pre-Smiths Morrissey pseudonym, taken from the film/ play The Man Who Came To Dinner.

## The Style Council
*Jazz! 'Satirical' films! Fluorescent shorts!*

*Great — Pretty Good — Average — Not Good — Awful*

So, Paul Weller bravely split The Jam, and paired up with keyboard man Mick Talbot to form the core of a shifting(ish) collective summed up by PW as 'a musical kama sutra'. And fair play: what with the top-hole first 45 Speak Like A Child and the aching disco ballad Long Hot Summer, the early singles and B-sides collected on **Introducing The Style Council** (1984) still sound pretty great.

As does some – but not all – of TSC's full-blown debut **Café Bleu** (1984), which had some ex-Jam disciples in a right old spin. Herein lay jazz instrumentals, one rap tune, a song crooned by Everything But The Girl's Tracy Thorn and much more exotica – though You're The Best Thing, Here's One That Got Away and Headstart For Happiness doubtless steadied some nerves.

## Mick Jones, post-Clash
*Tech-rock! Acid House! Chicken pox!*

*Great — Pretty Good — Average — Not Good — Awful*

In brief: in '83, Joe Strummer evicted Mick Jones from The Clash and MJ formed Big Audio Dynamite, W11's own peddlers of hip hop-influenced, sample-strewn tech-rock, including film-making Clash friend Don Letts. **This Is Big Audio Dynamite** (1985) was their opener: a bit patchy, but easily redeemed by its singles: The Bottom Line, Medicine Show, and the divine E=MC².

A contrite Strummer soon re-connected with Jones and crash-landed in the sessions for **No. 10, Upping Street** (1986), co-writing five songs ('We need some rock'n'roll,' he reckoned) and co-producing the lot. It's thus halfway to being the great lost Clash album, with songs as good as that implies: C'mon Every Beatbox, Beyond The Pale and Sightsee MC! in particular.

Wellerologists cite **Our Favourite Shop** (1985) as the Council's peak, and it probably is. A state-of-the-nation snap of Britain under Maggie Thatcher (the miners' strike, mass unemployment, you name it) that finds room for the odd love lyric, its themes soon dated it, but the songs were often great, and cheers from the provinces were heard at the complete absence of jazz pastiches. Yay!

Whereupon it all went a bit rum. By his own admission, Weller's relationship with Council singer Dee C Lee caused him to rather lose interest, and distractedly pilot **The Cost Of Loving** (1986), a melange of pop-soul that partly soundtracked a short 'satirical' film (JerUSAlem [sic] – have a look on YouTube). Heavens Above and the title track were good, but didn't save it.

By now, TSC were losing friends, and **Confession Of A Pop Group** (1988) duly tanked, but after 20-odd years, it may be time to state its case. The first half (aka – eek! – 'The Piano Paintings') is peppered with accomplishment and adventure, and Part Two – not least the sneering title track – is also no disgrace. Shame about the slap bass and gurgling synthesisers, but it was the '80s, right?

The '90s loomed, and Weller was enchanted by the more soul-y end of house music. Ergo **Modernism: A New Decade** (1989) – only available on their collected-works box set – which was knocked back by TSC's label, thus spelling their death. Note also their last UK gig at the Albert Hall, replete with Weller in fluorescent shorts and a baffled crowd. *La fin*, as they say in France.

There was no Strummer-aid on **Tighten Up Vol. 88** (1988) – though ex-Clash bass fella Paul Simonon did the sleeve art. The first song, Rock Non Stop, (All Night Long) rather sets the lukewarm tone by sounding like a Ladbroke Grove Chas & Dave. But! The Battle Of All Saints Road is a pretty glorious meld of reggae, country music and riot-memoir, for which BAD get ree-speck.

Whereupon Mick Jones caught chicken pox from his daughter, which turned into life-threatening pneumonia. BAD came back with the Acid-Housey and sample-packed **Megatop Phoenix** (1989) – flawed, but a glimpse of MJ's mythic London with real sparks of magic, not least on the soccer-themed Union, Jack: 'Make a stand before you fall/Your country needs you, to play football.'

Yet another twist: though Jones was an Acid House enthusiast, the rest of the band weren't. Thus, a split, and the founding of BAD II: Jones plus three new bods, including the ex-drummer with Sigue Sigue Sputnik. Their first proper album was **The Globe** (1991), a distinct two-half affair: four decent-ish opening songs – including the creditably catchy Rush – and much half-cocked filler.

Big Audio Dynamite became Big Audio, added a DJ and keyboard player Andre Shapps (strange fact: his brother Grant is a latter-day Tory MP), and made **Higher Power** (1994), proof that 1)the house thing was wearing thin, and 2)so were the songs. Then came **F-Punk** (1995), once again credited to BAD, and a plod back towards straight rock. And that was pretty much that.

# HEAVY MANORS

The classic album/rural hideaway interface, or how to 'get it together in the country'

**Bron-Yr-Aur**
*Near Machynlleth, Powys*
**Essential album**: Led Zeppelin, Led Zeppelin III (1970)
Remote(ish) Welsh cottage – the name means 'Golden Hill' – used and celebrated by Led Zeppelin. In spring 1970, Jimmy Page and Robert Plant came here (with Plant's wife Maureen and daughter Carmen, Page's girlfriend Charlotte and three roadies) to luxuriate in its rustic, *sans*-electricity vibes and create songs for Led Zeppelin III, duly commemorated as their 'folk album'. At least nine were written, including that album's Bron-Y-Aur (mis-spelled on the sleeve), and the more linguistically accurate Bron-Yr-Aur, included on Physical Graffiti. 'Zeppelin was starting to get very big and we wanted the rest of our journey to take a very level course,' said the reliably optimistic singer. 'Hence the trip into the mountains and the beginning of the ethereal Page and Plant.' Plus, it later transpired, one other creation: Page's daughter Scarlet, who was conceived here. Page and Plant came back in late 1970, and wrote – among other things – parts of Stairway To Heaven.

**Farley House**
*Farley Chamberlayne, Hampshire*
**Essential album**: Fairport Convention, Liege And Lief (1969)
The Queen Anne mansion rented for Fairport Convention by their renowned manager/producer Joe Boyd in 1969, partly to ape the bucolic Woodstock magic captured by The Band on 1968's Music From Big Pink. Still recovering from the horrific M1 car crash that killed drummer Martin Lamble and guitarist Richard Thompson's girlfriend Jeannie Franklyn, they retreated here soon after and worked on the music that would form that year's Liege And Lief, essentially the first English folk-rock album (pictures of their idyllic bolt-hole are all over its CD sleeve). 'Things started at around noon, and we worked till six,' says Thompson. 'There was a bit of football on the lawn; a bit of kite-flying up on Farley Mount, trips to the pub. And we did a bit of busking in Winchester, next

to the Cathedral. We discovered that we had an unpaid milk bill: £15, which seemed like a fortune. All of us piled off, and we played in the Cathedral close; the whole band. We raised about £30 in an hour – made a donation to the Cathedral restoration fund, paid the milk bill, and got a couple of rounds out of it.'

**Headley Grange**
*Headley, Hampshire*
**Essential album**: Led Zeppelin, Untitled aka Led Zeppelin IV (1971)
Built as an 18th-century workhouse – there were famous riots in November 1830 – before being first used as a private house circa 1870. Around a century later, it became a favoured recording/rehearsing retreat, used by the likes of Genesis, Bad Company, Fleetwood Mac, Peter Frampton – and Led Zep. With the aid of The Rolling Stones' mobile studio, it was used for Led Zeppelin III (during which infamous house-guest John Bonham chopped up part of a banister to make firewood), tracks from Physical Graffiti and, most famously, Led Zep's fourth LP. To get an idea of its cavernous acoustics, listen to When The Levee Breaks, whose booming drum part was recorded by putting John Bonham at the base of a stairwell.

*Hook End Manor: outbuilding contained giant pig*

**Hook End Manor**
*Checkendon, Berkshire*
**Essential album**: Pink Floyd, A Momentary Lapse Of Reason (1987)
Ten-bedroom, 16th-century pad – said to have been put up for the Bishop of Reading – that has long included a recording studio,

used by names as varied as Happy Mondays, Iron Maiden and Robbie Williams. In the late '60s, owned by Alvin Lee of blues-rock bores Ten Years After, and then sold to Pink Floyd's Dave Gilmour, who used one of its outbuildings to store Pink Floyd's famous inflatable giant pig. In the early 1990s, ownership passed to producer and Buggles co-founder Trevor Horn – who, in 2007, put it on the market for £12 million. Strange but true: now owned by one Mark White, solitary English member of a Russian band called Godnose.

### The Manor
*Shipton on Cherwell, Oxfordshire*
**Essential album**: Paul Weller, Wild Wood (1993)
Circa 1971, bought – in a semi-derelict state – by aspirant music tycoon Richard Branson, with a view to opening the first residential UK recording studio. During its first few years, guests included such far-out Virgin Records signings as Gong, Henry Cow, Krautrock kings Faust – and, perhaps most famously, Mike Oldfield, who recorded Tubular Bells here. By the early '90s it was the rural retreat favoured by Paul Weller, who praised it as 'a magical place, one of the last of the old-school residential studios where you could make it your own and go a bit barmy.' After the recording of the first album by Britpop participants Cast, closed in 1995, and now owned by the Seventh Marquess of Headfort. Which seems a shame.

### The Old Brewery
*Ewloe, North Wales*
**Essential album**: The Stone Roses, Second Coming (1994)
Converted ale-manufacturing centre turned into Angelshare Recording Studios circa 1993, and used by such acts as boozy folk-jazz titan John Martyn, West Country rock gurners Reef and Britpop fly-by-nights Mansun (it's since closed down). While it was still a 12-bedroom house, The Stone Roses – seemingly putting guitarist John Squire's Led Zep fixation into practice – came here for six weeks in March 1992, using The Rolling Stones' mobile studio to work on songs with producer John Leckie. The work came to precious little, though the horseplay sounds like a laugh. 'It was an egg

frenzy,' bassist Gary 'Mani' Mounfield later recalled. 'We'd wait for John Leckie to walk across this courtyard, then we'd egg him to fuck.' He went on: 'I remember the food was shit, as well. Anything you didn't eat the night before came back at you the next day with a layer of mash and melted cheese on it. We were fucking emaciated.'

*St Catherine's Court: ghostly vibes*

### St Catherine's Court
*Near Bath, Somerset*
**Essential album**: Radiohead, OK Computer (1997)
16th-century Tudor manor house near Bath, bought by Bond Girl actress Jane Seymour in 1984 for £350,000. Subsequently rented out for weddings, parties etc. – and, for recording purposes, to The Cure (for 1996's Wild Mood Swings) and Radiohead, who recorded seven songs here for OK Computer. 'Most of the time,' explained guitarist Jonny Greenwood, 'you go into a recording studio, and you can still smell the body odour from Whitesnake, or whichever band was in before you. It's just not a very creative place to be, so we used chose more neutral places.' As it turned out, however, the house had an unexpectedly unsettling effect on the band, who duly told stories about its ghostly ambience. 'Everything was just fear,' said Thom Yorke; for evidence, go straight to the downright creepy Exit Music (For A Film), with a vocal recorded – à la John Bonham – at the bottom of a stone staircase. Eight years later, New Order arrived to work on what currently stands as their last album, Waiting For The Sirens' Call – before Seymour sold the place in 2007 after running battles with irate locals over late-night noise. A headline from the Daily Mail: '"Neighbour from hell" Jane Seymour sells mansion after row with residents'. ☞

173

**Sheepcott Farm**
*Aston Tirrold, Berkshire*
**Essential album**: Traffic, Mr Fantasy (1967)
The origin of the British version of what
'60s types knew as 'Getting it together in the
country'. Owned in 1967 by one William
Piggott-Brown (a partner in Island Records
with label founder/boss Chris Blackwell),
who charged the freshly-formed Traffic £5 a
week to do their thing there. De facto chief
Trafficker Steve Winwood – who turned
20 that year – later reflected: 'The cottage
thing came about for practical reasons, really.
We were staying in a house in London and
whenever we wanted to play, the neighbours
would be banging on the walls. We wanted
somewhere where we could just play whenever
we wanted…It was very cut off with no road
to it, just a track, and there were only about
three weeks in the year when you could get
a car up there.' There were run-ins with the
estate's gamekeeper and locals who took
umbrage at Traffic's long hair, but all seems
to have been rural joy: a makeshift stage was
set up close to the house, and a never-ending
procession of droppers-in from London
included Pete Townshend and Eric Clapton.
Commemorated in the Traffic songs House
For Everyone and Berkshire Poppies.

**Stargroves**
*East Woodhay, Hampshire*
**Essential album**: The Rolling Stones, Sticky
Fingers (1971)
Owned by Mick Jagger during the Rolling
Stones' early '70s purple patch, and used – with
the aid, inevitably, of the band's mythic mobile
studio – for parts of Sticky Fingers, Exile
On Main Street and It's Only Rock'n'Roll.
Engineer Andy Johns later recalled: 'It was
a big mansion and a kind of grand hall with
a gallery around with bedroom doors and a
staircase…you could put Charlie
[Watts] in the bay
window. We did stuff
like Bitch there, and
on Moonlight Mile
when Mick is singing,
it sounds very live,
because it was four or
five in the morning,
with the sun about to
come up.' Most of The

Who's Won't Get Fooled Again was done here,
as well as some of Led Zep's Houses Of The
Holy and Physical Graffiti – along with the
outdoor scenes from the Doctor Who story
Pyramids Of Mars (1975), starring Tom Baker.
Now owned by Rod Stewart, who despite
his legendary supposed tightness, paid £2.5
million for it.

**Tittenhurst Park**
*Sunninghill, Berkshire*
**Essential album**: John Lennon, Imagine (1971)
'Imagine no possessions,' went John Lennon's
Imagine – a song put to tape, ironically
enough, at this droolsome Georgian pile,
bought by him and Yoko in 1969 for £145,000.
The Beatles' last photo session (only Paul
clean-shaven, and palpably grumpy vibes) was
done in the grounds and, thanks to a quickly
built in-situ studio called Ascot Sound, so was
part of the recording of 1970's John Lennon/
Plastic Ono Band and most of the following
year's Imagine; for the video for the album's
title track, John and Yoko sat at a piano in
the house's 'white room', after she'd opened
all the blinds. John and Yoko left for America
in August 1971, and in 1973 the property
was sold to Ringo Starr, who renamed Ascot
Sound Startling Studios, and filmed bits of the
T.Rex film Born To Boogie in the grounds.
Subsequent users of the recording facility
included Def Leppard, Whitesnake and Judas
Priest, who decided to move their kit into the
main house. Bought in 1988 by Sheikh Zayed
bin Sultan Al Nahyan, the top man in Abu
Dhabi, who died in 2004.

*Tittenhurst Park: 'Imagine no possessions' - arf!*

# HOW TO GET INTO CAN
... and speak 'the language of the Stone Age'. Warning: this may prove life-changing

**1** For beginners: Can were a German, Cologne-based quartet whose prime-period work (divided between two singers, American Malcolm Mooney and Japanese Damo Suzuki) represented the acme of so-called Krautrock, coolly messing with the rock form without tumbling into prog indulgence. A good starter: **Ege Bamyasi** (1972), a deliciously accessible Suzuki-era LP that's been known to change people forever.
**Song to start with**: I'm So Green, the blueprint for The Stone Roses' Fools Gold

**2** Next, a mind-expanding masterpiece: **Tago Mago** (1971), a double album that requires a bit more patience, but pays handsomely. And bear in mind: on this more than any other Can LP, drummer Jaki Liebezeit's groove-laden drum parts – as on, say, Mushroom – are both 1)perfect, and 2)crazily ahead of their time. Also, he kept such perfect rhythm that they could edit and re-edit insanely long jams with no bother at all. **Song to start with**: Halleluhwah – Happy Mondays did not nick the title for their 1989 single for nothing (even if it's spelt differently)

**3** Then back to the Malcolm Mooney period – which tends to be less streamlined and futuristic than the Damo Suzuki era (think the Velvet Underground c.1967), but remains way cool. **Monster Movie** (1969) was their debut LP and finishes with Yoo Doo Right – a super-long gem that foreshadows the groovesome Suzuki records. **Song to start with**: Father Cannot Yell

**4** **Soundtracks** (1970) anthologised Can's commissioned film music, bridging the Suzuki and Mooney phases. It ends with Mother Sky, which is as jaw-dropping a piece of experimental rock music as you may ever hear, not least because of Suzuki's compellingly out-there vocals. 'Sometimes it sounds like English, French or German,' he later explained. 'But really, it's the language of the Stone Age.'
**Song to start with**: Mother Sky

**5** **Future Days** (1973) was the last Suzuki record. He considered it 'boring' and 'not much of a freak out' and soon split – but it's better than that suggests: with the exception of the *motorik* Moonshake, an object lesson in how to evoke summer without falling into cliché (it was made during a particularly hot season in 1973). The review in the NME praised 'more positive energy to the square centimetre than three barrels of brown rice.' Nice.
**Song to start with**: Future Days

**6** And now you're out into the wild blue Krautrock yonder. **Delay 1968** (1981) was released some 13 years after it was made, and begins with Thief, covered live by Radiohead in 2001. Also try **Soon Over Babaluma** (1974) made after Suzuki's exit by Can's core quartet. NB: they finally broke up in 1979, though their final run of LPs should be approached with caution. **Songs to start with**: Thief, Dizzy Dizzy

*Can c.1972 with Damo Suzuki (2nd right)*

# BOB DYLAN'S BASEMENT TAPES: A HISTORY
### From Woodstock to the world, via Jagger, Clapton and The Byrds

**29 July 1966** Dylan suffers legendary 'Motorcycle Accident' while riding Triumph 500 along backroads of Woodstock. Injuries remain unclear, but projected gigs are cancelled, while a relieved Dylan spends time with family and thinks a lot.

**February 1967** Bob joined in Woodstock by four-fifths of backing band The Hawks, later called The Band: Robbie Robertson (guitar/chief songwriter), Richard Manuel (piano), Garth Hudson (organ/keyboards), Rick Danko (bass/vocals). Latter three are domiciled in a big pink house, quickly known as 'Big Pink'. 'Bob was OK,' Robertson later reflects. 'Except he had a big cast around his neck. A brace.'

*Dylan and Jagger: music from Big Pink spawned music from 'Big Brown'*

**December 1967** Dylan releases John Wesley Harding album, recorded in Nashville, and unrelated to Basement sessions, though pared-down sound, biblical vibes and folky ambience denotes similar approach.

**April 1968** Julie Driscoll, Brian Auger and The Trinity reach UK No 5 with pretty appealing treatment of This Wheel's On Fire, later used as theme tune for Absolutely Fabulous.

*Julie Driscoll*

**January 1968** Manfred Mann score UK No 1 with version of The Mighty Quinn, having heard Basement Tapes songs at offices of Dylan's British music publishers. In recollection of guitarist Tom McGuinness, 'We listened to a couple of songs, and Manfred *[Mann, keyboards]* said to Albert, "Why does Dylan get that fella with the funny voice to do his demos?" Albert looked at him with a slightly quizzical expression, trying to figure out whether it was a wind-up, and said, "That *is* Bob."'

**July 1968** The Byrds (briefly featuring Gram Parsons) release trailblazing country-rock LP Sweetheart Of The Rodeo, including two BTs songs: You Ain't Goin' Nowhere and Nothing Was Delivered. Freshly-renamed, The Band put out yet more influential debut album Music From Big Pink, including two Basement-born Dylan co-writes (This Wheel's On Fire, Tears Of Rage) and one Bob original, I Shall Be Released. Among musicians duly bowled over is Eric Clapton, who cites MFBP as one of the reasons he broke from Cream.

**December 1968** Rolling Stones release Beggars Banquet. Back-to-roots music betrays influence of Basement Tapes, and original cover – of toilet and scrawled-on bog wall – features giveaway graffiti 'Music from Big Brown'.

**Spring 1967** Robertson et al now casually rehearsing in basement of Big Pink, and Dylan begins to pay regular visits, joining them to play some new songs and endless cover versions.

**August 1967** 14 songs copyrighted, and put on acetate LP: Million Dollar Bash, Yea! Heavy And A Bottle Of Bread, Please Mrs Henry, Down In The Flood, Lo And Behold!, Tiny Montgomery, This Wheel's On Fire, You Ain't Goin' Nowhere, I Shall Be Released, Tears Of Rage, Too Much Of Nothing, Quinn The Eskimo (aka The Mighty Quinn), Open The Door Homer and Nothing Was Delivered.

**Summer 1967** Thanks partly to then-manager Albert Grossman's wish to keep money coming in by 'placing' songs with other musicians, Dylan begins taping new stuff with musicians in basement. 'The mood was never real serious,' says Robertson. 'He would say, in fun, "OK – That's a great one for the Everly Brothers."'

**October 1967** Hawks drummer Levon Helm finally moves to Woodstock. UK music magazine Disc And Music Echo prints letter from a worried Elaine Batten of Whitmore, near Leeds: 'Can you please, please, for the sake of my sanity, tell me what is happening in the world of Bob Dylan? Is he ill, well or in jail?'

**November 1967** Grossman-managed folk trio Peter, Paul & Mary have US hit with first Basement Tapes cover: Too Much Of Nothing. Meanwhile, Marianne Faithfull is given 14-track Basement Tapes acetate LP, taken on holiday with Mick Jagger to Brazil and the Caribbean. Same acetate is also brought to London by Grossman, swelling number of Basement Tapes covers throughout '68 and '69.

*Sandy Denny*

**31 August 1969** Dylan – with The Band – plays Isle of Wight festival. Set includes Quinn The Eskimo. Then all goes pretty much quiet. Until…

**July 1969** Having played Open The Door, Homer live, Fairport Convention include Million Dollar Bash on Unhalfbricking LP. Singer Sandy Denny will also cover Down In The Flood and Too Much Of Nothing.

**January 1969** While enduring sessions for Let It Be album and movie at Twickenham Film Studios, recent Woodstock guest George Harrison caught on tape playing snatch of Please Mrs Henry and asking Ringo Starr: 'Did you play those tapes?'

**February 1969** First appearance of Great White Wonder, Dylan bootleg containing seven Basement Tapes songs. Throughout year, rash of BTs covers appears.

**26 June 1975** CBS release 24-track album entitled The Basement Tapes. Spoiling the authenticity, among eight songs by The Band alone are some not recorded at Big Pink. Still, New York Times declares LP 'the greatest album in the history of American popular music.'

**October 2007** A footnote: release of Dylan-based movie I'm Not There; soundtrack features song of same name, hailed by Mojo magazine as 'The Basement Tapes' most legendary song'.

# THE GREAT ROCK'N'ROLL SWINDLES
## Twenty albums that should never, ever have been made

*Author's note: This is something much more than a selection of crap albums. These are what have come to be known as rock follies: largely the result of once-great talents stepping on creative banana skins, or misguided people trying to boldly push the artistic envelope and failing, albeit heroically (and often with the aid of drink, drugs and too much money). Now, read on...*

## Arcadia
**So Red The Rose** *1985*
Something of a toss-up here, in all senses. In 1984, Duran Duran had a sabbatical, during which Taylors Andy and John formed the Power Station with the inestimable Robert Palmer, and made an album famed for its quintessential '80s-ness. Worse followed: jolted into action, Simon Le Bon, Roger Taylor and Nick Rhodes momentarily traded as Arcadia, and made this. Like entries in an '80s paint catalogue, the song titles include Rose Arcana and Lady Ice, Sting and Dave Gilmour are on it, and Le Bon called it 'the most pretentious album ever made'. Soon after its release, Roger Taylor decided to become a farmer.
*Highest UK chart position:* 30

## Coverdale & Page
**Coverdale & Page** *1993*
The post-Led Zep manoeuvres of Jimmy Page included an aborted trio with two members of Yes called XYZ (ex-Yes/Zeppelin, see?), his team-up with ex-Free growler Paul Rodgers (until recently of Queen, or rather 'Queen'), soundtracks for two of Michael Winner's Death Wish movies – and this wheeze with the Whitesnake frontman damned as a cheapo Robert Plant. Plant's only comment: 'Jimmy Page always had a very bleak sense of humour.' (He had already referred to Coverdale as 'David Coverversion'.) Strangely, he and Page reunited the following year.
*Highest UK chart position:* 4

## Terence Trent D'Arby
**Neither Fish Nor Flesh** *1989*
For the benefit of younger readers: the man briefly so famous that he was briefly known as 'TTD' was raised in Florida, spent time with the US army in Germany, and made a humungous impact with the 1987 album Introducing The Hardline According To Terence Trent D'Arby (which was pretty good). The follow-up's accompanying notes thanked two wealthy Dubliners for 'not weeding out the mushrooms in your lovely garden' and featured TTD on kazoo, Irish 'boggle stick' and 'manifestations'. It tanked, and his career never recovered. In 2001 he changed his name to Sananda Maitreya after 'a series of dreams'. You would, wouldn't you?
*Highest UK chart position:* 12

## Deep Purple
**Concerto For Group And Orchestra** *1969*
The '60s were about to end. Proto-metal group Deep Purple had just hired singer Ian Gillan and bassist Roger Glover, and were about to create a titanic rock folly: a three-part concerto written by keyboardist Jon Lord, to be co-performed by the Royal Philharmonic Orchestra and conducted by esteemed baton-waver Malcolm Arnold. Gillan's only lyrics came in the second movement, were probably ad-libbed, and contained the telling question: 'How shall I know when to start singing my song?' At one point in rehearsals, Arnold told his orchestra they were 'playing like a bunch of cunts'.
*Highest UK chart position:* 26

## Duran Duran
**Thank You** *1995*
In early 1993, Duran Duran – yes, them again, by then down to just three of the original quintet – scored a global hit with Ordinary World. So what to do next? How about a covers album, including Bob Dylan's Lay Lady Lay, Grandmaster Flash and Melle Mel's White Lines (Don't Do It) and – no! – Public Enemy's 911 Is A Joke? There it was: white Brummie millionaires retooling a song about how black folks in the ghetto can't get the emergency services to come round. But never mind, eh? Lou Reed thought the version of Perfect Day was 'the best cover ever completed of one of my own songs'. He was lying.
*Highest UK chart position:* 12

## Bob Dylan
### Self Portrait *1970*
'We released that album to get people off my back.' Thus spake Dylan 21 years after the release of a true baffler, featuring such bamboozling low-points as a croonsome cover of Blue Moon, and a double-tracked Dylan having a go at Simon and Garfunkel's The Boxer. Rolling Stone's eminent critic Greil Marcus is famed for his florid, quasi-philosophical prose, but when it came to this album, his review famously opened in brutal Anglo-Saxon: 'What is this shit?'
*Highest UK chart position:* 1

## Bob Geldof
### Vegetarians Of Love *1990*
Having fed the world in 1985, Geldof released his first solo album the following year, but it tanked. This one did slightly better, though it still failed to revive his musical career. Tellingly, it was recorded in five days, and contained a tribute to unmanned space exploration called Thinking Voyager 2 Type Things which found the titular probe 'Looking back at home and weeping' and 'winding down and bleeping'. The world soon concluded that it could only tolerate him singing Rat Trap/I Don't Like Mondays (at a push).
*Highest UK chart position:* 21

## Goldie
### SaturnzReturn *1998*
Prior to his reinvention as a monarch of so-called 'reality' TV, the artist born Clifford Price enjoyed acclaim as the figurehead of the adventurous musical form known as drum'n'bass, swiftly followed by membership of the social circle commanded by Noel Gallagher and Meg Mathews. Such was the backdrop to his second album, an unbelievably indulgent effort built around Mother, a journey into his soul that lasted a full 72 minutes. 'The problem here is that his ambition far outstrips his talent,' said Rolling Stone magazine, 'making

him seem like the genre's Emerson, Lake & Palmer.' Ouch.
*Highest UK chart position:* 15

## Billy Idol
### Cyberpunk *1993*
Bob Dylan fell off his motorbike and invented country-rock: Billy Idol had an equally grave two-wheel tumble and got very into the first stirrings of the internet. The result: a 20-track future-gazing concept album and frantic talk about the ultimate computerised rock concert. One question arose: hadn't U2 just done this with Zoo TV? 'Whereas with U2 I think it all looks rather comfortable,' Billy responded, 'we want to push the technology so it's screaming! These computers will wish they never got involved with us! Ha ha!' He didn't make another record for 12 years.
*Highest UK chart position:* 30

## Mansun
### Attack Of The Grey Lantern *1997*
With Britpop going wobbly, the last musicians through the door – like this lot, a quartet from Chester – had to push beyond Oasis and Blur copyism or die. Ergo a conceptual debut album set in a fictional English town, starring a character called Mavis and her dad, a 'stripper vicar'. 'We want to make music that sounds like tomorrow,' they said. Brief success followed – though rock's subsequent big ideas did not include concept albums, or characters called Mavis. Or 'Stripper vicars'. After two more albums, they split in 2003.
*Highest UK chart position:* 1

*Duran Duran: White Lines?*
*Don't do it*

179

## George Martin
**In My Life** *1998*
The Beatles' producer marked his retirement with a collection of Fabs songs delivered by a motley all-star cast. Sean Connery turned in a spoken-word version of the title track ('And theshe memoriesh loshe their meaning…'), there were cameos from Goldie Hawn, violinist hottie Vanessa Mae and Celine Dion – and to cap it all, Jim Carrey did I Am The Walrus, with silly voices and everything. 'I needed someone to do a zany version,' Martin explained. Oh, *please*.
*Highest UK chart position:* 5

## Keith Moon
**Two Sides Of The Moon** *1975*
An interesting rock rule of thumb: covers of John Lennon's In My Life are often a sign of very bad things happening, as evidenced by Sean Connery (see above) and Twiggy on The Muppet Show (1976). So it also proved on Keith Moon's one and only solo album, effectively a portrait of being constantly off your head in LA. 'There were a lot of drugs, a lot of parties, and a lot of late-night stuff,' recalled one witness. Said Beatles cover is a sad disgrace, but arguably better than the treatment of Don't Worry Baby by Moon's beloved Beach Boys,

*Rick Wakeman: mind-numbing ludricrousness*

which was chosen as a single. By way of proof that some people will buy anything, a 'deluxe edition' was released in 2006.
*Highest UK chart position:* did not chart

## Oasis
**Be Here Now** *1997*
A big year, 1997 – the end of 18 years of Conservative government, the death of Diana, and this: Oasis's third album, received by the press as the work of Gods. It wasn't: 'We made the record to justify the drug habit,' admitted Noel Gallagher. Contains Magic Pie, arguably the worst song in Noel's oeuvre (if, in fact, he has an 'oeuvre').
*Highest UK chart position:* 1

## The Rolling Stones
**Their Satanic Majesties Request** *1967*
If the Aldi supermarket chain came up with a cut-price version of Sgt Pepper, this is what it would sound like: addled, half-finished, and replete with the mind-boggling sound of Bill Wyman unconvincingly pretending to go psychedelic on a song called In Another Land, which sounds like Trevor Brooking impersonating Syd Barrett. 2000 Light Years From Home and She's A Rainbow were OK, but the rest still sounds like borderline dreck. Manager/producer Andrew Loog Oldham quit when he scented disaster: 'My point of leaving was very simple. They asked me to pay £18,000 for the cover before they'd recorded the album.'
*Highest UK chart position:* 3

## Finley Quaye
**Vanguard** *2000*
Remember him? In 1998, Edinburgh-born Quaye won a Brit award on the back of a pleasant-if-meandering debut album titled Maverick A Strike. Its successor stiffed, and hurled its author to the margins, chiefly because it was – and how do you put this politely? – a right old barmy mess. By way of evidence, consider the lyrics of a song called Broadcast: 'No Glenn Hoddle/No supermodel/No Dennis Wise…No David Vine/No John Virgo/You love Greenpeace/I love Greenpeace/I love green pea.' Well, yes.
*Highest UK chart position:* 35

## Styx
### Kilroy Was Here *1983*
Only really known in Blighty for their 1979 soft-rock hit Babe, this Chicago troupe's crimes extended way beyond treacly AOR schmaltz. A case in point: this conceptual monster, made long after prog rock had passed from fashion, partly in response to the band's experience of being accused of concealing 'satanic' messages in their music by some very strange American people. The 'plot', such as it is: authoritarian Japanese robots take over the world and outlaw rock'n'roll, but one Robert Orin Charles Kilroy puts on – yay! – a rock show that somehow gets rid of the mechanised oppressors and liberates humanity. In the US it went platinum – and spawned the Top 10 hit Mr Roboto (chorus: 'Domo arigato/Mr Roboto'), which has some claim to being the worst single ever made. Seriously.
*Highest UK chart position: 67*

## Transvision Vamp
### Little Magnets Vs The Babble Of Bubble *1991*
Now *there's* a good title. Transvision Vamp (TV, see?) were a gloriously opportunistic West London wheeze whereby bottle-blonde siren Wendy James effectively sang the rock chestnut Louie Louie and a few T.Rex singles over and over again in ever-greater states of undress. 'I will be more famous than Madonna,' she assured us, and she also reckoned she'd eventually win an Oscar. Unfortunately, it didn't quite work out: their career peaked with the 1989 album Velveteen, whereupon this very confused follow-up was delayed by the record company and only released in the US. Still, you really should hear their cover of Bob Dylan's Can You Please Crawl Out Your Window?. Or there again, perhaps you shouldn't.
*Highest UK chart position: never released*

## Neil Young *&* Crazy Horse
### Greendale *2003*
Mid-way through a full-cast performance of this play/film/album in Los Angeles, Neil Young addressed his audience thus: 'I'd like to tell you what's going on, but I have no idea.' Neither did they, aside from some extremely vague stuff about green politics and George Bush's America and the killing of a policeman, delivered by an ensemble including 'Grandpa', 'Sun Green', 'Cousin Jed' and 'Officer Carmichael'. When the recorded version came out, he was given the full critical treatment: 'Nearly all of the songs plod along in a somnambulant blues slouch, punctuated with the most aimless guitar solos and fills of Young's career,' groaned one very unimpressed writer. 'And all drag on interminably, to nine, 10, 12 and 13 minutes in four cases.' Not exactly Harvest, then.
*Highest UK chart position: 24*

## Rick Wakeman
### The Myths And Legends Of King Arthur & The Knights Of The Round Table *1975*
Between 1973 and 1975 – during which time he quit prog-rock kingpins Yes, only to return in 1977 – Rick Wakeman made a mind-boggling conceptual trilogy: The Six Wives Of Henry VIII, Journey To The Centre Of The Earth, and this monstrosity (nailed by one US critic as follows: 'Here a kind of lumbering jazz, there a sort of jungle chant, then a tacked-piano nickelodeon ragtime in a sea of ego'). With an orchestra and cast of skating actors, it was delivered live at Wembley Arena, on ice – such an expensive wheeze that Wakeman went bankrupt. Such was rock's passage from stripped-down excitement to mind-numbingly ludicrous excess, and all in less than 20 years. Then punk came along – but unfortunately, the madness continued…
*Highest UK chart position: 2*

## Jeff Wayne
### War Of The Worlds *1978*
Thanks to a re-release in 2005, somewhat re-habilitated, but it hardly deserved it. Just to recap: a rock-opera treatment of the H. G. Wells novel, starring the thunder-voiced Richard Burton with bit-parts for '70s teen idol David Essex and Phil Lynott (who, in a fit of clever casting, played a vicar). To decisively nail that Edwardian alien invasion vibe, it also featured Forever Autumn, a quickly-ubiquitous AOR ballad crooned by The Moody Blues' Justin Hayward. The album spent 232 weeks on the UK charts, partly thanks to its status as a default Christmas present for male adolescents (imagine the yuletide scene: 'Here you are, Darren'; 'Oh wow! Jeff Wayne's War Of The Worlds. *Again*.')
*Highest UK chart position: 5*

## Morrissey's first solo decade

Great! Crap! Great! Crap! Then silence.

Great —

Pretty Good —

Average —

Not Good —

Awful —

A brisk start: no sooner had Morrissey called time on an abortive go at creating a Johnny Marr-less Smiths than he was back in the studio making **Viva Hate** (1988): written with sometime Smiths co-producer Stephen Street, it was received as proof that all was ship-shape in Mozland – as suggested by Suedehead and the super-bleak Everyday Is Like Sunday.

And it was going so swimmingly. The singles-only interregnum commemorated by **Bona Drag** (1990) (including The Last Of The Famous International Playboys and Interesting Drug) largely augured well, but then came **Kill Uncle** (1991): 38 measly minutes, largely done with an ex-member of the long-lost Fairground Attraction that – and let's not be coy – stank. Oh woe!

## David Bowie in the 1980s

He knew when to go out! He knew when to stay in! Get things done!

Great —

Pretty Good —

Average —

Not Good —

Awful —

With his Berlin Period over, DB glued artistic daring to a pop-oriented directness and came up with **Scary Monsters (And Super Creeps)** (1980) – the album still held up as his last great LP, and seen at the time as one in the eye for a new crop of Bowie disciples (e.g Gary Numan) – who were sent up on Teenage Wildlife. Also contains Ashes To Ashes, the kind of No 1 single no one makes any more.

After two non-album Gap Years came a ditching of musicians he'd long worked with and **Let's Dance** (1983), co-produced by ex-Chic fella Nile Rodgers and oozing a primped, professional feel that was the early '80s all over. 'You should be ashamed to say you do not love it,' yelled the NME, but there were drawbacks aplenty (e.g. his new canary-yellow barnet). Bluntly, it hasn't dated well.

**Your Arsenal** (1992) was made with a bequiffed new band, produced by Spider From Mars Mick Ronson, and v good – but bad vibes abounded. We'll Let You Know and The National Front Disco strayed into allegedly rum areas (as had Asian Rut and Bengali In Platforms), and Moz outraged the NME with a live show including skinhead imagery and a Union Jack. Oh woe! Again!

Some think **Vauxhall And I** (1994) remains his most perfect solo record. Wracked with grief over the deaths of three close friends and associates – including the aforementioned Ronson – Morrissey created an album full of poise, grace and the profundity of prime-period Smiths. But also note rib-tickling lyrics, e.g 'I will be/ At the bar/With my head on the bar.' What a wag!

*Naturellement*, it couldn't last. The whiffy compilation **World Of Morrissey** (1995) suggested something was up – and then Moz and his tough-looking lads swiftly made **Southpaw Grammar** (1995), which was no fun at all. Want a Morrissey album with a drum solo, two tracks lasting more than ten minutes and a witless throwaway called Dagenham Dave? You do not!

One more, and then seven years of silence. **Maladjusted** (1997) wasn't quite the wash-out that preceded it, but by now he was sounding bored – witness the single Alma Matters, which sounds like a work of sub-Moz music by someone else (as does the arguable all-time nadir Roy's Keen). The reviews were crap, the public reaction muted; Moz took the hint and vanished.

Neither has **Tonight** (1984), and it's a much weaker album, giving off a telling whiff of shiny trousers and Shock Waves hairspray (Iggy Pop was around, but the title track features the decade's obligatory Tina Turner duet). God only knows why DB covered The Beach Boys' God Only Knows, or made music damned as 'plastic reggae', although Loving The Alien wasn't too bad.

If an appearance in the Muppets-go-serious film Labyrinth and his crapola duet with Mick Jagger suggested the '80s were doing DB no favours, **Never Let Me Down** (1987) was incontestable proof. Bowie later said it was his 'nadir' – and note also the absurd, über-'80s Glass Spider tour, which drew this comment from guitarist Carlos Alomar: 'I hated all that dancing and shit.'

So what to do? Here was an idea: grow a beard, put on a suit, get in a man famed for playing his guitar with a vibrator, and pretend you're just one quarter of a kind of yuppie punk band. That's right! The self-titled **Tin Machine** (1989) might have briefly reached No 3 in the British charts, but it reeked, and there was really no excuse for a proto-grunge cover of John Lennon's Working Class Hero. At all.

In 1990, Bowie apparently called time on his past with the Sound And Vision tour, hyped by a wheeze whereby fans voted for which songs he would play on the understanding he'd never do his biggest hits again (he did, of course). Then came **Tin Machine II** (1991) which was as stenchy as the first one and sold even less. By now, things could only get better – which they did. Just about, anyway.

# IT'S A MIGHTY LONG WAY DOWN ROCK'N'ROLL, PART 2

The continuing history of albums, singles and the world in general, 1983-2008

## 1983

**BSS**: Karma Chameleon **Culture Club**
**BSA**: Thriller **Michael Jackson**
*Buoyed by the 'Falklands factor', Thatcher wins a landslide election victory. Microsoft Word is introduced, so cheers, Microsoft. The Chicken McNugget is introduced, so cheers, McDonalds.*
**GS**: Hand In Glove **The Smiths**
**GA**: Murmur **REM**

## 1984

**BSS**: Do They Know It's Christmas? **Band Aid**
**BSA**: Can't Slow Down **Lionel Richie**
*The world quietly celebrates the non-appearance of George Orwell's dystopia – though then again, things aren't exactly a breeze. In the UK, the miners' strike begins, and the IRA attempt to kill the entire cabinet; in Ethiopia, famine claims over a million lives, and prompts first Band Aid, then Live Aid.*
**GS**: Perfect Skin **Lloyd Cole & The Commotions**
**GA**: Purple Rain **Prince & The Revolution**

## 1985

**BSS**: The Power Of Love **Jennifer Rush**
**BSA**: Brothers In Arms **Dire Straits**
*The people's choice: Dire Straits decisively launching the CD age, or a very bad power ballad. The miners' strike ends; Mikhail Gorbachev becomes General Secretary of the Soviet Communist Party. Live Aid happens. Microsoft launches the first version of Windows.*
**GS**: When Love Breaks Down **Prefab Sprout**
**GA**: Hounds Of Love **Kate Bush**

## 1986

**BSS**: Don't Leave Me This Way **The Communards**
**BSA**: True Blue **Madonna**
*In the Ukraine, the nuclear reactor at Chernobyl explodes. The Challenger disaster kills seven astronauts aboard the Space Shuttle. The World Cup returns to Mexico, and Argentina take it home. Aerosmith remake Walk This Way with*

Run DMC, *and millions of white people belatedly become aware of hip hop music.*
**GS**: E=MC$^2$ **Big Audio Dynamite**
**GA**: Raising Hell **Run DMC**

## 1987

**BSS**: Never Gonna Give You Up **Rick Astley**
**BSA**: Bad **Michael Jackson**
*Margaret Thatcher wins her third British election. The Smiths split up. Lester Piggott is jailed for tax evasion. Guns N' Roses put out Appetite For Destruction. And a well-meaning though rather boring bloke from Newton-Le-Willows scores a hit in 17 countries (that's Rick Astley, incidentally).*
**GS**: (You Gotta) Fight For Your Right (To Party) **The Beastie Boys**
**GA**: Sign O' The Times **Prince**

*De La Soul: what the world was waiting for*

## 1988

**BSS**: Mistletoe And Wine **Cliff Richard**
**BSA**: Kylie **Kylie Minogue**
*Acid House prompts claims of a 'Second Summer Of Love', and for some people it's probably even better than the first. The Iran-Iraq war ends, with around a million lives lost. George Bush Sr is elected President of the USA. Top comedy oddball Kenneth Williams dies.*
**GS**: Wrote For Luck **Happy Mondays**
**GA**: It Takes A Nation Of Millions To Hold Us Back **Public Enemy**

## 1989

**BSS**: Ride On Time **Black Box**
**BSA**: Ten Good Reasons **Jason Donovan**
*The Stone Roses release their first album. Acid House continues, as evidenced by the year's No 1 45. The Berlin wall comes down. 'An underrated year', as a group called Gay Dad later put it.*
**GS**: Fools Gold/What The World Is Waiting For **The Stone Roses**
**GA**: 3 Feet High And Rising **De La Soul**

## 1990

**BSS**: Unchained Melody **The Righteous Brothers**
**BSA**: The Immaculate Collection **Madonna**
*Nelson Mandela is released from prison after 27 years of detention. Italy host the World Cup. England make it to the last four, Paul 'Gazza' Gascoigne cries, and Germany take the trophy. Iraq invades Kuwait; the Conservative Party topples Margaret Thatcher.*
**GS**: Been Caught Stealing **Jane's Addiction**
**GA**: Blue Lines **Massive Attack**

## 1991

**BSS**: (Everything I Do) I Do It For You **Bryan Adams**
**BSA**: Stars **Simply Red**
*Jesus! 16 consecutive weeks at No 1 for the theme from Robin Hood: Prince Of Thieves. Iraq is ejected from Kuwait, and the Soviet Union breathes its last. Nirvana release Nevermind, and the dread word 'grunge' goes global. The worldwide web becomes publicly available.*
**GS**: Smells Like Teen Spirit **Nirvana**
**GA**: Bandwagonesque **Teenage Fanclub**

## 1992

**BSS**: I Will Always Love You **Whitney Houston**
**BSA**: Stars **Simply Red**
*Jesus! Again! Mick Hucknall gets the BSA trophy for a second consecutive year (but take note, rock snobs: it's a genius LP). John Major unexpectedly wins the UK's general election, Bill Clinton is elected US President, and Benny Hill dies.*
**GS**: Motorcycle Emptiness **Manic Street Preachers**
**GA**: Dry **PJ Harvey**

*Jeff Buckley: groovier than the 'Jovi*

## 1993

**BSS**: I'd Do Anything For Love (But I Won't Do That) **Meat Loaf**
**BSA**: Bat Out Of Hell II: Back Into Hell **Meat Loaf**
*Jesus! Again! Really! Meat Loaf eats the charts, and millions wonder what 'that' is. In the former Yugoslavia, the siege of Sarajevo continues (it ends in 1996). Though they largely can't stand each other, two albums by Blur and Suede decisively invent Britpop.*
**GS**: Cannonball **The Breeders**
**GA**: The Infotainment Scan **The Fall**

## 1994

**BSS**: Love Is All Around **Wet Wet Wet**
**BSA**: Cross Road **Bon Jovi**
*Kurt Cobain commits suicide. Following the death of John Smith, Tony Blair becomes leader of the UK Labour Party. The USA hosts the World Cup, which is nice for them (Brazil win their fourth title). Blur put out Parklife, and Oasis release Definitely Maybe.*
**GS**: Loser **Beck**
**GA**: Grace **Jeff Buckley**

## 1995

**BSS**: Unchained Melody **Robson & Jerome**
**BSA**: Robson And Jerome **Robson & Jerome**
*Proof that Simon Cowell is death to music: it's his berrrr-illiant idea to make two blokes from Soldier Soldier pop stars. Blur battle Oasis for the No 1 position and win. Manic Street Preachers' Richey Edwards disappears.*
**GS**: Poison **The Prodigy**
**GA**: The Bends **Radiohead**

## 1996

**BSS**: Killing Me Softly **The Fugees**
**BSA**: Jagged Little Pill **Alanis Morissette**
*Bill Clinton wins a second term. Oasis sell out Knebworth, twice. The Prince and Princess of Wales are formally divorced. Tupac Shakur is shot in Las Vegas and dies six days later.*
**GS**: If It Makes You Happy **Sheryl Crow**
**GA**: A *[sic]* Ass Pocket Of Whiskey **RL Burnside**

## 1997

**BSS**: Something About The Way You Look Tonight/Candle In The Wind '97 **Elton John**
**BSA**: Be Here Now **Oasis**
*A big year. New Labour win by a landslide and Tony Blair moves into Downing Street. Radiohead release OK Computer. Diana, Princess of Wales, is killed in a car crash in Paris. Che Guevara's remains are returned to Cuba; Robert Mitchum and James Stewart die on consecutive days. Which is a bit weird.*
**GS**: Beetlebum **Blur**
**GA**: In It For The Money **Supergrass**

## 1998

**BSS**: Believe **Cher**
**BSA**: Talk On Corners **The Corrs**
*Bill Clinton denies he had 'sexual relations' with Monica Lewinsky, but is later impeached (though he's acquitted of all charges and survives in office). Politicians in Northern Ireland sign the Good Friday Agreement. The World Cup is hosted by France, who beat Brazil in the final.*
**GS**: Brimful Of Asha (Fatboy Slim remix) **Cornershop**
**GA**: The Three EPs **The Beta Band**

## 1999

**BSS**:…Baby One More Time **Britney Spears**
**BSA**: Come On Over **Shania Twain**
*In the midst of the crisis surrounding Kosovo, NATO bombs targets in Serbia. Napster begins operating and terrifies the music business. On New Year's Eve, millions party like it's 1999. Because it is.*
**GS**: Beautiful Stranger **Madonna**
**GA**: The Soft Bulletin **The Flaming Lips**

## 2000

**BSS**: Can We Fix It? **Bob The Builder**
**BSA**: 1 **The Beatles**
*Aka 'Y2K'. The Millennium bug fails to drop planes from the sky, break your cooker etc. Vladimir Putin is elected President of Russia. After controversy over vote-counting, George W. Bush becomes US President-elect. But never mind: by way of making everyone feel better, there's the first Coldplay album.*
**GS**: Feel Good Hit Of The Summer **Queens Of The Stone Age**
**GA**: Heartbreaker **Ryan Adams**

## 2001

**BSS**: It Wasn't Me **Shaggy feat. RikRok**
**BSA**: No Angel **Dido**
*In the UK, foot and mouth disease paralyses the countryside, and Labour win another landslide election victory, though all events are dwarfed by 9/11. George Harrison dies, aged 58.*
**GS**: Pyramid Song **Radiohead**
**GA**: Is This It? **The Strokes**

*OutKast: in a year of war and viruses, they shook it like a Polaroid picture*

# 2002

**BSS**: Anything Is Possible/Evergreen **Will Young**
**BSA**: Escapology **Robbie Williams**
*The Euro becomes a physical currency. South Korea and Japan jointly host the World Cup, and – well, yes – Brazil win it. Princess Margaret and The Queen Mother die; Britain and the US begin the build-up to war in Iraq.*
**GS**: Fell In Love With A Girl **The White Stripes**
**GA**: Up The Bracket **The Libertines**

# 2003

**BSS**: Where Is The Love? **Black Eyed Peas**
**BSA**: Life For Rent **Dido**
*What a difficult century so far. A million-plus people march in London against war in Iraq, but it starts soon after. The planet gets jittery about the SARS virus, and Nina Simone dies. But never mind, eh? BBC Choice becomes BBC Three, so what's with the moaning?*
**GS**: Hey Ya! **OutKast**
**GA**: Fever To Tell **Yeah Yeah Yeahs**

# 2004

**BSS**: Do They Know It's Chistmas? **Band Aid 20**
**BSA**: Scissor Sisters **Scissor Sisters**
*George W. Bush wins a second Presidential term. The European Union expands east. The 20th anniversary of Band Aid prompts the second revival of Do They Know It's Christmas?, allowing Joss Stone to sing, 'Fee-ya-eeed The Wuur-huurld', as she would. Thom Yorke plays piano.*
**GS**: Take Me Out **Franz Ferdinand**
**GA**: Hot Fuss **The Killers**

# 2005

**BSS**: Is This The Way To Amarillo? **Tony Christie feat. Peter Kay**
**BSA**: Back To Bedlam **James Blunt**
*A third term for Tony Blair, though he's already served notice that it will be his last, and the aftermath of the election sees ongoing wobbles. On 6 July London gets the Olympics; a day later terrorists attack public transport in London and kill 52 people. Hurricane Katrina decimates the US Gulf Coast.*
**GS**: Formed A Band **Art Brut**
**GA**: Funeral **Arcade Fire**

# 2006

**BSS**: Crazy Gnarls **Barkley**
**BSA**: Eyes Open Snow **Patrol**
*Germany hosts the World Cup and comes fourth; Italy win it. Nintendo release the Wii console, toughing out the fact that infantile British people will find its name at least slightly funny. James Brown dies on Christmas Day.*
**GS**: Rehab **Amy Winehouse**
**GA**: Whatever People Say I Am, That's What I'm Not **Arctic Monkeys**

*Klaxons: Skans rule*

# 2007

**BSS**: Bleeding Love **Leona Lewis**
**BSA**: Back To Black **Amy Winehouse**
*Microsoft releases Windows Vista. The Intergovernmental Panel On Climate Change says cglobal warming is 'very likely' to be caused by humans. The Millennium Dome reopens as the $O_2$ Arena. Gordon Brown takes over as PM from Tony Blair, which seems like a good idea at the time.*
**GS**: Golden Skans **Klaxons**
**GA**: The Good, The Bad And The Queen **Unnamed**

# 2008

**BSS**: Hallelujah **Alexandra Burke**
**BSA**: Rockferry **Duffy**
*Barack Obama defeats John McCain and is elected the 44th President of the United States of America. Fidel Castro announces that he's resigning as President of Cuba and hands power to his brother, Raul. Deaths include those of Heath Ledger and The Beatles' former associate Maharishi Mahesh Yogi.*
**GS**: American Boy **Estelle feat. Kanye West**
**GA**: Vampire Weekend **Vampire Weekend**

# Chapter 8

# THE BONUS TRACKS

A t the beginning of this book, there was a brief mention of the tendency of far too many musicians to utter such depressing words as, 'We just make music for ourselves, and if anyone else likes it, that's a bonus.' To end, we now return to the dreaded 'B' word, but thankfully in a completely different context – that of 'bonus tracks', as the music industry would have it.

On reissues of 'classic' albums – these days, in fact, of just about anything that has been released, ever – the original tracklisting is usually no longer enough. Now, once you're past the main event, there are miscellaneous add-ons, B-sides, curios and lost treasures. Only a few brave musicians hold out against this, and doing so is largely the preserve of rock'n'roll's royalty: albums by, for example, The Rolling Stones and Kraftwerk may have been buffed-up and remastered, but you must still consume them in the form they were created. At the time of writing, The Beatles were about to once again put out their albums (yet another re-re-release, if you will) in both stereo and mono versions, and 'embed' them with specially-filmed documentaries about the making of each one, but there was not a bonus track between them: the Fabs, it seems, do not stoop so low.

We, by contrast, are mere mortals, and this chapter is our own version of the codas-cum-epilogues that are such a central part of the modern music-buyer's life. It started as a run of items that didn't quite fit into the seven chapters that precede it – but then, rather spookily, the vague outlines of a subtext started to emerge: that of death, and rock'n'roll's rather sinister and stupid relationship with it.

You know the drill: 'Live fast, die young, and leave a beautiful corpse'. This is – obviously – a crock, not just because the fun of living fast soon gives way to grinding hangovers and horrible dysfunction (like most human beings, intoxicated rock stars are really no fun at all), but also because the 'beautiful corpse' bit usually turns out to be some way wide of the mark. Keith Moon died looking ten years older than he actually was. Elvis's cadaver was anything but pretty. The same applied to Jim Morrison. Even poor old Sid Vicious, dead at 22, had seen better days. In the last passages of their lives, none of them were happy, or productive, or much capable of their old creative feats (poor old Sid probably never managed many anyway). Their fate wasn't terribly romantic, or inspiring; theirs was not an example anyone in their right mind would follow.

But still, there is a grim fascination about what happened to them, evident every time people crowd into the 'meditation garden' at Elvis's renowned home Graceland, or drift into Père Lachaise cemetery, to stare at Morrison's marker and share the company of intense French people who tend to tug on their joints, mutter bits of old Doors songs, and thereby pay tribute to 'Jeem'. This writer, it has to be said, has often felt drawn to music's death-cults, and has spent time at the grave sites of such tragically-lost talents as Hank Williams, Nick Drake, and Gram Parsons (the blues pioneer Robert Johnson has three, which makes things that bit more interesting). Some of the thoughts that have thus come to mind are represented here, like this one: why do so many musicians die when they're 27? After that, in case anyone fancies setting off on the grave-trail, there is a guide to the relevant sites scattered around the UK, near such unlikely spots as Macclesfield, Cheltenham and Rushock, in Worcestershire.

Anyway, it's getting a little heavy in here. Well away from the dark stuff, this chapter also features an alternative history of British music television which includes both the late Peter Cook (death again, see?) and Keith Chegwin. There are reminders of history's greatest fictional bands, and the fondness of musicians for surmising that a normal name is no name at all and restyling themselves, from Ol' Dirty Bastard (RIP), through Buckethead and Palm Olive, and on to The Wonder Stuff's The Bass Thing – aka Rob Jones, who also died young, the reminder of which once again led to the feeling that this chapter was a little bit haunted. There is also a brief look at some of music's most unlikely collaborations, which includes the late Robert Palmer, something that nearly sent us over the edge.

Thankfully, as a means of cheering everyone up and looking to the future, there's also an item about notable rock offspring – because as well as dying, musicians manage to reproduce, and their story thus goes on, and on and on…

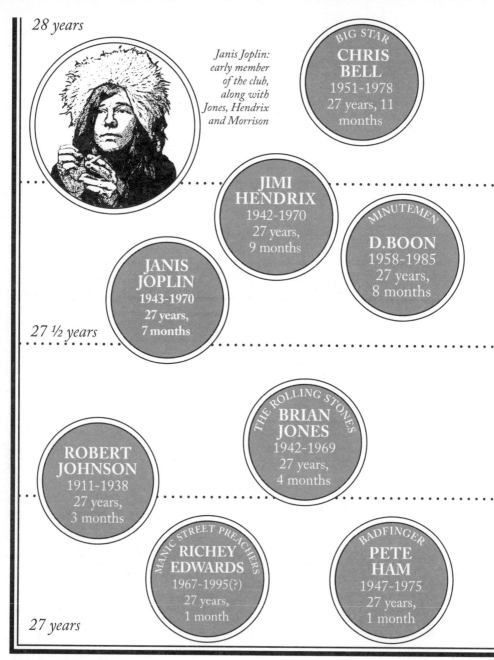

28 years

*Janis Joplin:*
*early member*
*of the club,*
*along with*
*Jones, Hendrix*
*and Morrison*

BIG STAR
**CHRIS
BELL**
1951-1978
27 years, 11
months

**JIMI
HENDRIX**
1942-1970
27 years,
9 months

MINUTEMEN
**D. BOON**
1958-1985
27 years,
8 months

**JANIS
JOPLIN**
1943-1970
27 years,
7 months

27 ½ years

THE ROLLING STONES
**BRIAN
JONES**
1942-1969
27 years,
4 months

**ROBERT
JOHNSON**
1911-1938
27 years,
3 months

MANIC STREET PREACHERS
**RICHEY
EDWARDS**
1967-1995(?)
27 years,
1 month

BADFINGER
**PETE
HAM**
1947-1975
27 years,
1 month

27 years

After Kurt Cobain's suicide in April 1994, his mother Wendy O'Connor said that she had told him 'not to join that stupid club' – an apparent reference to the 27 Club, a select organisation reserved for the remarkable number of musicians who've passed away at that age. Why? Big success tends to dawn in people's early-to-mid 20s and often goes sour and dysfunctional a couple of years later, though some people make a lot of 'Saturn's Return', an astrological

**PETE DE FREITAS**
ECHO & THE BUNNYMEN
1961-1989
27 years,
10 months

# THE 27 CLUB
**Much-missed musicians who died young – and the eerie theory of a numerological curse…**

**JIM MORRISON**
THE DOORS
1943-1971
27 years,
7 months

**RON 'PIGPEN' MCKERNAN**
THE GRATEFUL DEAD
1945-1973
27 years,
6 months

27 ½ years

*Kurt Cobain: joined 'that stupid club' despite advice to the contrary*

**ALAN CHRISTIE WILSON**
CANNED HEAT
1943-1970
27 years,
2 months

**KURT COBAIN**
NIRVANA
1967-1994
27 years,
1 month

**KRISTEN PFAFF**
HOLE
1967-1994
27 years,
21 days

**GRAM PARSONS**
1946-1973
26 years,
10 months

event that first occurs in your late 20s. To quote one stargazer, this is when 'things come to an end, hard realisations are faced, and the weight of the world is felt, very acutely.' So, some advice to twentysomething rockers who are feeling a bit peaky: Read your horoscope, and go easy on the drugs.

# BAD NEWS! DOOM! DROSS!

**Beyond the valley of Spinal Tap: fictional bands we have loved (and hated)**

## Animal Kwackers

Shameless British copy of The Banana Splits, invented by ITV in mid-'70s to brighten up young lives blighted by strikes, power cuts etc. Second-hand idea was glaring: whereas animal-based Splits were called Fleegle, Bingo, Drooper and Snorky, similarly faunal Kwackers went under names of Rory, Twang, Boots and Bongo. Strange fact: in first series, latter character was played by drummer Geoff Nicholls, subsequently one of three tutors on much missed BBC series Rockschool.

## Bad News

British metal band invented by three-quarters of The Young Ones – plus actor/writer Peter Richardson – under auspices of The Comic Strip, whose inaugural TV appearance went into production at same time as This Is Spinal Tap, creating impression of plagiarism. Not nearly as funny as the Tap, though character names (Vim Fuego, Den Dennis, Colin Grigson, Spider Webb) weren't bad. They managed two albums – and heroically played Monsters Of Rock festival in 1987 under a volley of urine-filled bottles. Some credit also for call-and-response chorus of Hey Hey Bad News: 'Hey hey, Bad News!'; 'Fuck off, Bad News!'

## The Banned

Six-piece group shoe-horned into script of EastEnders in 1986, built around characters of Sharon, Kelvin and Simon 'Wicksy' Wicks, played by Nick Berry. Managed by one 'Harry Reynolds', middle-class Marxist swiftly nicknamed 'Harry The Bastard' by NME. To cut to the quick: Harry clashed with Wicksy, Wicksy bailed (whereupon lachrymose Nick Berry single Every Loser Wins entered frame), and real-life Banned

single Something Outa [sic] Nothing – credited to Letitia Dean and Paul Medford, aka Sharon and Kelvin – eventually reached No 12 in UK charts.

## Breaking Glass

New Wave troupe at core of eponymous 1980 movie starring songstress Hazel O'Connor as 'Kate', whose career goes nuclear before turning to ash (strap-line on poster was 'The Rock'n'Roll Dream that couldn't last'). Also starred plenty of other talent: Phil Daniels, Jonathan Pryce, Jim Broadbent – and, as guitarist 'Tony', Mark Wingett from The Bill.

## Dr Teeth & The Electric Mayhem

Immortal band from The Muppets. Bandleader and keyboardist Dr Teeth modelled on New Orleans demi-god Dr John; lead guitarist Janis took name from Janis Joplin; ditto sax man Zoot and jazz-guy Zoot Sims. Name of bassist Sgt Floyd Pepper referenced obvious rock icons. Drummer Animal widely understood to have been based on Keith Moon, though creators denied any such intent; his parts were played by one Ronnie Verrell, British jazz drummer who died in 2002.

## Dross

Band inserted into script of Radio 4 soap The Archers in 2002, led by character of Fallon Rogers, also featuring ketamine-guzzling Jack 'Jazzer' McCreary, and pursued by fictional A&R man Curtis Morrison. Music was supplied by Birmingham indie-rock band The Def Offenders, never heard of since.

## The Jingles

Trio of puppet rats – named Stringy, Brassy and Windy – from utterly baffling CBeebies series Space Pirates, resident on illicitly-broadcasting spacecraft where they perform cover versions. Songs done up until March 2008 included

*Animal: the personification of 'Electric Mayhem'*

The Beach Boys' Fun Fun Fun, Booker T
& The MGs' Green Onions, and Van
Halen's Jump.

## The Little Ladies
All-female trio who formed basis of ITV show
Rock Follies (1976-77), treatment of the LLs'
ill-starred career with songs by Roxy Music's
Andy McKay. Parts of Devonia Rhoades, Anna
Wynd and Nancy Cunard de Longchamps
respectively played by singer/actress Julie
Covington, Charlotte Cornwell and Rula
Lenska, subsequently famed for encouraging
George Galloway's cat impression on Celebrity
Big Brother. Idea spawned one real-life Top 10
hit; second series also featured Bob Hoskins.

## Jim Maclaine & The Stray Cats
1974 rise-and-fall film Stardust was based
around rock star played by David Essex; band
– of no relation to '80s US rockabilly trio – was
composed of characters played by Brit comedy
perennial Paul Nicholas, Welsh rocker Dave
Edmunds, Keith Moon, Blue Peter bloke
Peter Duncan, and Karl Howman, best known
for '80s sitcom Brush Strokes. In film, band
get the hump with Maclaine's dominance,
whereupon he begins solo career and slide
towards decadence – and, eventually, death.

## The Maws Of Doom
Sub-plot in Jonathan Coe's 2001 novel
about adolescence in the 1970s, turned into
three-part TV series, finds key characters
Ben Trotter and Philip Chase attempting to
form progressive rock band in late 1976, and
convening rehearsal at which musicians are
invited to perform 'a rock symphony in five
movements'. Drummer and singer rebel, opt
instead for 'riotous three-chord thrash', and
thus accidentally form The Maws Of Doom;
what Trotter calls 'our school's first punk band'.

## The Partridge Family
Heroes of quintessentially '70s US TV show
(1970-74) in which single mum and offspring
tour America in garishly-painted bus. Sparked
rise of teen idol David Cassidy (aka Keith
Partridge), though arguably more notable for
presence of faux-bassist Danny Bonaduce
(Danny Partridge), whose subsequent life
amounted to cautionary tale about life after
child stardom, taking in drug abuse, two
divorces, and arrest for assaulting a transvestite.
He's now that bit more stable, with interests
including charity boxing: among his opponents
has been Donny Osmond (they fought in
1994; Bonaduce won).

## The Rutles
Well-covered stars of inspired Beatles spoof
at centre of 1978 TV movie All You Need
Is Cash – co-written by Python Eric Idle
and associate Python Neil Innes – with roots
in mid-'70s BBC series Rutland Weekend
Television. But note other made-up groups
referenced in script: Crosby, Stills, Nash,
Young, Gifted & Black, Punk Floyd, and Les
Garçons De La Plage (think about it).

## Stillwater
Stereotypical '70s rock band created for
autobiographical Cameron Crowe film Almost
Famous (2000), said to be an amalgam of Led
Zep, the Allman Brothers, Lynyrd Skynyrd
and The Eagles. Songs were written by Crowe,
wife Nancy Wilson (of big-haired sister act
Heart) and soft-rocker Peter Frampton. Part
of guitarist Russell Hammond – played by
Billy Crudup – was written for Brad Pitt, who
claimed he 'just didn't get it enough'. D'oh!

## The Thamesmen
Early name of Spinal Tap; in 1984's This Is
Spinal Tap, clip shows them playing Stones-
esque song Gimme Some Money circa 1965 –
bizarrely, song was later used for an American
Express TV ad. In footnotes of Tap legend,
there are at least four other band names: The
Originals, The New Originals, Anthem and –
maybe best of all – The Cadburys.

## The Wonders
Early '60s band whose story defines That
Thing You Do, throwaway 1996 movie written
and directed by Tom Hanks and centred
around Guy Patterson, jazz-loving drummer
who momentarily falls in with teen-pop
quartet before brief success – masterminded
by Hanks character Mr White – causes
terminal tensions, and he closes film on arm
of Liv Tyler character Faye Dolan. In real
life, Tyler soon took up with one Royston
Langdon, bassist/drummer with very un-
Wonders-like British band Spacehog; they
separated in 2003.

193

# THAT'S NOT MY NAME!

## A 19-stage masterclass in the art of the rock pseudonym. Sting? Schming!

**The Bass Thing** 1964-1993
*Real Name: Rob Jones* Bassist with Midlands indie specialists The Wonder Stuff between 1986 and 1989. Name seemingly came from knobbly-faced, dreadlocked, child-scaring appearance. Moved to the USA, where he died of a heroin overdose.

**Ariel Bender** b.1946
*RN: Luther Grosvenor* Native of Evesham, Worcestershire, who in 1973 replaced guitarist Mick Ralphs in Mott The Hoople. Thanks to contractual problems, needed a pseudonym – and Mott chief Ian Hunter remembered '70s songstress Lynsey De Paul coining name after watching Ralphs vandalising car aerials.

**Jello Biafra** b.1958
*RN: Eric Boucher* Founder of Californian punks the Dead Kennedys. Name combines the famous brand name of US gelatine products and the name of the would-be country at the centre of the Nigerian civil war of 1967-70, starved into submission by a blockade. Boucher chose it in 1978 after picking words at random, and later explained that he liked 'the way the two images collide in people's minds'.

**Buckethead** b.1969
*RN: Brian Carroll* Virtuosic guitarist and, between 2000 and 2004, member of in-limbo Guns N' Roses. Name comes from his insistence on wearing – along with a white mask – a bucket on his head, most famously from KFC, though these days he prefers a standard-issue hardware-shop number.

**Captain Sensible** b.1954
*RN: Raymond Burns* Stage names abounded in The Damned (see also Rat Scabies, below, guitarist **Brian James**, né Robertson, and singer **Dave Vanian**, né Letts), because of common punk syndrome whereby musicians wanted to avoid attention of DHSS. En route to the 1976 Mont de Marsan festival in South West France, Burns wore a shirt with epaulettes and pretended to be a pilot; another musician shot back, 'Oh, it's fucking Captain Sensible.' And lo, a legend was born.

194

**The House Of Lords** b.1976
*RN: Thomas Dartnall* Bassist with UK indie trio Young Knives, so named by his guitarist-vocalist brother Henry because 'he is the band's second chamber, constantly vetoing our great ideas'.

**Lydia Lunch** b.1949
*RN: Lydia Koch* Mouthy figurehead of New York 'no wave' scene and co-founder of Teenage Jesus And The Jerks, given name after she relocated to Manhattan from her native Rochester and regularly stole meals for friends.

**Meat Loaf** b.1951
*RN: Marvin Lee Aday* How to convert a schoolyard slur into a global(ish) brand. According to legend, around 1964 the already-sizable Aday trod on the foot of his high school football coach, who yelped, 'Get off me, you big lump of meatloaf.'

*Ol' Dirty Bastard*

**Ol' Dirty Bastard** 1968-2004
*RN: Russell Jones* Member of the Wu-Tang Clan, peppered with pseudonyms a cut above the hip hop norm (e.g. **Ghostface Killa**, **Inspectah Decks**). In keeping with WTC's love of martial arts, ODB took name from Guai Zhao Ruan Pi She, 1980 Taiwanese film whose title was translated for US market as 'Ol' Dirty And The Bastard'. Known to his mum as Rusty; died of a drugs overdose.

**Blackie Onassis** b.1967
*RN: Johnny Rowan* One-time drummer with Chicago indie ironists Urge Overkill. Stage names were a UO trademark (see also singer **National [or Nash] Kato**, aka Nathan Katruud). Rowan's paid homage to both ex-First Lady Jackie and W.A.S.P. heavy metaller **Blackie Lawless** (né Steven Duren).

**Palm Olive** b.1955
*RN: Paloma Romero* Spanish girlfriend of **Joe Strummer** (né John Mellor) and drummer with The Slits. Given name by Clash bassist Paul Simonon, renowned for fondness for nicknames (he gave Clash drummer Nicky 'Topper' Headon his because of Headon's resemblance to Micky The Monkey from UK comic The Topper). Nonplussed by her first name, Simonon used soundalike iconic soap brand. The Slits' first line-up was led by singer **Ari Up** (née Ariane Forster) and included guitarist Viv Albertine, which sounds like a stage name, but actually isn't.

**Porkbeast** b.1967
*RN: Alex Peach* Somewhat rotund bassist with Leicester 'grebo' band Crazyhead (line-up also included guitarist **Kev Reverb**, aka Kevin Bayliss, and drummer **Vom**, aka Robert Morris). Subsequently got a PhD in Social History, though still active in an East Midlands-based troupe called Stressbitch.

**Twiggy Ramirez** b.1971
*RN: Jeordie White* Bassist. Best example of wheeze whereby, in the mid-1990s, **Marilyn Manson** (né Brian Warner) insisted that his band members follow his lead and combine names of female icons and serial killers: see also **Madonna Wayne Gacy** (né Stephen Bier), **Ginger Fish** (né Kenneth Wilson) and **Daisy Berkowitz** (né Scott Putesky – we're short on space here, but this one fused Daisy Duke from TV's The Dukes Of Hazard and David Berkowitz, '70s murderer known as Son Of Sam). Ramirez stuck together British proto-supermodel and Richard Ramirez, an '80s killer who terrified Los Angeles.

**Zoot Horn Rollo** b.1948
*RN: Bill Harkelroad* Guitarist with best name in Trout Mask Replica-era incarnation of **Captain Beefheart**'s Magic Band, also including bassist **Rockette Morton** (né Mark Boston), co-guitarist **Antennae Jimmy Semens** (né Jeff Cotton), clarinet player **The Mascara Snake** (né Victor Hayden) and drummer **Drumbo** (né John French). In 1993, the Captain (né, of course, Don van Vliet) said this: 'I didn't care for their names. And they seemed to be related to their mama and papa. And I don't think I'd get along with their mama and papa. So I gave them the names.'

*Poly Styrene*

**Poly Styrene** b.1957
*RN: Marian Elliott* Kent-born singer with artful, saxophone-assisted punks X Ray Spex; her name reflected her fixation with 'plastic artificial living' (band also featured guitarist **Jak Airport**, aka Jack Stafford). Famed for braces on her teeth; in the 1980s, she became a Hare Krishna devotee.

**Rat Scabies** b.1957
*RN: Christopher Millar* Drummer with The Damned until 1996. Given name at pre-Damned rehearsals with The Clash's Mick Jones, when 1)Millar had scabies, and 2)Jones saw a rat. Simple, really.

**Johnnny Thunders** 1952-1991
*RN: John Genzale Jr* New York Dolls guitarist (they also featured co-guitarist **Sylvain Sylvain**, né Sylvain Mizrahi) who turned the Keith Richards drugs/falling over ethic into a cartoon, and then imported it into punk rock via his band the Heartbreakers. Name was nicked from Johnny Thunder, DC comics character created in 1940.

**Muddy Waters** 1915-1983
*RN: McKinley Morganfield* Blues god who was given name 'Muddy' by his grandma, thanks to childhood fondness for playing in rivers, streams etc. He added 'Water' as his renown spread through Mississippi. The finished article arrived after he moved to Chicago and made his second single for Chess records; a printer mistakenly put on the extra 's'.

**Jah Wobble** b.1958
*RN: John Wardle* Sex Pistols acolyte, close friend of **Johnny Rotten** (né Lydon), bassist with Public Image Ltd and eventual world music hybridist. Accidentally given name by a drunk **Sid Vicious** (né Simon Ritchie, later John Beverly) in 1976: slur his real name, and it all becomes obvious (clearly, the Lydon circle's obligatory love of reggae is in there too).

# 'It could be the perfect marriage...'
## 'Interesting' collaborations that you'd never have seen coming

### Paul Weller & Peter Gabriel (1979)

In mid-1979, Peter Gabriel's American record company heard a work-in-progress titled All Through The Wire, and asked him to make it sound 'more like the Doobie Brothers'. The ex-Genesis singer was having none of it – and seeing as The Jam were recording in an adjacent studio in Shepherd's Bush, he asked Paul Weller to contribute a scabrous guitar part. 'I just love watching him play,' said Gabriel. 'He's like liquid energy.' And what a surprise: the finished song sounded absolutely nothing like the Doobie Brothers.

*Palmer & Perry: 'too abstract'*

### Lou Reed & Kiss (1982)

By the early 1980s, the Kabuki-styled rock gods were fading fast. The solution: (Music From) The Elder, an esoteric rock opera set in a Tolkien-esque alternative universe. By way of outside input, they recruited producer Bob Ezrin (fresh from working on Pink Floyd's The Wall), and the stratospherically incongruous Lou Reed, who co-wrote three songs. When one of Kiss's management team heard the results, he said: 'The album doesn't sound anything like Kiss and no one is going to buy a Kiss album that doesn't sound like Kiss.' He wasn't wrong: it got no higher than No 75 on the US charts.

### Van Morrison & Cliff Richard (1989)

What larks: the legendarily grumpy Belfast blues-mystic roped in Cliff for a seasonal tribute to The Almighty entitled Whenever God Shines His Light, which reached No 20 in the UK charts, and was honoured with a spot on Top Of The Pops. 'He's a professional,' Morrison said of Richard. 'It's great working with somebody like that. He couldn't be around this long if he wasn't a great singer. I think he does himself down, though – underestimates himself.'

### Robert Palmer & Lee Perry (1978)

In 1978, the Batley-born lounge lizard travelled to Jamaica to work at the inestimable reggae producer Lee 'Scratch' Perry's Black Ark studio. 'You know those joke spliffs you see that are, like, nine inches long?' he later

196

recalled. 'They'd make them out of brown paper and just constantly smoke…It was quite an experience being in there, like, 10 hours a day.' They recorded four songs, but Palmer thought they sounded 'too abstract', and binned them – though one Perry track, Love Can Run Faster, appeared as a B-side. Jah evidently did not approve: within a year, the Black Ark had burned to the ground.

### Elton John & Eminem (2001)

No matter that Eminem's 2000 track Criminal contained the line 'Hate fags? The answer's yes' – these two paired off for a heartwarming rendition of Eminem's global hit Stan at the Grammy Awards in 2001. 'Let the Boy Georges and the George Michaels of the world get in a twist about it if they don't have the intelligence to see his intelligence,' said Sir Elt. So that was them told.

### Texas & the Wu-Tang Clan (1998)

Having re-established their career with 1997's White On Blonde, the Glaswegian troupe led by Sharleen Spiteri reworked their big hit Say What You Want with Method Man and RZA from the martial arts-obsessed hip hop collective. 'Method Man is just a wicked, wicked rapper,' said Spiteri. 'I can't wait to hear the combination of my vocals and his… I have a kind of sweet, virginal thing going on, and he's got this dirty sex vibe. It could be the perfect marriage.' It really wasn't, though in Holland, the 'wicked' new treatment was a bigger hit than the original. True!

# I'm a substitute for another guy
## Those injury-time members of classic bands

**Tetsu Yamauchi** *Faces*
Bassist who was fleetingly a member of Free before replacing Ronnie Lane in the Faces (also featuring Rod Stewart, obviously). He's on the fag-end live album Coast To Coast: Overture And Beginners (1973) and the singles Pool Hall Richard (1973) and You Can Make Me Dance, Sing Or Anything (1974). Has since spent his time playing jazz in his native Japan, including a stint with the gloriously named Kamadoma-Poly Breath Percussion Orchestra.

**Ray Wilson** *Genesis*
In 1996 Phil Collins left Genesis, so Tony Banks and Mike Rutherford got in the Scots singer with Stiltskin, whose Levi's-ad single Inside was a UK No 1 in 1994. There was one Wilson/Banks/Rutherford album, Calling All Stations, before it all went south in 1998. A decade on, he fronts a band called Ray Wilson and Stiltskin, and has also put in time with a project called Genesis Klassik, doing Genesis numbers with the Berlin Symphony Ensemble. Form an orderly queue, etc.

**Blaze Bayley** *Iron Maiden*
Born Bayley Cook, in case you were wondering. For a taste of this Birmingham-born metaller's genius, go back to page 51. Having done ten years with the inestimable Wolfsbane, he was chosen to replace the departed Bruce Dickinson in Iron Maiden: two underwhelming albums followed and, by 2000, Dickinson was back, leaving BB 'bitterly disappointed'. Has since sounded more upbeat: 'Iron Maiden are the most important heavy metal band in the history of the world and I was a part of that.'

**Robbie Maddix** *The Stone Roses*
In late 1994 the Roses released Second Coming but didn't do much to support it, and in March 1995, drummer Alan 'Reni' Wren mysteriously went on his way, replaced by 25-year-old Maddix, a former drummer with long-lost British rapper the Rebel MC. He stuck with the Roses through their career-killing show at Reading '96 until their final split, a few weeks later. Has since attempted a solo career; in 2007, he supported Ian Brown on a UK tour.

**Nick Sheppard & Vince White** *The Clash*
Along with drummer Pete Howard, servants of 'the Cut The Crap Clash', named after the cruddy album of the same name. Sheppard had played with punk also-rans The Cortinas; the real name of 'Vince' was actually Greg, considered non-U by bassist Paul Simonon. By late 1985, it was over (though Simonon and manager Bernie Rhodes are said to have auditioned singers for a post-Joe Strummer Clash, surely not one of history's better ideas).

**Doug Yule** *The Velvet Underground*
The man who replaced John Cale in The Velvet Underground, played – and sang – on their third and fourth LPs (and 1985's reclaimed collection VU), and even piloted a last-ditch line-up featuring no original members – witness the 1973 album Squeeze. Subsequently worked as a carpenter, and was passed over for their big 1993 reunion. 'I don't know without being asked, but I'm pretty sure I would've said no,' he reckoned. Yeah, *right*.

*Faces with Tetsu (far left): next stop, the Kamadoma-Poly Breath Percussion Orchestra*

# GET YOUR ROCK'S OFFSPRING

**Talented(ish) spawn of some of music's greatest stars. And Bob Geldof**

**Rolan Bolan** *b.1975*
Only son of Marc Bolan and Gloria Jones, singer of the original Northern Soul version of Tainted Love (1964). When he died, she and Bolan senior weren't married: their son's childhood was thus threatened by 'virtual poverty', though he says David Bowie generously chipped in (e.g. paying for a private education). As of 2007, he's seen some Bolan-related cash, which may be just as well: a low-profile musical career (and yes, he doesn't mind playing some of Dad's stuff) presumably doesn't cover that much food, fuel etc.

**Jakob Dylan** *b.1969*
Youngest sprog of Bob and Sara Dylan, a union that also produced Jesse, Anna and Samuel. Despite spurts of solo activity, still seemingly in charge of mainstream Americana-ish troupe The Wallflowers. Their 1996 album Bringing Down The Horse 'did' six million copies worldwide, though inevitably it didn't compare to the best Dylan senior LPs. Still, he's long since adjusted to all that: 'If the barometer for all songwriters was to match his body of work, then anyone you might mention alive or dead is a failure. But I've learned to not be too hung up on what's fair or not fair.' And fair play to him, eh?

**Liam Finn** *b.1983*
Eldest son of Crowded House lynchpin Neil Finn, with one album currently to his name: 2007's I'll Be Lightning, in roughly the same vein as the late US singer-songwriter Elliott Smith. His closest collaborator is Eliza-Jane Barnes, daughter of Aussie rock star Jimmy Barnes (Google him, mate). Has toured with the 'House since their 2007 reformation, but perhaps deserving of most respect for his own pretty accomplished stuff, and a voluminous beard.

**Peaches Geldof**
*b.1989*
Not a musician, though she does DJ as part of a duo called – oh, go on then – the 'Trash Pussies'. Aside from her Dad, has links to rock via relationships with Faris Badwan of Goth-ish indie-rock

troupe The Horrors, the irksome Donny Tourette of Towers Of London, and one Max Drummey, of the not-exactly-happening US duo Chester French (the latter was married to PG for six months). As well as the obligatory Reality TV and modelling, in 2006 she presented a Channel 4 programme called The Beginner's Guide To Islam, which eased global tensions at a stroke. Possibly.

**Julian Lennon**
*b.1963*
Son of Beatle John and mum Cynthia, and a fleeting pop star twice – in 1984 (when Too Late For Goodbyes

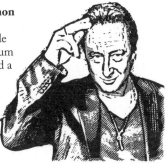

reached No 6 in the UK), and 1991 (the rather icky eco-ballad Saltwater, No 6 again). A few years later, he claimed that Lennon Senior 'could talk about peace and love out loud to the world, but he could never show it to the people who supposedly meant most to him', though by 2009 he had seemingly mellowed: 'I have nothing but love for him now,' he said. Now lives in Northern Italy, claims to be 'a happy camper', and says his once-extremely-difficult relationship with Yoko Ono is 'OK'.

### Sean Lennon *b.1975*

Son of Beatle John and mum Yoko, with a solo catalogue numbering three albums. Has also played with Japanese-American duo Cibo Matto, The Strokes' Albert Hammond Jr – and his mother. Somewhat rum fact: as well as starring in Michael Jackson's film Moonwalker, spent time as a child at Jacko's home, along with his friend, future DJ/producer Mark Ronson, who has since claimed that they illicitly watched TV porn, but what with him being such a responsible sort, the 'King Of Pop' disapproved.

### Ziggy Marley *b.1968*

Eldest son of Bob and Rita Marley, officially named David. Along with siblings Cedella, Stephen and Sharon, formed Ziggy Marley And The Melody Makers, who had a solitary burst of UK success in 1988 when the single Tomorrow People made it to No 22. Now on to his third solo album, but the MMs are still going. Note also their half-brother Rohan Marley, married to the ex-Fugee Lauryn Hill, with whom he has five kids.

### Lisa-Marie Presley *b.1968*

Only child of The King – and Priscilla, obviously – whose personal life has been rather lively: at the time of writing she was on to her fourth marriage, past husbands having included that well-known Elvis fanatic Nicolas Cage – who filed for divorce after 108 days – and the late Michael Jackson ('If you lined up all the men I've been with in a row, you'd think I was completely psychotic'). After long making music in private, began her singing career aged 35, and has thus far put out two albums of achingly safe radio-rock, delivered in a strangely deep voice. Oh, and she's a Scientologist, obviously.

### Chris Stills *b.1974*

Dad is Stephen Stills, as in Crosby, Stills, Nash (& Young). Partly raised in Paris by his French mother; in 1990s New York he briefly served in a band with Adam 'Son of Leonard' Cohen, before opting for a solo career (of sorts), and releasing an album called 100 Year Thing in 1998. It didn't do much and, at the time of writing, he was in France, playing Julius Caesar in a rather naff rock musical version of Cleopatra (in French, obviously).

### Teddy Thompson *b.1976*

Eldest of two kids born to folk-rock luminaries Richard and Linda Thompson (younger sister Kamila is also a musician), whose very early years were played out in a spartan London Sufi Muslim commune. Has played with both ma and pa, though his solo career is the main event. His fourth album, A Piece Of What You Need (2008) was praised to the skies, and deservedly so: in his own quietly-spoken way, he just about transcends his parentage (unlike, say, the aforementioned Ms Geldof). NB: he's also pally with this pair…

### Rufus & Martha Wainwright *b.1973 & 1976*

Brother and sister brought into the world by US singer-songwriter Loudon Wainwright III and Canadian folkie Kate McGarrigle. Rufus has managed a productive and pretty successful career since 1998. Martha's oeuvre (two albums, at the time of writing) has been a bit more erratic: her self-titled first album (2005) was pretty great, though 2008's I Know You're Married But I've Got Feelings Too didn't quite match it. For a glimpse of the worst kind of father-daughter relations, have a listen to her infamous song Bloody Mother Fucking Asshole, which Loudon must have been thrilled with.

### Dweezil Zappa *b.1969*

What a card the late Frank Zappa was: with his second wife Gail, he fathered daughters named Moon Unit (later shortened to 'Moon') and Diva, and sons Ahmet and Dweezil – though the latter's name was initially registered as Ian because an LA hospital refused to play ball. Dweezil later had the 'D' word officially recognised and set out on a career path split between acting (e.g. his cameo role in 1986's Pretty In Pink) and being a musician. Since 2006 he's been in charge of a touring tribute to his dad called Zappa Plays Zappa. His name, incidentally, comes from a nickname good old Frank had for one of his wife's toes. Brilliant!

# THE ALTERNATIVE HISTORY OF MUSIC TV

## Cue David Essex! Cue 'Cheggers'! Cue some bloke off Basil Brush!

**Six-Five Special** BBC1 *(then known as BBC TV)*, *1957-58*
Auntie Beeb's first attempt to get with the rock programme. 'Time to jive on the old six five,' said host and DJ Pete Murray, before introducing the hard-rocking likes of Cleo Laine, Lonnie Donegan and early Brit-rocker Marty Wilde – who, relative to most of his company, must have looked like Sid Vicious. Producer Jack Good soon jumped to ITV to invent the superior Oh Boy!, whereupon the BBC haughtily canned SFS and left rock'n'roll pretty much alone until the advent of Top Of The Pops.

**Thank Your Lucky Stars** *ITV, 1961-66*
Reasonably long-running pop-fest, forever overshadowed by the infinitely cooler Ready Steady Go!. Fair play, though: The Beatles made their national TV debut on TYLS, as did the Stones. Note also the famous 'Spin-a-disc' section, in which one DJ and three kid-on-the-street-type adolescents reviewed and rated new releases, which briefly made a star of 16-year-old Midlander Janice Nicholls, author of the catchphrase 'I'll give it five' (or 'Oi'll give it foive'). She made a novelty record of the same name. It was not a hit.

*Keith 'Cheggers' Chegwin: after playing pop, he rested*

**Supersonic** *ITV, 1975-77*
Subtly strange kids' music programme that achieved its brief glory phase on weekday afternoons, though it started and finished in Saturday morning slots. Silver-haired director/producer Mike Mansfield (later responsible for peak-period Adam And The Ants videos and the soporific in-concert series Cue The Music) doubled as a low-key presenter, sitting in the control room and uttering such lines as 'David Essex, Rock On, cue music.' It managed two series: in among Slade, Mud, Marc Bolan et al were three appearances by Albert Hammond, dad of the same-named Strokes guitarist.

**Get It Together!** *ITV, 1977-81*
Pop-centred children's show that seems like something from the 19th century. Co-hosted by sometime Basil Brush sidekick Roy North (that's his second mention in this book, for some reason), who introduced a grim selection of bands – e.g. the fag-end Bay City Rollers – and closed the show with an unnecessary rendition of a current hit, as well as singing the title tune: 'Get it together/Everybody now, let's have a good time/Put your hand together with mine.' Grim, in a word.

**Rock Goes To College** BBC2 *1978-81*
Oooh! Clever title! Straightforward enough wheeze whereby 'album-orientated' groups familiar with the University/Polytechnic circuit had between eight and 15 (approximately, obviously) songs screened on TV. Initially, given the non-invention of stereo television, it was simultaneously broadcast on Radio 1 FM, so viewers could turn the sound down and put the speakers either side of their 'set'. Highlights: John Martyn, AC/DC, The Specials. Low points: fusioneers Spiro Gyra, grunt-rockers The Climax Blues Band, vapid early Paul Young vehicle the Q-Tips.

## Revolver *ITV, 1978*

Lasted a mere eight episodes. Produced by music svengali Mickie Most, who aimed at something very different from Top Of The Pops-esque light entertainment and fancied a bit of the upsurge by then curdling into 'New Wave'. Hosted by Peter Cook, who played the manager of the venue where it was set, and camply affected to loathe a lot of what was on. His introduction to The Stranglers ran thus: 'It is very seldom that you come across a group you really like – and this group are no exception. I really don't like them at all.'

## Cheggers Plays Pop *BBC1, 1979-86*

Afternoon kids' creation that lasted a TV lifetime, hosted by Swap Shop mainstay Keith Chegwin and based around a three-way package: mimed performances by often desperate groups, a central pop quiz segment, and inexplicable 'games' in which schoolkids got waylaid on huge inflatables and covered in foam. Incidental fact: though not selected for games/the quiz, the author of this book was on it, cheering on his school in May 1982, in a show that featured faux-rockabilly chancers Coast To Coast and pseudo-world music troupe Monsoon, both promoting singles that completely stiffed.

## Gas Tank *Channel 4, 1982-83*

A genuinely weird one. Hosted by sometime Yes keyboard man Rick Wakeman and Tony Ashton (1946-2001, co-founder of '70s trio Ashton, Gardner & Dyke) and built around an in-studio 'jam' heavy on booze and cigarette smoke, and seemingly always featuring raddled figureheads of the pre-punk era, e.g. The Who's John Entwistle, Deep Purple's Ian Paice, Ten Years After's Alvin Lee. It couldn't last, and it didn't.

## The Roxy *ITV, 1988*

Ill-starred attempt to break the mainstream dominance of Top Of The Pops by – that's right! – making a crap version of it. Co-hosted by sometime Radio 1 DJ David 'Kid' Jensen and Irishman Kevin Sharkey (these days, a successful painter), and filmed in Newcastle, which may have caused its quick death: for too many sensitive artists, the prospect of travelling 'oop North' for a three-minute mime slot apparently proved too much.

## Snub TV *BBC2, 1987-89*

Half-hour, none-more-indie show – part of Janet Street Porter's early-evening 'Def II' package – in which up-and-coming sensations on the music press/toilet venue treadmill did their musical thing and were interviewed. The voiceovers – mainly by producer Brenda Kelly – had a strangely bored quality; the show featured such acts as Primal Scream, Manic Street Preachers, the Sugarcubes, fleetingly-big Mancunian rapper MC Tunes and good old Dog Faced Hermans.

## Rapido *BBC2, 1988-92*

Another Def II mainstay: actually created in France, and syndicated to around 14 countries. In the UK version, borderline unbearable but somehow very funny host Antoine De Caunes (who later hosted the woeful Eurotrash) simply did his thing in bad English, which was all part of the fun. The recipe was simple: a handful of items in which behind-the-scenes reportage was mixed with interviews. Most legendary film: The Stone Roses in 1989, spending ten minutes being impossibly bored (sample quote from Ian Brown: 'It's hard for us to act interested when we're not, innit lads?')

## Naked City *Channel 4, 1993-94*

It's-all-happening weekly show with an indie-rock tilt, hosted by then-18-year-old future Times writer Caitlin Moran and a presenter-at-large role for soon-come Big Breakfast presenter Johnny Vaughan. Ticked most of the 'yoof TV' boxes – as proved by, say, an interview with long-lost shoegazers Curve in a sex shop ('The underlying current of sex is to express love to somebody else,' said singer Toni Halliday). Caught the first stirrings of Britpop, but was cruelly axed before it all got going.

## The Jo Whiley Show *Channel 4, 1998*

Slightly irksome 'post-pub' show – now pretty much airbrushed from history – in which the breathy Radio 1 DJ attempted interesting conversations with a three-strong panel (e.g. Suede's Brett Anderson, John Power out of Cast and Neneh Cherry) about the current state of rock, with the odd live performance as a bonus. A typical moment: The Divine Comedy's Neil Hannon scandalising fellow guests by claiming that Aqua's Barbie Girl was a work of genius. Oooh! Controversial!

# DON'T BE CRUEL!

## We won't. But when it comes to Elvis's 31 screen roles, it's a bit tempting...

**Love Me Tender** *1956* **Elvis plays:** *Clint Reno* Set in the US Civil War, with plot revolving around a robbery and a love triangle. Elvis dies at the end; mum Gladys was reportedly very upset. **Is it any good?** It's alright(ish).

**Loving You** *1957* **EP:** *Deke Rivers* His first colour movie. Boils down his early career into a tangled plot whereby Elvis is fancied by two women, joins a travelling musical roadshow and alerts white squares to rock'n'roll. **ISAG?** A stop-gap, frankly.

**Jailhouse Rock** *1957* **EP:** *Vince Everett* B&W again. Elvis/Vince is jailed, but develops his musical talent and stars in a TV broadcast. When he's out, he becomes a star, but things get very complicated. **ISAG?** A pretty great R'n'R period piece.

**King Creole** *1958* **EP:** *Danny Fisher* Based on a Harold Robbins novel. B&W, and set in New Orleans, mixing up Elvis/Danny's singing talent with gangland intrigue. Also stars Walter Matthau. **ISAG?** It really is.

**GI Blues** *1960* **EP:** *Tulsa McLean* Bland Elvsploitation, in colour (as are all films from hereon in). First of nine Elvis movies directed by one Norman Taurog, and aimed at dramatising his time in the army. **ISAG?** Endurable rather than enjoyable.

**Flaming Star** *1960* **EP:** *Pacer Burton* Much better: almost song-free Western about the tensions between Native Americans and white ranchers, with Elvis caught in the middle as a mixed-race character. **ISAG?** Yes!

**Wild In The Country** *1961* **EP:** *Glenn Tyler* Serious screenplay by leftie US dramatist Clifford Odets: Elvis plays a damaged youth, placed in the care of a psychiatrist, and troubled by family dysfunction. **ISAG?** Better than some of his films, but very flawed.

**Blue Hawaii** *1961* **EP:** *Chad Gate* Norman Taurog returns, with plot revolving around love, swimming trunks and Elvis/Chad avoiding a job in his parents' pineapple cannery. **ISAG?** What do you think?

**Follow That Dream** *1962* **EP:** *Toby Kwimper* A dirt-poor family pitch up in Florida but are hindered by local busybodies, including a social worker romantically spurned by Elvis/Toby. **ISAG?** OK, but not quite Steinbeckian.

**Kid Galahad** *1962* **EP:** *Walter Gulick* Despite obligatory song segments, his last real stab at serious acting: a remake of a 1937 Bogart-starring drama involving boxing and the corruption therein. **ISAG?** Middling.

**Girls! Girls! Girls!** *1962* **EP:** *Ross Carpenter* More N. Taurog stuff. Elvis plays a fisherman, whose travails are – no, really – slotted into wafer-thin romantic sub-plots. Includes a musical number called Song Of The Shrimp. **ISAG?** Rubbish! Rubbish! Rubbish!

**It Happened At The World's Fair** *1963* **EP:** *Mike Edwards* Go, Taurog! Elvis is a crop-dusting pilot who goes to the titular event in Seattle and takes a shine to a local nurse, before the story tumbles into stuff about smuggling illegal furs into Canada. **ISAG?** Well, no.

**Fun In Acapulco** *1963* **EP:** *Mike Windgren* Mexico-centred comedy vehicle involving predictable mixture of girls and sun-soaked locations. Also stars Ursula Andress, fresh from Dr No. **ISAG?** Not much fun at all.

**Kissin' Cousins** *1964* **EP:** *Josh Morgan & Jodie Tatum* US Air Force are set on putting a missile base on a Tennessee mountain. Josh is a lieutenant dispatched to convince a mountain-dwelling redneck family to play ball; Jodie (Elvis again, with different hair) is a young hillbilly whose resemblance to Josh points up complicated family ties. **ISAG?** Kitschly diverting, but hardly art.

**Viva Las Vegas** *1964* **EP:** *Lucky Johnson* Elvis/Lucky dreams of winning the Las Vegas Grand Prix. Flame-haired vixen Ann-Margret plays a swimming instructor; she and Elvis cop off and he achieves pole position. Kind of thing. **ISAG?** Again, kitschly diverting etc.

**Roustabout** *1964* **EP:** *Charlie Rogers* Title is the US equivalent of 'odd-job man'. Elvis/Charlie is hired to work for a travelling funfair, before jumping ship to another one – and then returning to save the day. **ISAG?** Not quite The Deer Hunter, really.

**Girl Happy** *1964* **EP:** *Rusty Wells* A balsa-wood plot: Elvis/Rusty is in charge of a band who travel from Chicago to Florida, where he pulls his manager's daughter. **ISAG?** 'Rusty Wells'? Come on.

**Tickle Me** *1965* **EP:** *Lonnie Beal*
More Norman Taurog bollockry: rodeo-centred Western with a buried-treasure storyline, and girls, fighting etc. **ISAG?** No!

**Harum Scarum** *1965* **EP:** *Johnny Tyrone*
The tag-line read: 'Elvis brings the big beat to Bagdad [sic] in a riotous, rockin', rollin' adventure spoof.' He plays a film star on tour in a Middle East awash with crap racial stereotypes. **ISAG?** To paraphrase Donald Rumsfeld, shocking and awful.

**Frankie And Johnny** *1966* **EP:** *Johnny*
Loosely based on the early 20th-century American song of the same name: Frankie (a woman) and Johnny are a singing duo on a Mississippi riverboat, and he has a gambling problem. Cue all sorts of rum doings. **ISAG?** He did worse, actually.

**Paradise, Hawaiian Style** *1966* **EP:** *Rick Richards* Oh lord. Elvis/Rick is a recently-sacked airline pilot who goes back to his native Hawaii to start a helicopter-flight business with a friend called Danny. But then woman trouble makes everything a bit messy. **ISAG?** *[Pained silence]*

**Spinout** *1966* **EP:** *Mike McCoy* The return of N. Taurog. By now, recycling had set in: Elvis/Rick is in charge of a band (à la Girl Happy) and fond of motor racing (see Viva Las Vegas). He eventually bags off with a drummer called Susan. **ISAG?** Bilge, really.

**Easy Come, Easy Go** *1967* **EP:** *Ted Jackson*
Elvis is a 'navy frogman' who finds – oh yes – some buried treasure. Cue a race for the prize, with a sub-plot about hippies. **ISAG?** Contains a song called Yoga Is As Yoga Does. Which may tell you something.

**Double Trouble** *1967* **EP:** *Guy Lambert*
A Taurog one. Partly set – but not filmed – in London, and based around Elvis's travails as a singer whose life goes wrong en route to Belgium. Also features Norman Rossington, who appeared in The Beatles' A Hard Day's Night. **ISAG?** 'Rather dull,' said one review, politely.

**Clambake** *1967* **EP:** *Scott Hayward*
Elvis's rich-kid character swaps places with a Miami ski instructor so he can see how the other half lives. He also pulls. NB: a clambake is a beach barbecue. **ISAG?** A burned sausage, metaphorically speaking.

**Stay Away, Joe** *1968* **EP:** *Charlie Lightcloud*
A la Flaming Star, Elvis plays a Native American, though the comparisons stop there. Elvis/Charlie is a study in racist stereotyping, and the most notable sub-plot involves cows. **ISAG?** Moooo!

**Speedway** *1968* **EP:** *Steve Grayson* One more for Norman Taurog. Elvis is a stockcar racer, travelling the US with Bill Bixby (also in Clambake) who played Dr Bruce Banner in TV's The Incredible Hulk. Nancy Sinatra is a tax inspector; Elvis gets off with her. Obviously. **ISAG?** Moooo! Again.

**Live A Little, Love A Little** *1968* **EP:** *Greg Nolan* The last Taurog film. Involves Elvis playing an LA photographer and getting involved with a woman called Bernice, who seems to have a personality disorder. Great. **ISAG?** Even fans say this may be his worst.

**Charro!** *1969* **EP:** *Jess Wade* 'A different kind of role,' said the posters. A Western set on the US/Mexican border, and not a musical: Elvis/Jess is accused of theft and decides to prove his innocence by tracking down the guys who did it. **ISAG?** Better than Clambake, anyway.

**The Trouble With Girls** *1969* **EP:** *Walter Hale*
Involves a travelling show who pitch up in Iowa, where Elvis/Walter stumbles upon a murder mystery. Not many songs. **ISAG?** In context, not that bad.

**Change Of Habit** *1969* **EP:** *Dr John Carpenter*
To finish: Elvis is an urban GP, who works with three women, including Mary Tyler-Moore. Why won't she get off with him? Because she's a nun! Chances of Elvis/Mary romance are unclear, even at the end. **ISAG?** Worth watching, in a weird way. Really.

*Elvis and Mary Tyler-Moore: 'Is this as bad as Clambake?'; 'No, you're fine.'*

# WHERE'S YOUR HEADSTONE AT?
### The UK's most notable music-related gravesites

*Note: Though the USA is peppered with rock gravesites, Britain contains surprisingly few, partly because many of our most renowned musicians have resting places that are either known only to their family, or no such site at all. This applies, for example, to such figures as George Harrison, Syd Barrett, Joe Strummer and Sid Vicious.*

## Dusty Springfield 1939-1999
*St Mary's Church, Henley-on-Thames, Oxfordshire*
Springfield died of breast cancer, and her funeral took place in her adopted hometown of Henley-on-Thames. Some of her ashes were scattered off the Cliffs of Moher in County Clare, Southern Ireland, and the rest were laid here, commemorated by a very modest stone that simply features Springfield's name and dates (and the fact that she received an OBE). Fans tend to congregate here on or soon after their annual 'Dusty day', held on the Sunday closest to the date of her birth – 16 April, if you're interested.

## Nick Drake 1948-1974
*St Mary Magdalene Church, Tanworth-in-Arden, Warwickshire*
Drake was killed by an overdose of antidepressants; the coroner recorded a verdict of suicide, which has since been disputed. He was cremated, and his ashes were scattered under an oak tree in the village where he both grew up and spent his last years. The rear of his gravestone is inscribed with the words, 'Now we rise and we are everywhere', in tribute to From The Morning, the last song on his last album, Pink Moon. For the last seven years, each summer has seen the obligatory 'Nick Drake gathering' in Tanworth-in-Arden, and the inevitable graveside tributes. Says one of its organisers: 'People touch it and move their hand over it. It's the closest thing they can think of to meeting Nick and saying thank you.'

## Ian Curtis 1956-1980
*Macclesfield Cemetery and Crematorium, Cheshire*
As portrayed in the films 24 Hour Party People and Control, the Joy Division singer killed himself at his marital home in Macclesfield, and was cremated nearby. For 27 years, he was commemorated with a very modest marker featuring the words 'Love will tear us apart' – but in July 2008 it was stolen and quickly replaced with a new one. 'I'm speechless,' said Joy Divison and New Order drummer – and fellow Macclesfielder – Stephen Morris. 'You couldn't sell it on eBay – it's ridiculous and very upsetting.'

## Sandy Denny 1947-1978
*Putney Vale Cemetery, Stag Lane, London SW15*
The folk-rock pioneer, one-time member of Fairport Convention and woefully underrated singer-songwriter died of a brain haemorrhage, a month after falling down a flight of stairs at a holiday cottage in Cornwall. She was buried close to her family home in Wimbledon, next to the A3: a report of her funeral in Melody Maker described 'the wind whipping across Putney Vale Cemetery, blowing the noise of the nearby dual carriageway away in gusts of sudden silence.' Her rather ostentatious headstone features the two-word legend 'The Lady', a reference to a song from her 1972 album Sandy.

## Keith Moon 1946-1978

*Golders Green Crematorium, Hoop Lane, London NW11*

After years of problems with drink, drugs and out-there behaviour, Moon was killed by an overdose of the sedative Heminevrin. He's one of scores of famous people whose ashes are either stored, or were scattered, at the UK's first crematorium. A small part of the huge lawn received Moon's ashes, and it's numbered 3P. According to the staff, Moon's reputation for out-of-control behaviour is occasionally reflected in some visitors' inappropriate antics. Says Eric Willis, the on-site Head of Maintenance: 'Some do the windmill guitar thing; other people will stand there, and then do a silly jump. The thing is, you're standing on people's ashes, aren't you? So we politely ask them to leave the lawn and go back to the path.' NB: in a summerhouse at the gardens' southern tip, there's also a small wooden plaque dedicated to the Free guitarist Paul Kossoff, who died of drug-related heart failure in March 1976.

## Brian Jones 1942-1969

*Priory Road Cemetery, Prestbury, near Cheltenham, Gloucestershire*

Freshly fired by The Rolling Stones, Jones drowned – somewhat mysteriously – in the swimming pool of Cotchford Farm, the Sussex pile once owned by Winnie The Pooh's creator, A. A. Milne. In his hometown of Cheltenham, because his death was considered a possible suicide, the Church of England declined to find burial room, so Jones was interred at this municipal cemetery, in a hole said to be 12 feet deep, lest anyone tried to dig him up (it's plot number V11393). Fans pay a mass visit here each February and July, to commemorate his birth and death respectively.

## Marc Bolan 1947-1977

*Golders Green Crematorium, Hoop Lane, London NW11*

T.Rex disciples who want to either pay tribute or come over all macabre can do so at two sites: the spot on Barnes Common where he was killed when the Mini driven by his partner Gloria hit a tree, or at the aforementioned Golders Green 'crem', which offers three focuses of remembrance. There are two plaques in the West Memorial Court, one of which was erected in 2002 by his fan club, and also a rose bush in the West Statue Beds, marked by a small plastic sign. On 16 September each year, fans come to North London to mark Bolan's death, bearing flowers, poems, letters and, in tribute to the 1970 hit Ride A White Swan, the bird-shaped vases that line the walls of the crematorium's tea rooms.

## John Bonham 1948-1980

*St Michael's Church, Rushock, near Droitwich Spa, Worcestershire*

Led Zeppelin's drummer died on 24 September 1980, after a day-long alcohol binge (in)famously involving around 40 measures of vodka. He was cremated, and his gravestone sits in a churchyard near his one-time home of Old Hyde Farm. When the author paid a visit, a mountain of mementoes included 80 drumsticks, a copy of Led Zeppelin II and, oddly, a Red Hot Chili Peppers all-areas tour pass. Rushock residents are used to visitors: 'One little Japanese girl came all the way from London, in a black cab,' marvels one. 'What people usually comment on is how quiet it is.'

# SOURCES

This book draws on interviews by the author with John Lydon, Richard Thompson, Mark E. Smith, Liam and Noel Gallagher, David Gilmour, Roger Waters, Paul Weller, Lemmy, Billy Bragg, Francis Rossi, Rick Parfitt, John Coghlan, Alan Lancaster, Rick Nielsen, Dave Rowntree, Alex James, Dave Hill, Noddy Holder, Jim Lea, Ringo Starr, Paul McCartney, Gary 'Mani' Mounfield, Andy Partridge, Robbie Robertson and Tom McGuinness. Some of the items were adopted from articles originally written for Q, Mojo, Rolling Stone, The Times and The Guardian. In addition, tribute should be paid to Uncut, The Word, NME, Select, Creem, and the estimable archive of music journalism collected at www.rocksbackpages.com.

Should you wish to develop an interest in the stuff detailed in Chapter 3, the following books are recommended without hesitation: Totally Guitar (Tony Bacon and Dave Hunter, Backbeat, 2004), Star Sets (Jon Cohan, Hal Leonard, 1995), and Guitar Effects Pedals: The Practical Handbook (Dave Hunter, Backbeat, 2004).

Also, hats off to a handful of indispensable reference books: The Great Rock Discography (Martin C. Strong, Mojo Books, 2000), The Great Alternative & Indie Discography (Martin C. Strong, Canongate, 1999), British Hit Singles & Albums (edited by David Roberts, Guinness World Records, 2004), and The Guinness Top 40 Charts (Paul Gambaccini, Tim Rice, Jonathan Rice, Guinness, 1996). Much appreciation also to the Oxford English Dictionary, the relevant edition of which, like so many good things, dates from 1989 (we think).

For more information about Hywel Harris's design and illustration work, visit www.hywel.biz

# ACKNOWLEDGEMENTS

First of all, huge thanks to Ginny Luckhurst, not just for the idea that sparked this book, but her love and support. We also owe a huge debt of gratitude to our agent, Jonny Geller, and Antonia Hodgson, for her belief, vision and encouragement. Among the biggest thanks of all go to Linda Silverman, who tirelessly researched the sources for the illustrations, and didn't mind emails requesting images of Henrik Ibsen, Joe Strummer and Karen O, even at the weekend. Massive appreciation to Andy Fyfe for so expertly editing the book, Sean Garrehy for his work on the cover, and Tamsin Kitson for her work on press and publicity, Tamsyn Berryman for Herculean work on the text, and Marie Hrynczak for similar feats with production.

In addition, thanks to: Morlais Harris, for patience and good advice; the staff of Q magazine, the very generous and always-insightful Steve Lowe, Melissa Pimentel, Phyl Mighall, Lois Wilson, Hilary Reeman, Mark and Sharon Shotton, James, Monica, Claire, Mark, Karen and Sarah Bradshaw, Alex James, the staff of Hay on Wye library and the town's booksellers.

To finish, two mentions in print for James and Rosa Harris. Now, to bed…

John Harris and Hywel Harris, July 2009

# IMAGE REFERENCES

Adrian Sheratt/ALAMY 172; AKG images 175; Camera Press 14; Empics Entertainment/PA Photos (Sheila E. image) 63; Kerstin Rodgers 101; LFI 51, 112, 136; Photoshot 157; Pictorial Press (Jim Lea image) 111

Corbis
62 (John Bonham image: Neal Preston, Ginger Baker image: Michael Ochs Archive)

Getty Images
32 (Popperfoto), 52, 72 (George Martin: Michael Ochs Archive), 120 (Paul Stanley image), 120 (Vinnie Vincent image: Michael Ochs Archive), 137, 138 (Alma Cogan image: Popperfoto)

Redferns
8, 18 (Howard Barlow), 19 (Robert Knight), 22, 23, 24, 25 (Erica Echenberg), 27, 30, 31, 33 (top image), 39, 41, 42, 43 (Phil Dent), 44, 47 (Robert Knight Archive), 49 (Estate of Keith Morris), 63 (Clyde Stubblefield image), 64, 78, 79, 81, 82, 87, 89, 102, 104 (Michael Stipe image: Mike Hutson), 104 (Robert Smith image: Ebet Roberts), 105, 106 (Mick Hutson), 107 (Mick Hutson), 110, 111, 112, 113 (Dr John image), 114 (Labelle image: Colin Fuller), 114 (Angus Young image), 116 (Flavor Flav and Madonna images), 117 (Slipknot image: Mike Hutson), 117 (Karen O image: Tabatha Fireman), 119, 120 (Peter Criss image), 121 (Gene Simmons and Ace Frehley images), 121 (Eric Carr image: Ebet Roberts), 122 (Henry Rollins image: Martin Philbey), 124 (Phil Oakey image), 125, 126 (Keith Flint image: Mick Hutson), 126 (The Police images), 128, 135, 141, 142 (Tom Hanley), 143 (David Redfern), 148, 150, 152 (GAB Archive), 153 (Ron Howard), 158 (Giles Petard), 161, 164 (Neil Young image), 167, 177 (GAB Archive), 170 (The Style Council and Mick Jones images), 174, 179 (Mick Hutston), 180 (GAB Archive), 182 (Morrissey and David Bowie images), 184 (Ebet Roberts), 185 (Mike Linssen), 187 (Mick Hutson), 190, 191, 194, 195, 197, 198 (Jakob Dylan image), 199, 200, 203

Retna
16, 113 (Peter Gabriel image)

Rex Features
20 (CSU Archives/Everett Collection), 28 (Erik Pendzich), 40, 50 (Issac Hayes and Jesse Jackson images: Everett Collection), 55, 84 (Brian Rasic), 88 (Alex James image), 93 (Ibsen image), 93 (Rosa Parks image: Everett Collection), 100 (Neil Kinnock image: Brian Harris), 100 (Lenin image), 101 (Karl Schoendorfer), 105 (Adam Ant), 106, 115, 118, 122 (Liam Gallagher image), 123 (Travis Barker image), 123 (Tommy Lee image), 123 (Amy Winehouse image: Richard Young), 124 (Sinead O'Connor image: Richard Young), 127 (Limahl image: Brian Rasic), 127 (Amy Winehouse image: Richard Young), 132 (Brian Rasic), 138 (Barry Peake), 139, 140, 141 (Maureen Starkey/Starr), 164 (Murray Joe), 173, 176 (Harry Goodwin), 186 (Dave Allocca), 192 (David Dagley), 196 (Bleddyn Butcher), 198 (Peaches Geldof and Julian Lennon images)

Urbanimage.TV/Adrian Boot
33, 88 (Paul Simonon image)

WireImage
159 (Ron Galella), 160 (Chris Walter), 161 (Blondie image: Tom Hill),

*Every effort has been made to credit all copyright holders of images used for this book but any omissions will be rectified in the next edition.*